Henry M'Cormac

Aspirations from the Inner, the Spiritual Life

Aiming to Reconcile Religion, Literature, Science, Art, with Faith, and...

Henry M'Cormac

Aspirations from the Inner, the Spiritual Life
Aiming to Reconcile Religion, Literature, Science, Art, with Faith, and...

ISBN/EAN: 9783337091446

Printed in Europe, USA, Canada, Australia, Japan

Cover: Foto ©Thomas Meinert / pixelio.de

More available books at **www.hansebooks.com**

ASPIRATIONS

FROM

THE INNER, THE SPIRITUAL LIFE,

AIMING TO RECONCILE

RELIGION, LITERATURE, SCIENCE, ART,

WITH

FAITH, AND HOPE, AND LOVE, AND IMMORTALITY.

BY

HENRY M'CORMAC, M.D.

LONDON:
LONGMAN, BROWN, GREEN, AND ROBERTS.
1860.

PREFACE.

SOME twenty years since, in a work on the philosophy of our common nature,[1] I essayed to set forth the range of our faculties, their relations human and divine, and now, with, I trust, augmented insight, increased experience, and unabated hope, resume the task.

This is not a sectarian book. It is simply the inculcation of spiritual truth, a spiritual religion and a spiritual God, aspirations[2] from the inner life, the life we do not see, but which, not the less, resumes our experience here, and, in a degree, the experience which is to come. For the earthly is in correspondence with the celestial life, and the spiritual truths of the present are also true for ever.

There is not a principle, a fact, in our moral nature, which is not in strictest subservience to interests that cannot die. For the better intelligence, in all their simplicity and all their grandeur, of God's adorable laws, their beauty, their holiness, their truth, would approve religion's mighty unity and infinitely benefit our kind.

I would develop the great ideas of faith, and hope, and love, and immortality. I would plead for humanity, the elevation

---

[1] *The Philosophy of Human Nature.* Lond. 1837.
[2] Ἀγάπη, χαρὰ, εἰρήνη, μακροθυμία, χρηστότης, ἀγαθωσύνη, πίστις, πρᾳότης, ἐγκράτεια.

of the masses, the integration in life and action of the heaven-imparted immunities of our kind. And thus would I realise the mighty spiritual freehold and thrice divine reality, that through aspiration and effort, not otherwise, rectitude is achieved, in brief the power of being and doing good, for the sake of goodness and truth alone.

I would urge unity of faith, the amalgamation of creeds, on the basis of God's truth and love, and raise or strive to raise, each weary anxious heart straight to highest heaven.

I would unite the beautiful, the elevated, the good, the pure, reconcile religion, literature, science, art, nay every precious and excellent thing, too much estranged, with religious trust and religious truth. For there is not a folly, a forfeit, or a crime, which has not its origin in ignorance or neglect of the great laws which regulate our human nature, and more especially, deficient culture of the intelligence and of the spiritual affections, inner jewel and cornerstone of the angelic world where souls find rest for ever.

Love it is, not fear, the end not merely the means, accurate discernment and pervasive enlightenment, hope not despair, which, heaven's very essence, exclude alike menace, and arrogance, and gloom. Since the spiritual kingdom, and truth, and purity, with all gladness, are indeed within, and the divine is never far.[1] For there is but one God, as there is but one desert, one obedience, one love, divinest principles, great with glorious augury to man. And each celestial affection approaches us to the divine, and conjoined with science, also divine, opens a path to the stars.

---

[1] Καίτοιγε οὐ μακρὰν ἀπὸ ἑνὸς ἑκάστου ἡμῶν ὑπάρχοντα.

In other respects, the physician is brought so in contact with the more solemn instants of life and death, when all disguise disappears, and the soul in all its littleness and all its greatness stands revealed, that he perhaps of all men, has facilities for appreciating the value of influences coextensive with the world, deep as human feeling, pervasive as human thought. If I should be so fortunate as to realise, or help to realise for others, aspirations which comprise my heart, my soul, my convictions, and my trust, if I might soothe but a single suffering, abate a single care, confirm truths which must endure for ever, it would prove a grateful return for hours of earnest inquiry and prolonged reflection.

HENRY M'CORMAC, M.D.

BELFAST, *Dec.* 1859.

CONTENTS.

BOOK I.

	SEC.		SEC.
Moral Courage,	1	The True Light,	28
The End and the Means,	2	Incorporate Religion,	29
Waking up the Affections,	3	Love an Inspiration,	30
Love begets Love,	4	The Real Eden,	31
In the Name of God,	5	Life Unending,	32
Man and God,	6	True Safety,	33
One Truth,	7	The Road to the Stars,	34
Providence,	8	The Letter and the Spirit,	35
One Life, One Light,	9	Glimpses of Paradise,	36
The Law of Duty,	10	The Comforter,	37
Divine Intelligence and Love,	11	Realisation of the Ideal,	38
The Price of Living,	12	Liberty, Necessity,	39
Love Divine,	13	Spiritual Progress,	40
Eternal Progress,	14	The Unseen Presence,	41
The Law of Progress,	15	Love Conquers Death,	42
The White Stone,	16	The Better Affections,	43
The Harps of God,	17	The Angel by our Side,	44
Divine Consolations,	18	Subjection of Matter,	45
The Light and the Darkness,	19	The Disinterested Affections,	46
The Mighty Transition,	20	Faith in the Unseen,	47
Religion and Reason,	21	What we Find and what we Bring,	48
Putting down Evil,	22		
Nature a Hymn,	23	Creation our Care,	49
The Great Dragon,	24	The Good Physician,	50
A Divine Friend,	25	Heart's Nurture,	51
Heart's Treasures,	26	Physical and Moral Culture,	52
The Ladder of the Spirit,	27	The Tree of Life,	53

BOOK II.

	SEC.		SEC.
Truest Innocence,	54	The Incarnate Angel,	80
The Divine in Man,	55	Devotion and Belief,	81
Unreal Crimes,	56	Manners,	82
The Pure Affections,	57	Man and Brute,	83
Life through Death,	58	Training,	84
The Seen and the Unseen,	59	Progressive Religion,	85
Cumulative Influences,	60	The Christian Ideal,	86
The Eden of Life,	61	Price of Liberty,	87
Man, as Man,	62	Desert,	88
Earth's Salt,	63	A Divine Environment,	89
The Heavenly Light,	64	The Current of Existence,	90
Man's Hand,	65	Working with God,	91
Undine,	66	Providence,	92
Tolerance,	67	Dignity of Human Nature,	93
True Nobility,	68	Youth Eternal,	94
Divinity of Love,	69	Divinity of Beneficence,	95
Real Courtesy,	70	To Seem and to Be,	96
The Whole Man,	71	Disinterested Affection,	97
Order Divine,	72	Church of the Future,	98
The Shagreen Skin,	73	The Bridge,	99
Absence of the Divine,	74	Spiritual Influences,	100
Asceticism,	75	The Charities of Heaven,	101
True Nobility,	76	Great Thinkers,	102
Force and Tenderness,	77	The Curate of Meudon,	103
Seed of Heaven,	78	The Divine Kingdom,	104
Unity of Religious Truth,	79		

BOOK III.

Training Souls for God,	105	Living Day by Day,	110
One Providence, One Inspiration,	106	A Just Appreciation,	111
		True Precision,	112
Religious Truth,	107	The Seraph Within,	113
The Spirit of the Universe,	108	The Soul in the Voice,	114
Moral Death,	109	The Tree of Life,	115

		SEC.			SEC.
A Noble Book,	.	116	The Soul's Permanence,	.	138
Looking Heavenward,		117	Faith, of Heaven,	.	139
Effort,	. .	118	The Inner Life,	.	140
Shadows,	. .	119	Loftiest Aims,	.	141
Life no Dream,	.	120	Reciprocal Development,	.	142
The Faithful Dead,	.	121	Force of Character,	.	143
To Know, to Be, and to Do,		122	Genius, Divine,	.	144
A Divine Ideal,	.	123	The Corrective of Evil,	.	145
Impulse and Principle,	.	124	Love Casts out Fear,	.	146
Woman's Grace,	.	125	The Intent and the Act,	.	147
Moral Conquest,	.	126	Death a Symbol,	.	148
A Soul,	.	127	Testimony of Christianity,	.	149
A Confession,	. .	128	The Mighty Reversion,	.	150
Kepler,	. .	129	A Divine Initiation,		151
The Body,	. .	130	Unity with God,	.	152
The Divine Everywhere,	.	131	The Process of Assent,	.	153
Celestial Law,	.	132	Harmony of Divine Truth,		154
Soul-Culture,	.	133	The Safe Road,	.	155
Duties, Ours,	.	134	True Affection Unselfish,	.	156
To Confer Happiness,	.	135	Compassions, Divine,	.	157
Faith and Works,	. .	136	Children of God,	.	158
Testimony of the Plants,	.	137	The Business of Age,	.	159

BOOK IV.

The Inner Voice,	. .	160	Introspection,	.	173
The Veiled Life,	. .	161	Divine Adjustments,	.	174
Action and Reaction,	.	162	Unity with the Divine,	.	175
Evil of Fear,	.	163	Partings, .	.	176
Insistence of Purpose,	.	164	The Highest Wisdom,	.	177
The Divine Want,	. .	165	Sin and Suffering,	.	178
Heaven at our Doors,	.	166	Contending with Evil,	.	179
The Paradise of Childhood,	.	167	Physical Neglect,	.	180
Divine Unities,	. .	168	Needfulness of the Affections,		181
Man and God,	.	169	Seeds of Holiness,	.	182
Medisance,	. .	170	Fellowship with God,	:	183
Association of Ideas,		171	Spiritual Treasures,	.	184
Aspiration,	. .	172	A True Faith,	: .	185

CONTENTS.

	SEC.		SEC.
Our Real Birth-place,	186	The Mountain Side,	197
True Science, Divine,	187	A Twofold Life,	198
Conscience,	188	Esoteric, Exoteric,	199
The Great Realities,	189	Materialism,	200
Looking Inward,	190	Music Culture,	201
Earth a Paradise,	191	A Divine Transfiguration,	202
Goldsmith,	192	Life's Healing,	203
Art, Divine,	193	The Stars of Spiritual Truth,	204
The Roman and the Greek,	194	Freedom in Obedience,	205
The Revelation of Poesy,	195	Heart's Culture,	206
Uhland's Dream,	196		

BOOK V.

Angelic Communion,	207	Confiding in the Divine,	232
The Purpose of Nature,	208	Philosophy and Faith,	233
Man and Brute,	209	Revelation of the Beautiful,	234
Speculation,	210	Genius,	235
The Inner Power,	211	Poetry,	236
The Magical in Nature,	212	Spiritual Safety,	237
Evolution of the Divine,	213	The Pitcher of Tears,	238
Seeds of Paradise,	214	Spiritual Reclamation,	239
Evil, to be Overcome,	215	Providence, of Heaven,	240
The Angel on Guard,	216	The Queen of Nature,	241
Prayer and Praise,	217	The Lower Animals,	242
Effort and Development,	218	Palaces, Divine,	243
The Object and the Pursuit,	219	The Voices of the Telegraph,	244
Progression,	220	Transfiguration of Love,	245
The Morning Stars,	221	The Heaven in our Path,	246
The Spirit in the Flesh,	222	True Reform,	247
Nil Desperandum,	223	Turning to God,	248
Our Very Best,	224	Genesis of Souls,	249
The Affections,	225	A Mind Diseased,	250
Faith and Fact,	226	To-Pan,	251
The Formula and the Truth,	227	Swift,	252
Divine Consideration,	228	The Soul's Healing,	253
Perfect Love,	229	Progressive Purity,	254
Culture and Self-Culture,	230	He Liveth Best who Loveth Best,	255
Heart's Influence,	231		

BOOK VI.

	SEC.		SEC.
Angelic Lineaments,	. 256	Aspiration and Realisation,	279
Sympathy, Divine, .	257	Flowers of Paradise,	. 280
Freedom through Genius,	. 258	Keepers of the Gates,	. 281
The World's Loveliness,	. 259	Associate Angels, .	. 282
The Grave, no Resting-Place,	260	A Real Faith, .	. 283
A Charter of Freedom,	. 261	Spiritual Influence, .	. 284
No Concession to Evil,	. 262	Divine Efficacy, .	. 285
No Ontology, .	. 263	Heavenly Earnest, .	. 286
A Nation's Greatness,	. 264	Road to Paradise, .	. 287
Universal Inspiration,	. 265	Truth, Trust, Love,	. 288
The Petrel of the Deep,	. 266	Faith and Reason, .	289
The Pure Affections,	. 267	Masculine Development,	. 290
Circumstances, .	. 268	Progressive Opinion,	. 291
Truthful Intuitions,	. 269	Introspection, .	. 292
The Evil and the Good Seed,	270	No Partial Culture, .	. 293
Safety for All, .	. 271	Unity of Nations, .	. 294
Self-Respect, .	. 272	Mental Soundness, .	. 295
The Religion of the Soul,	. 273	Love a Faculty, .	. 296
The Inner Mansions,	274	Utterances of Literature,	297
True Greatness, .	. 275	The Angel in Humanity,	. 298
The Virtues of no Sex,	. 276	Divine Truthfulness,	. 299
A Just Asceticism, .	. 277	The Higher Life, .	. 300
The Carriage of our Souls, .	278		

BOOK VII.

Self-Sacrifice, .	. 301	Human Dwellings, .	. 310
The Nirvana, .	. 302	Lost is Lost, .	. 311
A Nation's Hope, .	. 303	Municipalities, .	. 312
The World a Paradise,	. 304	The Holiest Air, .	. 313
Conversion, .	. 305	A Wise Ignorance, .	. 314
Human Nature, .	. 306	A Golden Thought, .	. 315
Purpose, .	. 307	The Exhibition, .	. 316
Swedenborg, .	. 308	Dogmatic Theology,	. 317
Love and Fear, .	309	Disease and Decay,	. 318

CONTENTS.

	SEC.		SEC.
The Insane,	319	Real Growth,	337
The Marseillaise,	320	Grotius,	338
Fear, a Blight,	321	A Progressive Light,	339
The Navigators of Old,	322	Death, Life,	340
Money,	323	Constancy,	341
Guardianship of Souls,	324	Art's Realities,	342
Filiation of Crime,	325	A Progressive Faith,	343
The Visible World,	326	Harmony of Existence,	344
Life's Mission,	327	The Religion of the Soul,	345
Pious Frauds,	328	Mental Science,	346
Psychology,	329	The Oppressor and the Oppressed,	347
Purification through Love,	330		
Growing Old,	331	Life a Religion,	348
Sincerity a Test,	332	Spiritual Renewal,	349
A Mighty Aim,	333	A True Ideal,	350
Conscience,	334	The Angel of Death,	351
The Price of Progress,	335	Hidden Influences,	352
Saving Angels,	336	A Discourse with God,	353

BOOK VIII.

San Januarius,	354	The Soul's Bravery,	370
Human Victims,	355	Living for God,	371
No Sin, no Soil,	356	The Real and the Ideal,	372
Religious Persecution,	357	Up and Doing,	373
Protestantism,	358	Pearls and Diamonds,	374
Children,	359	A Night at Sea,	375
Truthfulness,	360	Philosophy and Religion,	376
Death,	361	Living for Ever,	377
Renunciation,	362	Mother and Child,	378
Roads to Excellence,	363	Warring with Despair,	379
Art,	364	Progressive Influences,	380
Divine Energy,	365	Knowledge and Faith,	381
The Best of Men,	366	Remorse and Superstition,	382
House of Truth,	367	Faith and Love,	383
Broad Principles,	368	The Soul's Liberation,	384
Needful Effort,	369	The Hand,	385

	SEC.		SEC.
Necessity and Free-Will,	386	Spiritual Life,	396
Truth never Trite,	387	Love of Order and of Truth,	397
The Intent of Death,	388	Men of Progress,	398
True Nobility,	389	Conception of the Divine,	399
A Ravelled Skein,	390	The Better Life,	400
Courage at Heart,	391	Excellence of no Sex,	401
Poverty of Soul,	392	The Divine Treasury,	402
The Life Within,	393	The Past at our Door,	403
Modern Speculation,	394	The Crown,	404
Creative Power of Love and Art,	395		

BOOK IX.

Speculation,	405	Pictures,	429
Outward Objects,	406	Music's Efficacy,	430
The Promised Shore,	407	English Characteristics,	431
Ideas never Die,	408	Receptivity of Man's Soul,	432
To be Greatly Good,	409	Culture,	433
A Great Soul,	410	Amalgamation of Creeds,	434
To Know God,	411	Religious Essentials,	435
Life's Treasures,	412	The Divine in Art,	436
Torn Away,	413	Genius,	437
Humanity, One,	414	Heart's Co-operation,	438
Youth, Innocence,	415	Glorious Trilogies,	439
Music, Divine,	416	The Higher Life,	440
A Thought of God,	417	Our Outer Existence,	441
Speculative Ability,	418	Life, Spiritual,	442
The Angels by our Side,	419	The Will of God,	443
The Highest Beauty,	420	Spiritual Constancy,	444
Divine Progress,	421	Trust and Truth,	445
Spiritual Parentage,	422	Solidarity of Man,	446
Fixity of Opinion,	423	Ecstasies,	447
True Causation,	424	One Reason,	448
The Road to Greatness,	425	Sculptured Excellence,	449
Nature, Man, God,	426	The Soul's Impress,	450
Taking the Veil,	427	Charlotte Bronte,	451
Unseen Enemies,	428	The Paradise Within,	452

BOOK X.

	SEC.		SEC.
Nature's Rest,	453	A Thanksgiving,	477
One Faith, One God,	454	Religion, Faith, Philosophy,	478
The Highest Trust,	455	Doing Aright,	479
Life, a Sacred Experience,	456	A Healthy Soul,	480
Overcoming Evil with Good,	457	Mental Affluence,	481
The Inner Kingdom,	458	Religion, Past and to Come,	482
Charlotte Montefiore,	459	True Genius,	483
Antoninus, Epictetus,	460	Fear, not Religion,	484
Spiritual Unity,	461	Man's Capacity,	485
Shelley, Rousseau,	462	Suffering Terminable,	486
Elevation of the Masses,	463	Abelard,	487
Standing Armies,	464	The Pure shall See God,	488
A Prayer,	465	A False Security,	489
Eternity,	466	Leopardi,	490
Key to Heaven,	467	The Dead Children,	491
Self-Esteem,	468	God's Provident Love,	492
A True Revealing,	469	Godwin, Roland, Fuller,	493
The Great Reality,	470	Culture's Object,	494
The Secure Haven,	471	Augustin, Calvin,	495
Spindrift of Time,	472	Woman's Wrongs,	496
Socrates,	473	Celestial Armies,	497
Jean Paul,	474	Insanity, Crime,	498
The True Paradise,	475	The Test of Existence,	499
Medisance,	476	Law, Divine,	500

ASPIRATIONS

FROM

THE INNER, THE SPIRITUAL LIFE.

BOOK I.

FROM such a chaos as this, the mind turns anxiously to a future which must assuredly arrive. *Incende quod adorasti, adora quod incendisti.* Many a revolution, social and political, must first pass over the European world. In religion, in ethics, in mental science, men's minds must long continue to oscillate, as they do now, between the most abject superstitions, the wildest infidelities, and find scanty resting-place in the intervals. So it must be until some one speaking with authority shall rouse them once more, by collecting all that is true in modern philosophy, and incorporating it with the one leading principle of man's relation to God, as creature to Creator, subject to sovereign, responsible agent to his master, weak and imperfect nature to him who can purify and exalt it. But the hour is not yet come nor the man. *Edinburgh Review.*

We have spoken from a profound conviction that there is a truth as lofty as ever council decreed, an image of Christianity as holy as ever won the admiration of saint or martyr, the moral and spiritual character of religion itself. *Id.*

ASPIRATIONS.

1. MORAL COWARDICE.

MORAL cowardice is the source of every mean and pitiful thing, renders a man afraid of duty, afraid of death, so that when the moment for action arrives, he equivocates, intreats, fears.[1] Moral courage is religion in action, moral cowardice is religion in defeat. Oh brother, exclaims a strenuous thinker, never strike sail to a fear, come greatly into port or sail with God the seas. Without courage, the courage of the heart, no one can be truly great. This is a courage that does not depend on thews or sinews, but on the soul. It animated the patriots and martyrs of old, as it animates the patriots and martyrs of to-day. Moral courage makes the man, the absence of it the knave, the driveller, and the fool. It is to the age's dishonour that its intellectual tendencies are marked with the characters of fear.[2] Yet courage must be guided by purity and truth, since divested of these, it is shorn of half its strength.

2. THE END AND THE MEANS.

No end is secure without well-digested means. Now, the great end is present and eternal progress, the means

[1] Tergiversatur, timet, plorat. *Senecae Luc. Ann. Epist.*
[2] Martineau, *Prospective Review*, Feb. 1846.

never-ceasing action, heaven-ward and God-ward. I would not, observes Kant, give one of Kepler's discoveries for a principality. What principality indeed, could equal the eternal principality which science realises in the empire of thought. No wisdom equals that which reveals man to himself, teaches him to regard social institutions, nay his whole life, as the possible means of unfolding and exalting the spirit within.[1] Then let us cherish angelic thoughts, the fellow-workers whom some day we must let go that angels may come in.[2] And thus shall we further the divine, thus realise the conception of that eternity whose nigh approach illumines life's close, as the rising sun illumines the glad expanses of the sea.

3. WAKING UP THE AFFECTIONS.

If only the thrice-precious affections could be reproduced at will, it would convert this life into heaven. More permanent if less intense satisfactions, however, are placed within control.[3] Our happiness is consulted in the main,[4] while the actual subsistence of the better affections, assures us of that loftier destiny wherein they shall flourish and expand for ever.

4. LOVE BEGETS LOVE.

The sentiment of love is realised by love. We cannot know God except by becoming the image of

[1] Channing, *Spiritual Freedom*. [2] Emerson, *On Compensation*.
[3] *Tucker's Light of Nature*, Mildmay, Vol. II. p. 577.
[4] Ad prudentem gubernatorem pertinet negligere aliquem defectum bonitatis in parte, ut faciat augmentum bonitatis in toto. Aquinas, *Contra Gent.*

God.[1] Indeed only in so far as man is thus, thinks thus, can he give the reason of anything that God has made.[2] Spiritual truth is apprehended by being spiritual.[3] The flight from evil, says Plato, consists in resembling God, in becoming holy, just, and wise.[4] The mind, observes Channing, alone is free, which, instead of stopping at the material and making it a prison wall, passes to its author beyond, and finds in the radiant signatures of the infinite, helps to its own enlargement.

At times we are as very angels, till things inferior steal in upon us and rob us of our better selves. In truth, we are of a spiritual nature, however much that nature may be dimmed, and the reality of virtue fills the heart with ineffable joy.[5] But the bondage of matter falls away one day, and the soul, rich in spiritual wealth, and coming to rely upon itself, proceeds heaven-ward, fit associate for angels indeed, all the sons and daughters of God.[6] When gifts celestial descend upon the soul, then do we discern what it is to be of the divine image, and of the spiritual nature which never dies.

[1] *Orr's Theism*, Lond. 1857.
[2] Swedenborg, *passim*.
[3] Non possumus loqui recté de numine divino nisi simus illustrati lumine ejus. Iamblichus, *De Myst.* Cap. 18.
Ille honorat Deum optimé qui quantum fieri potest, facit mentem suam similem Deo. *Sexti Empirici Sentent. Opera*, Lipsiae, 1718.
[4] *Theaetetus*.
[5] *Hampden's Lectures on Moral Philosophy*, Lect. III.
[6] Animal, providum, sagax, multiplex, artium memor, plenum rationis et consilii quem vocamus hominem, praeclara quadam conditione generatum esse a supremo Deo. Cicero.

5. IN THE NAME OF GOD.

In the name of the ever-compassionate and merciful God,[1] from whom all certainty and truth do spring.[2] This indeed is an invocation which might well preface every serious thought and action of our lives. It would leave scant harbourage for evil, would not concentrate the sanctities of life on days, forms, shred of the beauty of holiness.[3] It would not concede authority to interpreters between conscience and the divine, erect tribunals that fail to recognise the spiritual equality and brotherhood of man, or suffer us to abnegate faith in the celestial obligations of justice, and truth, and love. For, thus, O God most merciful and compassionate, should we not be merciful even as thou art merciful.

6. MAN AND GOD.

It is with man in a degree as with God, though infinity separate them.[4] For as the divine excellence shines through the material creation, the rising and setting sun, the flowing waters, the undulating sea, the spiritual radiance of the flowers, so is the countenance transfigured by a well-disciplined temper, a

---

[1] *Al-Koran*, Sale.
[2] Itaque plane video omnis scientiae certitudinem et veritatem ab una veri Dei cognitione pendere. Descartes, Lond. 1664. *Med.* V.
[3] *Dial*, Boston, Oct. 1840.
[4] Itur ad astra frugalitate, temperantia, fortitudine aliisque virtutibus. Dii non sunt fastidiosi, non invidi. Admittunt nos et porrigunt manum ascendentibus. Imò Deus venit ad homines et in homines. Mens bona nulla est sine Deo. *Senecae Epist.*

heavenly will, and man, as Seneca tells us, becomes as a ministering angel, emulous indeed of heaven.[1]

7. ONE TRUTH.

As there is but one physics, one mathematics, in short one universal material law,[2] so there is but one universal moral law, one rule of love, in fine one esoteric truth, although there be many exoteric forms. Error in speculation, however, does not exclude intensity of devotion, precise action. The image, the relic, and the formula worshipper, may yet vie in veneration and love. Have I not seen the Moslim on his mat of prayer, as the perception of a higher power streamed in upon his consciousness, entreat heaven with intensest fervour beneath the cathedral of immensity. For love casts a halo not merely on a pure and upright faith, but even on partial errors and superstitions themselves.

8. PROVIDENCE.

There is a providence extending to the whole and also to the parts.[3] It does not provide at one time and fail to provide at another, does not lavish favours on one nation or individual, to the prejudice or exclusion of other nations and individuals. It is a constant, not an interruptive providence. It is the best conceivable providence. It is the providence of God.

[1] Vir bonus non tantum Dei discipulus et aemulator, sed etiam vera progenies est. *De Providentia.*
[2] Cumberland's *Law of Nature*, Tower's tr. Dublin, 1750, § IX, *Prolegomena.*
[3] Mundus administrator providentia Deorum, iidemque consulunt rebus humanis nec solùm universis, verum etiam singulis. Cicero.

9. ONE LIFE, ONE LIGHT.

There is in truth, but one life, the life of the soul. The life here and the life hereafter, are not so much two lives as one life. The loves, hopes, aspirings which we cherish now, we shall cherish always. For consciousness is the life of man. The body with its wondrous mechanism, is but an accessory, the mould of the material. It might be likened to the parasitic cloud which clings to the mountain's brow. The mountain is as the permanent soul, the cloud is as the perishing frame. The present and the future indeed, are embraced by one consciousness, except in so far as accruing knowledge and renewed affections, shall augment the old knowledge and the old loves.

10. THE LAW OF DUTY.

The law of duty is the law of this and of the unseen life. Like the divine of which Seneca speaks, it meets one at every turn. Duty involves the moral law, the moral law involves duty, charity to our neighbour, purity of soul. Conscience, the inner light, is not indeed innate, but the capacity of realising it is so. As objects appear to us under the form with which our sensuous nature compels us to invest them, so ideas and emotions must seem and be, according to the mode in which our spiritual nature constrains us to accept them.[1] Thus, faith in God and in the unseen, is in relation with our moral consciousness, growing as it grows, expanding as it expands, in sympathy and unison together.

[1] Phenomenon, noumenon.

11. DIVINE INTELLIGENCE AND LOVE.

Sweetest flowers, blossoms like diamond crowns, rich with the richest odours, fair beyond the imagination to conceive, adorn the wilderness. There, do we find the liquid crystal of the antelope's eye, the glittering hues of reptile, insect, and bird, the seraphic sunrise and sunset glow of the tropics, the rapt gaze of the Indian or African mother, as she fondles her sable offspring, lovely in her own eyes and in the eyes of all who respect the handiwork of God. Wherever we survey creation, in whatsoever direction we turn, there also do we discern intelligence and love, traces, as Cicero divinely expresses it, of one God, ruler and architect of the world.[1]

12. THE PRICE OF LIVING.

If we would live we must pay the price of living, pay it in its pains and its sufferings, as in its joys and its satisfactions.[2] We have indeed realised a lofty proficiency, cheaply compassed, because cheap at any price, a glorious gain. Yet man too often values what he has not, and what he has he values not, though it comprise present, and the reversion of eternal life and felicity.

A cloud, exclaims Fenelon, covers for a moment our feeble vision, but thy rays, O truth eternal, have pierced

[1] Pulchritudo mundi, ordo rerum coelestium, conversio solis, lunae, siderumque omnium, indicant satis aspectu ipso ea omnia non esse fortuita—Cum autem nec mens, nec potestas humana possit hoc efficere, Deus unus potest esse architectus et rector tanti operis et muneris.

[2] Οὐδὲν προῖκα περιγίνεται. *Epicteti Enchiridion*, Foulis.

this cloud.[1] In aiming at the divine, the philosopher of Stagira is indeed in unison with the Christian saint, in that the dignity of a being augments with his duties, and measures itself by the greatness of his task.

13. LOVE DIVINE.

True love bears fruitage unto immortal life. To live in truth, is to exist in the purer affections, without which existence would be valueless, a sorry void. It has been conceived that of beings spiritual, there were some that loved only, and some which only thought. Yet how could there be existence without this great, redeeming affection, existence without love. If, as the Christian apostle has said, we could but realise the love which the great spirit has shed upon our hearts, it would renew the world. For this is the real, the spiritual revival, which commends itself to our souls. And he that loveth not, knoweth not God, for God is love.[2] Love indeed, realises that which else is inconceivable to the heart of man. For faith is love, and God is love, love for the infinite hosts of sentient beings whose father, preserver, and creator he is. If in any wise we are to resemble him, it must also be in respect of this affection, which in veriest truth bears fruitage unto immortality.

14. ETERNAL PROGRESS.

As a mark, observes Epictetus, is not set up to be missed, so neither is evil the intent of providence in

---

[1] Je vous avais donc perdu de vue pour un peu de temps, un nuage avait couvert nos yeux pour un moment, mais vos rayons, O vérité éternelle ont percé ce nuage. *De l'Existence de Dieu.*

[2] Ὁ μὴ ἀγαπῶν οὐκ ἔγνω τὸν Θεόν, ὅτι ὁ Θεὸς ἀγάπη ἐστίν.

the world. The divine purpose can never fail.[1] The law of progress which is also the law of liberty, includes all spiritual beings. To doubt it indeed, were to doubt the mercy of God. Duty urges progress in ourselves, its furtherance in others. It is a law which includes not only the intelligent and the good, but also the unintelligent and the bad, for they too must rise from the slough. The moral nature is so constituted as to render it impossible to remain in blindness and perversity for ever. Then peal it forth, there is progress for all. The glad waters of the river of life shall irrigate every soul. As intelligence has been made to bear on the idiot, goodness to glow in the heart of the debased, so purity and truth, with all excellence, in virtue of the conditions of our being, shall sometime take possession of every consciousness for ever.

15. THE LAW OF PROGRESS.

The law of progress renders all men brothers, all women sisters. The heavenly mansions indeed, loom brighter, clearer, because nigher, to some than to others. The requirements of progress, in truth, are inexorable. Reason and religion are in strictest accordance in defining them. For purity of soul is in perfect keeping with good sense, and no sense is too good for goodness. The heavenly soul is simply the best soul not only for the future, but for the subtle, shifting present, that decides on issues to come. In this life, as in the next, there are not two great classes merely, the elect and non-elect, but shades innumerable as engendered by con-

[1] Αει ευ πιπτουσι οι Διος κυβοι.

duct, position, character.[1] Although the most exalted devotion relate to high aims, religion comes also in contact and sympathy with the common springs of life and action. Soon or late, perfection must be approached by all. Our belief in God and in the spirit-life, alike involves this mighty consummation. We are associated on the onward path, a path which by a blessed necessity, each soul must traverse to the end.

16. THE WHITE STONE.

I know one who as a child, sat with his sister reading the apocalyptic lines of John. To him that conquereth I will give to eat of the manna that is hidden, I will give him a white stone.[2] Then his heart welled up with deep emotion, as he became conscious of the divine presence, and God's gentle kingdom, the surpassing value of desert, and of the better life to come. And he to whom that dream of beauty came, has not forgotten the hidden manna or the white stone, and yet hopes to compass them ere he die.

17. THE HARPS OF GOD.

Angels, to us invisible, are everywhere about us, hymning, as with harp and psaltery, the infinite perfections, the adorable goodness, of God. Within us and around, divinest harmonies, indeed harps of God, are continually sounding for those who have ears to hear and to apprehend.[3] Such are audible in the

---

[1] Martineau, *Miscellanies*.

[2] Τῷ νικῶντι δώσω αὐτῷ φαγεῖν ἀπὸ τοῦ μάννα τοῦ κεκρυμμένου, καὶ δώσω ψῆφον λευκήν.

[3] Ἔχοντας κιθάρας τοῦ Θεοῦ.

nightly murmurs of the rushing stream, the ripple on the beach, the fitful winds, the countless laughter, as the poet with unsurpassable beauty has worded it, of the ocean wave.[1] They are heard in the birds' song, the cries of the children in the spring, in fine in every joyous, heartfelt utterance of nature and of man. Sometimes indeed, one hears air-borne symphonies, one knows not whence they come, as if trumping seraphs were hurrying by.

In the magical recesses of Africa and Asia, rife with glorious beauty, a ceaseless pealing hymn, rising and falling with glad diapason, issues from the animated world. One listens with a sort of ecstasy, by wild Irish or Scottish strands, or in some great American sea-bay, to the voices of carolling birds, sweeter far than any flute. In fine, the denizens of land and sea unite with man's great soul in jubilant utterances, in veriest truth the harps of God.

18. DIVINE CONSOLATIONS.

In those wondrous fragments whose mysterious splendour overtops even eastern imagery, it is said with surpassing sweetness and truth, and God shall wipe away all tears from their eyes, and there shall be neither sorrow, nor suffering, nor death any more.[2] Such indeed is the aspiration of every believer in the compassionate mercies of God. In the hidden life, hidden from the eye of sense, but not from the

---

[1] Ποντίων τε κυμάτων ἀνήριθμον γέλασμα.
[2] Καὶ ἐξαλείψει ὁ Θεὸς παν δάκρυον ἀπὸ των ὀφθαλμῶν αὐτῶν και ὁ θάνατος ουκ ἔσται ἔτι.

spiritual eye, we have the unassailable assurance that a clearer insight will be afforded us, and that our longing hopes and fond desires shall not be frustrated for ever.

19. THE LIGHT AND THE DARKNESS.

That he who is himself bereft of spiritual insight, the inward revealing, shall fail to discern it in another, is unhappily too true. The light indeed shines in the darkness, but the darkness apprehends it not.[1] And thus has the letter come to trench upon the spirit. Yet of what avail is the letter without the spirit. It is of no avail at all. We may not play fast and loose with eternal verities, employing the counters termed words. The word is a breath, a pulse, the utterance of the moment, but truth is everlasting. As the bodily eye is needed to discern the sun's light, so is the spiritual eye to discern the light of the spirit, the truths of God. This, indeed, is the glad awakening in which not only man and angels, but the one great cause by whom the universe and conscience itself are called into being, rejoice.[2] For God is its source. His is the true light which lights up the moral world, rescues man from darkness and from sin. His, is the wisdom which regulates, the power which produces, the providence which orders all things.

[1] Καὶ τὸ φῶς ἐν τῇ σκοτια φαίνει, και ἡ σκοτία αὐτὸ ου καταλαβειν.

[2] C'est la même sagesse infinie de Dieu qui a tout reglé, et qui parait non seulement dans l'excellence de ses ouvrages, mais beaucoup plus dans la simplicité des voyes par lesquelles il les construit. Malebranche, *Recherche de la Vérité.* Paris, 1712. T. iv. p. 605.

20. THE MIGHTY TRANSITION.

How complete is the transition to the life unseen. Nor house, nor land, nor jewels, nor dignities, accompany us there. The so-styled material realities of this life are shadows indeed, flitting matters borrowing significance from higher things. But love, and hope, and charity, with magnanimity and disinterestedness, in fine all the sweet family of the virtues, are the great, the enduring realities, and so shall remain to the close.

21. RELIGION AND REASON.

Pure ethics, observes Kant, are the supreme judge of belief. The criterion which they furnish is indeed divine. They vindicate the soul's jurisdiction in her own cause, assert the supremacy of the inner court of appeal in all questions involving purely spiritual interests.[1] Moral science is one thing, popular opinion may be, often is, another. There are many formulas, there can be but one rule of right, the pure ethical belief. If we do not test the formula by the rule of right, the pure ethical belief, we incur the risk of missing its vital import, the truth-kernel embodied within.

The adherents of a certain faith adopt a different standard. They would subject the intellect to authority, one man's intellect to another man's authority.[2] What is their argument, however, but a paralogism, their narrower standard but the crystallisation of a thought, the unprogressive, imperfect utterance of bygone ages,

[1] Wilson, *Spiritual Catholicity*, Preface.
[2] Balmez, *European Civilisation*, Chap. iv. *Id.* Chap. lxix.

which, for convenience sake, and to preclude discussion, they assume to be infallible. Yet all the sects are more or less liable to the charge of paralogism, all would assume infallibility, all debar discussion. Man's thought, however, will not be always crystallised. Reason is progressive as it is divine, and cannot be safely discarded from ethical, from religious considerations. Religion, indeed, is the precious jewel, reason the golden setting. For the base metal of unreason, however garnished with the plea of infallibility, only desecrates religion, which it yet farther serves to hide and obscure.

22. PUTTING DOWN EVIL.

All evil is imperfection and made to be overcome. It is indeed to be subdued within the soul, true arena of man's activity, for else are the intentions of providence thwarted, and the heart becomes a blight.

23. NATURE A HYMN.

Nature, in all her kingdoms, sends forth a pealing hymn, a ceaseless message from God to man. Of her perpetual freshness we never tire, the infinite solace, which, speaking through no interpreter, gently steals us out of our humanity, giving us a foretaste of that more diffused disembodied life which may hereafter be ours.[1] Let the spring with its wealth of greenery and flowers recur never so often, we welcome it with renewed ecstasy. To the wash of the waters on the shingle beach or at the bark's prow, the aeolian murmurs of the winds and waves, we would listen for ever.

[1] Mrs. Jameson, *Commonplace Book.*

The various earth, the lustrous stars, the faces and labours of our kind fill us with unabated delight. For a spiritual unity underlies them all, with utterances fresh from heaven. They assure us that we are God's children, creatures of his adoption, that he means well by us, and that he is leading us step by step, and hour by hour, to yet loftier fruitions and the better life to come.

24. THE GREAT DRAGON.

The difference in men's spiritual states is greatly referable to habit. Effort, indeed, is essential at once to body and soul. By so much as we overcome inertia, the dragon which devours the moral purposes of our kind, by so much do we approximate to God, our mighty exemplar, and the angels of humanity, who, having slain the dragon, inertia, have won their way to a higher state, and to that spiritual energy which is itself a condition and forecast of heaven.

25. A DIVINE FRIEND.

Would we have a divine friend, let us be a friend to the divine. For the love which we tender heaven, flows back with double measure on ourselves. Here, if anywhere, love is not barren. The self-sacrificing affections suffice unto themselves. The soul that loves God, seeks no higher reward. For here, to love and to be beloved, are, indeed, necessarily and indissolubly one.

26. HEART'S TREASURES.

He who would enrich himself merely, is not rich unto God, for where the treasure is, will the heart be also.[1] It is the grand distinction, that while material wealth, as such, perishes, spiritual wealth endures for ever. Material wealth, indeed, is consecrated, when it becomes the agent and the exponent of genius, and thought, and love, else, as was said long years ago, it is neither of God nor of heaven.

27. THE LADDER OF THE SPIRIT.

There is a spiritual ladder which shall conduct us from height to height, and from infinity to infinity, if we will. The child, indeed, dwells very nigh the spiritual life, but with the advance of years, he too often comes to lose the consciousness of its exceeding nearness and accessibility. We may not all, perhaps, reach the summit of the ladder, but if we only persevere, we shall gaze on the celestial fields at last, gain gleams and glimpses of the sunny heavens.

28. THE TRUE LIGHT.

And this, says John, is the true light.[2] It is, indeed, the light spiritual, which appeals to every understanding, every heart, pronounces for purity, self-renunciation, and truth, which converts the unregenerate into the regenerate man, leads us to the truth which it divests of the un-truth, cleanses the soul from evil thoughts and foul desires, realises God, and providence, and futurity, evokes the angel in the breast, the inward, the sure revealing, with every sweet and precious thing, alike for earth and heaven.

---

[1] "Ὅπου γάρ ἐστιν ὁ θησαυρὸς ὑμῶν, ἐκεῖ ἔσται καὶ ἡ καρδία ὑμῶν.
[2] Ἦν τὸ φῶς τὸ ἀληθινόν.

29. INCORPORATE RELIGION.

True religion, of which the great fountain is God's revealings, is incorporate with all the just actions and affections of our lives. Is not the mariner religious, when, his life suspended by a thread, he clings to the lee yardarm, and, wet with drift and spray, dips deep into the trough of the surging, seething sea. Is not the physician religious, when, heedless of risk, he sits by the couch of the pestilence-stricken, presses the burning hand, smoothes the terror-distorted features, promises, ay, and imparts relief. Is not the lawyer so, when, forcefully and truthfully pleading, he preserves from the grasp of fraud and chicane the widow's portion, the orphan's inheritance. Is not the patriot religious, when, at every hazard, he stands up for the interests of his country and his kind. And is not the mother so, when, night after night, she watches untiringly by the couch of her suffering offspring. In truth, our whole nature, our affections, and our best interests alike, are knit up and at one with the divine.

30. LOVE AN INSPIRATION.

In labours of love we improve as we advance. For love is truest inspiration, dips in celestial hues the artist's pencil, points, as with a diamond, the writer's pen, transfigures the sluggard, fills the else apathetic heart with new-born ecstasy. Many a saintly being, animated by divine love, has passed with angel tread, often bruised but bruising never, right across this joy-strewn but also tear-sprinkled earth, to the immortal shores, and among the celestial inmates of the highest heavens.

31. THE REAL EDEN.

The good is ever nigh,[1] in our very midst if we will.[2] Celestial influences, indeed, spring up within us, are evoked by delicacy and truthfulness of soul, the vigilant discharge of duty, living this life aright, preparing for the life which is to come. For this is to realise the Eden of our hopes, causing heaven, that nigh heaven, which, in truth, is everywhere, to sit upon our threshold and midst our very floors.

32. LIFE UNENDING.

Eternal life, as Paul has urged,[3] is to all who by patient well-doing, seek honour, glory, immortality. It needs, indeed, material culture to abate physical wretchedness, as it needs moral and religious culture to set aside spiritual destitution and decay. And so surely as the gnomon tracks the sun, our divine capacities can only experience development, in virtue of suitable opportunity and fitting training.

33. TRUE SAFETY.

In Roman-Catholic communities the heart, in Protestant ones the intellect, each severally, is almost exclusively appealed to. And, although we may demur

[1] "Εγγικι γὰρ ἡ βασιλεία των ουρανων.
  Gottes Gut ist nimmer fern.
[2] Ἡ βασιλεία του Θεοῦ ἐντὸς ἐστίν.
[3] Τοῖς μὲν καθ᾽ ὑπομονὴν ἔργου ἀγαθοῦ δόξαν και τιμὴν και αφθαρσίαν ζητοῦσι ζωὴν αἰώνιον.

to consider a woman a divinity, we can at least sympathize with the love and reverence displayed in the worship of the Virgin,[1] since it embodies in a degree our sense of the obligations which we owe the sex, that sex to which in very truth all who suffer belong.[2] Sweetly has the subject, divinely poetic in itself, been adverted to by Heine in his pilgrimage to Kevlaar.[3]

34. THE ROAD TO THE STARS.

God is love.[4] In him the spiritual affections reach their climax and perfection. Love, indeed, is the actuating principle of all religion, as fear is the actuating principle of all superstition. For love, in a sense, is the sum of existence, and it is only according to our measure of it, that we become accessible to religious truth, or indeed to truth at all.[5]

---

[1] O du Heilige,
Hochbeneidete,
Süsse Mutter der Liebe.
Trösterin im Leiden,
Quelle der Freuden,
Hilf uns, Maria.

[2] La femme a cela de commun avec l'ange que les êtres souffrants lui appartiennent. *Eugenie Grandet.*
Vincent de Paul n'a inventé qu'un uniforme, car il y a dans la femme de tout rang et de tout âge l'étoffe d'une soeur de charité. E. About.

[3] Am Fenster stand die Mutter,
Im Bette lag der Sohn,
Willst du nicht aufsteh'n Wilhelm
Zu schau'n die Prozession.

[4] Ὁ Θεὸς ἀγάπη ἐστίν.

[5] *Perthes' Life*, tr. Vol. ii. p. 146.

35. THE LETTER AND THE SPIRIT.

The very gospel of God, would that it were preached to all, is, that just deeds and pure affections confer happiness, and that the good which we do, is its own great and enduring reward. The conviction that some written formula, only, can save, and that the unwritten formulas of holiness, and truth, and love, were they even those of an angel, are else of no avail, is one rife with misery and ill. More developed affections, a better cultivated reason, will indeed one day cease to tolerate the virtual exclusion of the wise and good, the errors and misconceptions of teachers dead and gone, as well as lead to the universal adoption of the heaven-born formula here set out with.

36. GLIMPSES OF PARADISE.

Like Paul, we too are sometimes caught up, obtaining far-off glimpses of the sunny heavens and palaces of ecstasy, gilding, oftener than is thought, the poor man's lot, inspiring the poet's measures, the speculations of the philosopher, nay, even childhood's happy dreams. Like the saint of Tarsus, the Swedish seer visited, he assures us, the starry mansions, but never, since his final journey, has he returned to verify the tale, and his celestial arcana remain arcana indeed. For as Paul himself said, eye hath not seen, nor ear heard, nor indeed hath man's heart conceived, what God designs for those who love him.[1]

---

[1] "Ἆ ὀφθαλμὸς οὐκ εἶδε, καὶ οὖς οὐκ ἔκουσι, καὶ ἐπί καρδίαν ἀνθρώπου οὐκ ἀνέβη, ἅ ἡτοίμασιν ὁ Θεὸς τοῖς ἀγαπῶσιν αὐτόν.

37. THE COMFORTER.

The Holy Spirit,[1] the paraclete of the Greek Church, emphatically the Comforter, is, of all titles, most divine. For God, is in truth, our father, comforter, and friend, as will be felt and known, better and better, more and more, as men themselves increase in goodness, and holiness, and truth.

38. REALISATION OF THE IDEAL.

Consciousness is king and lord of the human breast. Its elevation and purification, therefore, are above all things desirable. Now, by a law of the moral nature, the realisation of our ideal, calls for successive efforts, fresh ideals. In virtue of this, the good man becomes better, the wise man wiser, the able man yet more able.[2] But by another law, habit lays hold of us, we are stranded, perchance, on the shelves of formalism, carried round in the eddies of routine. The only issue, then, is to conquer fresh domains for the legitimate empire of habit, to compass yet other ideals, successes on successes for ever.

39. LIBERTY, NECESSITY.

Each true obligation is divine. No honest effort, no virtuous impulse, ever yet fell through. For it is only by obedience that we overcome difficulties, realise the divine. Here, indeed, conformity breeds ability, non-conformity disability to conform. We are only at

---

[1] Τὸ ἅγιον πνεῦμα.
[2] Animus hominis quidquid sibi imperat obtinet. *Pub. Syri. Sentent.*

liberty to do what is right, to work for, and with God. The controversy as to liberty and necessity, reminds one of Kant's antinomies. One can arrange it, either way, for or against, by dexterous shifting of the terms. We act according to our intellectual light, our habits, requirements, and sense of moral truth. Yet, the consciousness of intention, the compound nature of motive, the play of the feelings and affections, all combine to produce the sense, and, indeed, the reality, of liberty, as confined to the range of man's control.

The author of the disquisition on matter and spirit, has urged the doctrine of necessity as founded on the nature of cause and effect.[1] To live within its dictates, he affirms, would be to live within the gates of heaven, to see God's finger in every event. The important actions of our lives, the strong workings of our affections, are evidently determinable.[2] Philosophical liberty, therefore, does not subsist, liberty does not require it, and the liberty of indifference becomes absurd.[3] But man's real field of empire is the soul. It is indeed his place. Here lies his only secure possession, true arena of moral effort and moral liberty, his victories and his defeats. All others, in comparison, flit and flit for ever away.

40. SPIRITUAL PROGRESS.

Only by degrees can we ascend to heaven, though fain to reach it at a bound. For spiritual discernment, even with our best efforts, is of tardy growth. Yet, as mountain guides climb loftiest Alps, by steps secure

[1] Priestley.   [2] Hartley, *On Man.*   [3] Edwards, *On the Will.*

though slow, so the daily footfall, if we only persist, shall conduct us to highest empyrean at last.

41. THE UNSEEN PRESENCE.

Like heaven itself, spiritual existence is in our midst. It is here, it is there, it is everywhere. For God and the better life are the very, the real presence, a hierarchy of intelligence and love commensurate with all creation. It exists in every sun, it is present in every star, nay in those far-off nebulous masses whose lagging light consumes long ages ere it can arrive.

42. LOVE CONQUERS DEATH.

Love conquers death, subdues it in truth for ever. Would only that each soul were filled, each breast were animated by it. For life, a life of sacrifice, subduing death in love, alone suffices, alone can enable us, with the poet, to say,

> Thou art life's shadow, and as the tree
> Stands in the sun and shadows all beneath,
> So in the light of great eternity
> Life eminent creates the shade of death.
> The shadow passeth when the tree doth fall,
> But love shall reign for ever over all.

The angelic, the spiritual affections know nor dread nor fear. They lend the soul supremacy over death, have done so and will do so, while heaven and earth endure.

43. THE BETTER AFFECTIONS.

The Author of our best affections experiences them best. This must be so, for God is love. Here, and here only, is anthropomorphism conceivable, since in holiness and goodness, so far at least as it is possible for the creature to approach the Creator, man perfected and God are as one.

44. THE ANGEL BY OUR SIDE.

How many pass through life without becoming even dimly conscious that angels house beside them, that in some devoted wife, fond child, or self-denying mother, a spirit ministers to all that is precious and excellent in man. For love abates all false, degrading distinctions, makes us, in truth, free of the hierarchy of heaven.

45. THE SUBJECTION OF MATTER.

Matter obeys God as the body obeys the soul. Every human act, unless it become automatic, demands a distinct volition, whereas the divine impress suffices, apparently without further intervention. The lovely flowers bloom, richest perfumes flow, the lofty trees wave, the swift light speeds, with obedient spontaneity, for ever. Matter, in all its phases, obeys with unfaltering accuracy the primal command. To the supreme will, it would seem an equal effort to float an atom as to poise a world.

46. THE DISINTERESTED AFFECTIONS.

The disinterested affections yield loftiest evidence of infinite tenderness and love. And thus disinterested, through a provision most divine, are the affections required to prove. They are, indeed, jewels of price, the very fragrance and cynosure of heaven.

47. FAITH IN THE UNSEEN.

That faith, the worship of spirit by spirit, is indeed the substance of things hoped for, the evidence of things not seen,[1] is of all utterances most elevated, most true. Mightiest principles indeed are involved in the belief of the unseen. They are preached by all our affections, all our intelligence.[2] And thus the inner life is fostered, with reverence, and hope, and love, raising us to some parity with the spiritual hosts, the mighty community of heaven.

48. WHAT WE FIND, AND WHAT WE BRING.

The perception of religious truth, as of all excellence, varies with the culture of the inner nature and the prescription of the age. It is not only what we find in religion, but also what we bring. Like refinement, religion creates, because it discovers moral beauty. Spiritual poverty, indeed, seeks refuge in forms and ceremonies, whereas spiritual truth, with all the affections, must be seated in our heart of hearts, and in our soul of souls.

49. CREATION, OUR CARE.

God commends the world to our care, and like a father rejoices in the happiness and perfection of his creatures.[3] Models of divinest perfection subsist around.

---

[1] Εστι δὲ πίστις ἐλπιζομένων ὑπόστασις πραγματων, ἔλεγχος οὐ βλεπομένων.
[2] *Hazlett's Essay on Painting.*
[3] Bester, geliebtester Vater, erwächst nicht dem Schöpfer desto mehr Veherrlichung aus seiner Schöpfung, je vollkommener, je glücklicher seine Geschöpfe sind. *Schleiermacher's Leben in Briefen*, Band I. s.s. 56. 98.

What disinterestedness, and, so to speak, self-sacrifice, does creation not display. The affections incite us to imitate the divine, and, so far as may be, to render our conduct its very reflection and counterpart.

50. THE GOOD PHYSICIAN.

The good physician is among the truest servants of a compassionate God. Acting up to his sacred mission, he relieves the suffering, comforts the perishing and the sorrow-laden, allays the pangs which often times it is humanity's lot to endure. Endless almost, are the benefits which accrue from the conscientious exercise of medical skill. The wise and good physician vindicates God's ways, and in countless particulars approves himself the preserver and benefactor of his kind.

51. HEART'S NURTURE.

There are eyes, indeed, that beam of love, faces which nature charges with a meaning and a pathos, not belonging to the single human soul that flutters beneath them, but speaking the joys and sorrows of foregone generations, just as a nation's language may be instinct with a poesy unfelt by the lips that utter it.[1] For man cannot long abide among the dry bones of the intellect, but needs continual pasture in the feelings and affections. The affections, indeed, are as the red, red gold, they are rubies bright, they are pearls, they are divine.

Once I saw a son, a good and gentle son, one that was good unto his father, as became a son. And the

---

[1] *Adam Bede.*

father held his son's hand, and kissed it, and again kissed it. Emotion exhaled from every feature. And he said, in tones that were calculated to move an angel's sympathies, my son, my son. I find it impossible to convey in words, the impression which this scene from heaven made upon my heart, and which nothing shall efface for ever.

52. PHYSICAL AND MORAL CULTURE.

The moral loss ascribable to physical mismanagement and neglect, is indeed enormous. One gazes with painful interest on Schiller immured in his little chamber at Wiemar. The ceiling is low, the precincts are narrow and confined, and consumption, from the respiration of an ill-renewed atmosphere, is imminent. Of consumption, in effect, this magnificent man, as Goethe well terms him, died in the very flower of his years.

53. THE TREE OF LIFE.

Progressive development, with the appreciation of spiritual truth, is of moment, indeed. Unless a man be, as it were, born anew, he can hardly visit the celestial shores.[1] For how shall spiritual things be discerned, if spiritual discernment, itself, subsist not. Spiritual insight is but the soul's emancipation, the perception of the so nigh world of holiness, and faith, and truth, and love. By slow degrees, only, in this life, or were it in the next, is the shelter of the tree of life and of things spiritual, to be realised. For, whether

[1] 'Εὰν μή τις γεννηθῇ ἄνωθεν, οὐ δύναται ἰδεῖν τὴν βασιλείαν τοῦ Θεοῦ.

we live, or whether we die, it can, in this respect, make no difference, seeing that we are alike in the presence of God.

Francis of Assisi, founder of the mendicant order which bore his name, is said for fifty years to have fulfilled the resolves he made at twenty-one. Yet is it vigorous effort, not mendicancy, that is needed. For every attempt to realise some great and good ideal, in very truth, brings nobility along with it, and, as the poet sings,
> A life that bears immortal fruit,
> In such great offices as suit,
> The full-grown energies of heaven.

ASPIRATIONS

FROM

THE INNER, THE SPIRITUAL LIFE.

BOOK II.

THE polity of the Roman Church was perfect for its own purposes. It grasped the whole body of the state, and left no grade or member uncared for. But when heresy broke into the fold, and conviction instead of submission was made the basis of the new church, uniformity became impossible and sects inevitable. Then arose the proverb, *ubi una, ibi nulla*. And if a civilised community is ever again to be one fold, under one shepherd, it must be by getting through the sectarian stage, as the individual man can best do, and resolving moral, as well as material phenomena, into general laws and a universal providence. *Edinburgh Review*.

God and God's truth, need no *suppressio veri*, for reason is the field of human things, whose fruitful study brings insight into things divine. By tedious discipline, indeed, by slow providence, by inspirations addressed to the seeking intellect of the philosopher, the yearning imagination of the poet, the ardent piety of the prophet, by the sympathy of religious natures with each other, the common reason and conscience of all men, has the divine spirit sought to drive away the mists that dim our human vision. *National Review*.

ASPIRATIONS.

54. TRUEST INNOCENCE.

To be wise as serpents, harmless as doves, was Christ's emphatic counsel.[1] It was in truth the most perfect counsel. We cannot be too good or too wise. And those who would oppose it, from the first spiritual enemy to the last, they know not what they do. Then let the friends of truth be wise. But the highest wisdom is truthfulness, adhesion to those eternal interests, which nothing should be suffered to thrust aside. The individual, indeed, may be crushed, humanity outraged, but when the lamp falls another takes it up, trims the wick, replenishes the oil, in short, sustains the bright effulgence for all the coming generations of men.[2]

55. THE DIVINE IN MAN.

Well indeed has Cicero said, that in every great and good man there houses some ray of the divine.[3] One thus lighted up, becomes in veriest truth a Pharos to

---

[1] Φρόνιμοι ὡς οἱ ὄφεις, καὶ ἀκέραιοι ὡς αἱ περιστεραί.

[2] *Et quasi cursores vitaï lampada tradunt.* Sumtum à ludis quos faciebant Athenienses, in quibus is qui currebat, lampada tenebat, et cursu confecto, ei qui postea cursurus erat, lampada tradebat. *Lucretii de Rerum Natura*, Lib. ii. Francofurti, 1583.

[3] Nemo magnus sine aliquo afflatu divino unquam fuit. *De Natura Deorum.*

his kind. It must needs be so, for goodness and greatness come from God alone, alone can be realised by daily effort and care.

56. UNREAL CRIMES.

Crimes that are no crimes, connected with belief and unbelief, have been set up in every age and time. Yet belief and unbelief, if the profession be sincere, have nothing in the world in common with crime. If belief and unbelief, observes Bailey, be involuntary, to apply rewards and punishments to opinion, were absurd as to raise men to the peerage for being ruddy, to hang them for scrofula, or to whip them for the gout.[1] To set up as objects of praise and blame, things that really involve neither praise nor blame, is but to undermine the principles of morality, to play fast and loose with the best interests of our kind. All truth, conceptions the most spiritual and elevated, are self-evident and demonstrable, need, indeed, no extraneous aid or sustentation whatever. The idolatry of forms, and opinions, and times, irrespective of right and wrong, is only less reprehensible than the worship of stocks and stones.

57. THE PURE AFFECTIONS.

It is quite impossible to exaggerate the unspeakable grace and loveliness of the spiritual, the purer affections. They alone can successfully combat base addictions, earth-born passions. Beacon-lights and solace of humanity, they convert the heart in which they dwell, into a very hostelry of heaven.

[1] *On the Formation and Publication of Opinions*, Lond. 1826.

58. LIFE THROUGH DEATH.

The child within us, says Socrates, dreads death. Yet in the current of my experience I have ever found that the child proper, does not dread death at all. Through the infinite tenderness and compassion of God, death, for the most part, comes upon him like sleep or some sweet dream. If indeed there be anything touching, anything that speaks to the heart's deep fountains, it is the passing away of some gentle, innocent child.[1]

Death, in truth, is not the pit, the grave, the closed eye merely, much less the cessation of deep love, the loss of consciousness. No, it is a provision full of angelic significance, one for exalting, not debasing humanity, working out great spiritual ends, realising disinterestedness. Suffering, like some white-winged dove, oft brings down the peace of heaven on many a shattered soul. No one, indeed, can gaze upon the faces of the faithful dead, without feeling his heart yearn within him towards that purer, loftier state, which death's evangel so surely typifies and prefigures.

59. THE SEEN AND THE UNSEEN.

The intense overpoweringness of the immediate, the visible, too often obscures the appreciation of the impalpable and the unseen. Some portion at least of our consciousness should be reserved for developing the germs of spiritual life, the sustentation of the divine flame, which one day we are to light afresh upon the

---
[1] Ὸν οἱ θεοὶ φιλοῦσιν ἀποθνήσκει νέος.
Muor giovane colui ch'al cielo e caro. *Leopardi.*

altars of the invisible. Man, indeed, is placed over this lower world, but by so much as he looks forward to the future and the enduring, does he transcend creatures to whom it has not been given to aspire to a world unseen.[1]

60. CUMULATIVE INFLUENCES.

If men had but adequate faith in the mighty efficacy of cumulative influences, their constancy would more rarely flag. The difference between an elevated and an inferior race, indeed, resides in the possession of a purpose, as distinguished from mere impulse. Strenuous efforts directed to worthiest objects, liken man, in a degree, to the ineffable Essence, to whom the universe indeed is a purpose, and its perfection a never-ceasing end.

61. THE EDEN OF LIFE.

Each man, each Adam, comes into life's Eden, pure, fresh, and innocent of guile. There he remains till, as the subtle allegory has it, the Serpent, that is to say man's inferior passions and addictions, holds out the apple of sensuality and invites him to partake. If he consent, the spiritual life dies within him, at least, until happily, compliance with the moral law and the spiritual affections restore him to the Eden of his hopes, and the better life be renewed again. For moral death is death indeed, the only death which sin introduces or can introduce into this world. Here, and here only,

---

[1] Nullum est animal praeter hominem, quod habet ullam notitiam Dei. Cicero, *De Legibus*.

in man's very soul, is the celestial garden, paradise indeed, abode of truth, and love, and all the affections, else it is a Hades of evil, and misery, and despair.[1]

62. MAN AS MAN.

Morally and intellectually, if not physically, the black man and the white, the red man and the brown, are one, capable of culture and introspection, of all the spiritual affections, the great ideas of duty, and of a moral head and governor of the world. There are, in truth, many races, but humanity is one. That we are indeed one, that everywhere man is man, shall one day find acceptance on earth, as it has already found acceptance in heaven.

63. EARTH'S SALT.

Ye are the world's light, the earth's salt.[2] Such are the emphatic utterances in which the Founder of Christianity addressed those who were to transmit divinest effluences to the hearts and souls of their kind. Oft, while sympathising with those who suffer in humanity's sacred cause, we, too, would shoulder the cross with Christ, would drink the hemlock with Socrates, ascend the pile with Servetus, languish in the dungeon with Galileo, traverse the brine with Priestley, yet not the less do we crucify, poison, burn, imprison, banish, in the gentler forms, indeed, which the charities of modern life alone sanction, the man at our very doors who fain

---

[1] Fragt ihr wo Höll' und Himmel sey
 Uns wohnen beide in und bei.
      Herder, nach Swift.

[2] φῶς τοῦ κόσμου, ἅλας τῆς γῆς.

would sprinkle a little salt on the weeds of human error, venture to shed some rays of light on the yet abounding darkness. Yet, oh brothers, true associates and dear friends, faint not nor hesitate by the way. To-morrow, ye embark on the broad ocean of eternity. Ye, too, shall be revered while others fill your place. Nor is there a jewel however bright, or glorious secret, which, in the transit of the ages, ye shall not lay bare before the enraptured gaze of rescued, rejoicing humanity.

64. THE HEAVENLY LIGHT.

Prayers and praise should rise heaven-wafted towards the Infinite, and hope unbounded cling to every breast. We should have faith in God, whose silent influence is indeed everywhere, as in a parent, and in the illimitable to come. Therefore, dear heart, have courage. For see, the sun of truth gleams brightly in the darkness, grows larger, and yet larger, till it shall envelop thy whole being in the heavenly light which shines for ever and for ever.

65. MAN'S HAND.

How wondrous is the hand of man. To what moral, as well as material uses, is it not subservient, uses calculated, were they only well considered, to move us, as Galen[1] has grandly said, to hymns of deepest thankfulness. Well fare, indeed, the hand of human beneficence and mercy, and symbol, best and loftiest, the hand of God.

---

[1] Ὁν ἱστάμενοι πρὸ τῶν βωμῶν ᾖδον, ὥς φασιν, ὑμνοῦντες τοὺς Θεούς. Περὶ χρίας τῶν μορίων. *Galeni Opera,* Lipsiae, 1822.

66. UNDINE.

Undine, by the Baron de la Motte Fouqué, is the history of a soul in its passage through this superterrene life. Undine is that soul, rife with every spiritual affection, in its primal innocence and purity, as free from earthly dross and stain. The unutterable grace and loveliness of a heart untrammelled by convention or deceit, are there. There, too, are the sweetness and the excellence of truest, best womanhood, the most exalted humanity. Undine is as a flawless gem. All falsity, and soil, and unworthiness, like the ocean in conflict with some granite rock, foam, froth, and break upon her faithfulness and her truth in vain. The glory and the gorgeousness of worldly things pale before her unfaltering constancy. She is not simply of earthly, but of celestial purity and perfection. Like every great, and good, and noble spirit, hers, indeed, was a link between earth and heaven. Her trust, without reserve, or reticence, or alloy, questions nothing, doubts nothing, but is all sacrifice, and submission, and love. Undine is not perhaps higher than humanity, but she is a very lofty ideal of human virtues and perfections.

67. TOLERANCE.

The Mayflower, as has been said by the Edinburgh Review, carried to new shores the germ of a great nation, a spiritual venture, universal toleration, latent in the most inhuman of school-born theologies, universal religion in a husk of Calvinism.[1] For tolerance is a true moral

[1] Vol. xcii. p. 341.

principle, but tolerance at least implies counter-tolerance. If a man firmly conceive that he is right, surely it yields grounds for every reasonable indulgence and concession to others. A rational conviction can only spring from the exercise of reason, a loving conviction from the dictates of the heart. Heaven itself constrains not opinion.[1] For God has made free the human soul, and respects the dignity of man. Even those who would shackle it, must still appeal to that reason which they else affect to decry. Alas for those in error, yet condemn them not. For them, too, the great effulgence must one day brightly shine. Tolerance, happily, advances with the ages. Material flames have ceased to shrivel up the shrinking frame, and one day calumny, and detraction, hardly less scathing, must also cease to shrivel up the genial sympathies of the soul. Man will live more and more with God, more in accordance with the dictates of those precious capacities and spiritual affections, of which the sedulous culture alone inspires truest toleration in, and by all.

68. TRUE NOBILITY.

Such is the heaven-born nobility of our nature, that from our apparent weaknesses oft-times springs our greatest strength. The manliest, are ever the gentlest of men, and this is only consistent with moral courage and the spiritual affections, the truest and most exalted of all. The best of both sexes, indeed, approach most closely in loveable endowments. It must be so, for the virtues are of no sex. There are men, in truth, who

[1] *The New Philosophy*, London, 1853.

evince almost feminine tenderness and compassion, as there have been, and are, women of loftiest courage under circumstances the most calculated to appal. Mrs. Jameson,[1] citing Swift in corroboration, enlarges, with not less force than truthfulness, on the solidarity of all the virtues in respect of one and the other sex.

69. DIVINITY OF LOVE.

Love is humanity's greatest need. But true love, inner jewel and perfume of the soul, is also divine. For love is the seed of progress, of all excellence.[2] Through it, indeed, must men be saved. This exalted affection has no thought of self, only seeks happiness in another, and to exhale its sweetness into the soul of the beloved. It is the link of eternity, binds us at once to nature and the world. No stain in truth, may soil the pinions of the seraph. No degradation, no impurity, is compatible, or indeed possible, with true love, which, proclaiming our immortal destinies, raises us on wings of truth, and trust, and tenderness, to heaven.

70. REAL COURTESY.

There is something surely very admirable in the courtesy and devotion of knight-errantry. It was a defiance cast down to selfishness and brutality, worsting them indeed, with their own material weapons. Chi-

[1] *Ethical Fragments.*
[2] Qui vous rend un juge si sévère pour vous-même, qui vous fait penser que vous ne serez jamais assez grand, assez noble, assez dévoué, assez brave, assez désintéressé, que deux yeux s'arretent sur vous un instant.

valry, in the narrower sense, may indeed disappear, but it is well replaced by the pure life, lofty bearing, refined courtesy, and higher culture of modern times. True chivalry, else, is of no age or time, and seated in our being's depths, can never die. Other Bayards, yet other Sidneys, there are, and shall be, while earth and man endure.

71. THE WHOLE MAN.

The perfect man is the whole man. A narrow rule of life is impracticable as it is undesirable, has no sufficient hold on the inner sympathies which unite a moral purpose with a lofty aim. Spiritual religion is compatible with every exposition of the divine, the highest aspirations, the loftiest motives, the soul's eternal peace.

72. ORDER DIVINE.

We are yet greatly deficient in respect of the extreme order, neatness, and purity incumbent upon us as creatures of God. For these are a debt, a moral conquest, in truth, which civilisation owes as a just tribute to self, and a lesson to barbarism. There is evidence, indeed, that this form of regeneration also, has begun. We shall one day witness over earth's wide domain, the material welfare and moral culture, of which each is to the other the only certain and enduring correlative.

73. THE SHAGREEN SKIN.

Life, in certain respects, may be likened to the shagreen skin in the romance.[1] Each day, each hour,

[1] *Peau de Chagrin*, Balzac.

curtails its fair dimensions, brings it to a close. In the tale, indeed, the author makes the hero abuse his unexampled opportunities, lapse into a pitiful egotism, revealing a sorry conception of the intention of existence. Alas, it is too often so in this rich and various life, so abounding in jewels beyond measure or price. We perish miserably on the very brink of the waters of life and truth.[1] The rarest opportunities, boundless capacities, the loveliest affections, affections worthy indeed of earth and heaven, are flung aside or trampled upon, as if they were very dross.

74. ABSENCE OF THE DIVINE.

Professing atheists, for many reasons, must ever be few. Atheism, indeed, is a moral distortion, produced by oblique, equivocal culture, too often a narrow if not tortuous heart. Like insanity, crime, poverty, it is the disease of civilisation, or rather of what we so term. It is the mock antithesis of superstition. I would rather, says Plutarch, men should affirm there was no Plutarch, than that they should affirm I was a naughty Plutarch.[2] The atheism, however, of which I would speak, is of a yet more disastrous stamp, acknowledging God but loving him not, professing charity but evincing none, admitting God's existence with as little feeling as it is denied by some, the atheism of the heart, in short, if not the atheism of the understanding.

[1] Emerson, *The Poet*.

[2] "Ἔγωγ' οὖν ἄν ἐθέλοιμι μᾶλλον τοὺς ἀνθρώπους λέγειν περὶ ἐμοῦ, μήτε γεγονέναι τοπαράπαν μηδὲ εἶναι Πλούταρχον, ἤ λέγειν ὅτι Πλούταρχός ἐστιν ἄνθρωπος ἀβέβαιος. *De Superstitione*.

75. ASCETICISM.

To wrestle with virtue,[1] was the Stoics' maxim. They professed, indeed, not so much the regulation, as the extinction of the passions and affections, very grace and glory of the world. Stoicism, however, with all its shortcomings, was a noble cultus, prescribed moral development, and not merely the mortification of the living frame.

Like the Stoics, Spinoza esteemed virtue and good fortune as one,[2] and found the way, he conceived, in submission to God and the death of the passions.[3] This lofty egotism, however, which followed nature as its sovereign good,[4] has yielded to yet diviner lights. Stoicism, indeed, insisted on self-sacrifice, but the spiritual affections, which Stoicism did not sufficiently recognise, take us out of ourselves, and insist on sacrifice for others as well. Stoicism sacrificed the passions to the principle of perfect rectitude.[5] Death was esteemed a gate, and as Porphyry,[6] and certain Christian mystics had it, a two-fold outlet, at once from human passion and the world. The fortitude of

---

[1] Ἀσκεῖν ἀρετήν.

[2] *Ethics*, Lib. v. § 42.

[3] Spinoza zeigt dass Tugend und Glück dasselbe sind, und nur in der Liebe zu Gott, und der Tödtung aller Leidenschaften bestehen. *Ree, Wanderungen eines Zeitgenossen*, Hambro, 1857. B. i. S. 25.

[4] Etenim quod summum bonum a Stoicis dicitur, convenienter naturae vivere. Cicero, *De Officiis*, Lib. iii. cap. 3.

[5] Ἀπάθεια. Impatientia, qua animus invulnerabilis et extra omnem patientiam positus dicitur. Seneca, *Epist.* ix.

[6] Ὁ γοῦν θάνατος δυπλοῦς. *Sententiae*, ix. Cantab. 1655.

the adherents of Stoicism,[1] its bear and forbear, were in truth, admirable, paved the way for a sublimer creed and yet higher excellence, at a time when brute constraint and violence well nigh ruled the world.

76. TRUE NOBILITY.

There is something surpassing, nay, divine,[2] purest aspirations, ineffaceable tenderness, heroic devotion, consummate truth, in the great deep heart of man. Were not these displayed when Socrates stepped forward to rescue his pupil in the fight. Was it otherwise, when, greatly daring, Arnold of Winkelried, at never-to-be-forgotten Sempach, uttered the memorable words, which peal, and shall for ever peal, across the ages. Dear, true confederates, he cried, foster my wife and children, behold I clear a path for you,[3] grasping as he spoke, and burying in his breast, a sheaf of Austrian spears. Him, as Vattel said, while the centuries roll, shall Switzerland remember.[4] But patriotism, with all the virtues, never shall be wanting, while humanity endures.[5]

'Tis liberty alone that gives the flower
Of fleeting life its lustre and perfume,
And we were weeds without it.[6]

[1] 'Ἀνέχου καὶ ἀπέχου. *Sustine et abstine*, Epictetus.
 'Οἰστέον καὶ ἐλπιστέον. *Tolerandum et Sperandum*, Euripides.
[2] Est aliquid divinum.
[3] Treue liebe Eidgenossen, sorget für mein Weib und für meine Kinder, ich will euch eine Gasse machen. Müller, *Geschichte*. Band. xxi. S. 22. Tübingen, Cotta, 1816.
[4] *Law of Nations, On Noble Citizens.*
[5] Sag' an Helvetien, du Heldenvaterland,
 Wie ist dein altes Volk dem jetzigen verwand. *Haller.*
[6] Cowper.

77. FORCE AND TENDERNESS.

There are two principles in man's nature, force and tenderness. If the latter be cultivated to excess, it degenerates into weakness, if the former, into brutality. Yet heaven lends strength for the fit discharge of every task, and sweetness enough to temper it. And never was there lofty soul which had not ample admixture of both.

78. THE SEED OF HEAVEN.

The seeds of all true, and pure, and beautiful, and heavenly things are in God, that God whose silent image is everywhere. They spring from him, because they are in him, and of him, and from him. He is the very fountain of honour, and loveliness, and progress, and truth. Beauty is his quintessence, his the mother's ineffable tenderness, the father's fondness, the infant's winning smile. He is courageous with the patriot, hopeful with the philanthropist. His, is the flower's aroma, the solace of the tepid breeze, the cadence of the running stream. He smiles in the sculptor's studio, on the painter's frescoed wall. The choral voices of the children and of the birds are his, neither is he absent in the ecstasy of love, nor in any gracious, or exquisite, or ravishing thing. In fine, wherever there is light, and life, and love, there also is He, and will be, so long as man's soul endures.

79. UNITY OF RELIGIOUS TRUTH.

Religion is spoken of under various names, as if there were, or could be, any religion but One. For religion is goodness, and truth, and love, an infinite, a progressive revealing, indeed the house of God, the very gate of heaven. It is belief in the one fountain of science, and truth, and love, as well as in man himself, counterpart and image of the divine. For belief in the earnest will, the living mind, belief in a personal God, is the very kernel of the true life of man.[1] And much of religious error, as has been said, consists in making the symbol too stark and strong, so that sense, and often feeling also, are lost in sound.

80. THE INCARNATE ANGEL.

Some, nay many women and men, walk through life as angels walk in heaven. All the better spirits, intelligence, appreciation, courtesy, grace, love, with every truthful, spiritual essence, attend and mark their path. It is alike visible in what they do, as in what they leave undone. Their rectitude is, as it has well been called, a perpetual victory. And, thus, is the road to the stars. For every sweet affection, gentle word, and noble deed, and worthy thought, lend aid in building up the spiritual house, furthers the road to heaven.

81. DEVOTION AND BELIEF.

Just conclusions, feelings deep and true, coupled with the loftiest standard of self-restraint and moral earnestness, are needful indeed to man. The spiritual affections are the very guardian angels of the soul. A pseudocreed complicates, and needlessly deranges, human duties. Such, however, are nature's divine compensa-

[1] Letter from Dr. Baird.

tions, that the sincerest devotion is not incompatible with utterest error. Yet, the holder of the most perfect creed may be cold and apathetic as the stone, so that, in very truth, it imports us yet more to love than to know.

82. MANNERS.

A work, or rather series of works, on the illustrious women of the Seventeenth Century, has recently emanated from Victor Cousin's pen.[1] Angels, rather than women, sweetly justifying Dante's magnificent apostrophe,[2] seem to speak from every page. An admirable commentator on this work, again and again adverts to the surpassing charm of truly noble manners, as exponents of spiritual loveliness and grace.[3] It is an art, he truly says, for manners too are an art, the only one perchance, cultivable in earth and heaven, the highest indeed, because imitating nothing but God.

> Instructed by the heightening sense
> Of dignity and reverence
> In their true motions found.[4]

Manners in truth make us free of the angelic kingdom, and founded on goodness and love, imply the very courtesies of heaven. For, if we shall but reflect, the essential happiness of this life and of the life to come,

---

[1] *Etudes sur les Femmes Illustres du* xvii. *Siecle.* Paris, 1854.
[2] In te misericordia, in te pietate,
   In te magnificenza, in te s' aduna
   Quantunque e in creatura di bontate.
[3] *National Review*, Oct. 1856.
[4] Ben Jonson.

must needs include the commerce, itself celestial, of natures progressively elevated, with each other and with God. In the particular instances cited, beauty, station, wit, courage, magnanimity, in short, every factitious distinction and natural grace, unite, so that with excusable hyperbole the writer adverted to, has added, it seems scarcely possible, the celestial inmates themselves, should shine with brighter, purer lustre.[1]

83. MAN AND BRUTE.

The possession of an inner consciousness, and more or less perfect self-direction, by the brute, suggests very serious reflections. He owns, indeed, intellectual, and even moral capabilities, susceptible of a certain culture. In the brute, also, the phenomena which we style sensations and ideas, would seem modifications of a thinking principle.[2] In respect of self-sacrifice and attachment, the lower animals sustain advantageous comparison even with man. There is, in short, that about them, which should secure our provident sympathy and care. If not, as Cowper says,

> To feed upon immortal truth,
> To walk with God and be divinely free,

the lower tribes furnish, not the less, boundless illustration of unspeakable goodness and love.

[1] A trente-cinq ans Mme de Longueville a dit adieu au monde. Et pourtant elle est toujours la même, aussi gracieuse que majesteuse, et quelquefois aussi fière, aussi énergique et aussi sublime que Jacqueline Pascal et Angelique Arnauld. V. Cousin, *Mme de Sablé*, Paris, 1854, p. 8.

[2] Weder das Körperliche noch das Geistige als das Wahrhaft Seiende betrachten, sondern ein Drittes, von dem jede beiden nur Attribute, nur Erscheinungsweisen sind. Rée, *Wanderungen*.

84. TRAINING.

Lunacy, want, crime, disease, are terrible indications of indifference and neglect. Judicious, sufficing care, acting on a naturally sound organism, realises bodily health, not less securely than does sufficing mental and moral culture, not omitting the affections, a healthy soul. Pauperism, lunacy, crime, could not, indeed, subsist in the face of prudence and intelligence, any more than could plague, cholera, scrofula, fever, consumption, idiotcy, subsist along with bodily health. The culture of the young is the basis of all good government,[1] and we owe it at once to heaven and ourselves, to inquire into every preventible evil, whether moral or physical, and to apply the fitting remedy.

85. PROGRESSIVE RELIGION.

Religion, reconciling reason and love, the law of nature and the law of God, should be progressive, even as man's soul, his heart, his truth, his faith, his love, is progressive. Else, indeed, what were it to me?[2] Art, religion, poesy, unlike physical science, seek outward expression as regards the inner life and thoughts of God. For religion is not hope or fear merely, but spiritual beauty, and goodness, and trust, and love. It seeks the unseen, which lies behind the seen, that which includes all reality and all truth, the great ideal, archetype and earnest of heaven, which is at once the foundation of the universe and basis of the invisible.[3]

---

[1] Ἀρχὴ πολιτείας ἁπάσης νέων τροφά. Diogenes Laertius. [2] Τί πρός μέ.
[3] Wenn wir betrachten die sichtbare Welt und das Leben der Crea-

Day by day, the conviction more freshly presses, that there are indwelling principles in man and nature, absent from no place, and continually made manifest in holiness, beauty, and truth. For every doctrine that is opposed to the law of love, the law of love condemns. These are the divine, the celestial realities, which must eventually do away with all absurd, fanatical, superstitious, atheistical, heathenish dogmas and practices, bring men round to elevated conceptions, and uniting our highest nature with the infinite, the everlasting, and the unseen, for ever reconcile the soul to God and to itself.[1]

86. THE CHRISTIAN IDEAL.

How lofty was Christ's ideal of holiness, and faith, and love. Deep and all-pervasive was the religious sentiment within him. It was the devotion of a life, a soul mighty to realise the divine in man, the spirituality of religion, the religion of the heart. His was intensest sympathy, because of his conviction of the infinite value of life and of the spiritual in humanity. In him, too, was life spiritual. He strove indeed, for

turen, so finden wir darinnen das Gleichniss der unsichtbaren geistlichen Welt welche wie die Seele im Leibe in der sichtbaren Welt verborgen ist, und sehen daran das der verborgene Gott allem nahe und durch alles ist, und dem sichtbaren Wesen ganz verborgen. Jacob Boehme.

[1] Das Zeugniss des Geistes in letzer Instanz ist immer nur Bezeugung der Wahrheit durch das eigne Gewissen, das innere Wahrheitsgefühl des Gläubigen. Der einfache unabweisliche Grund dafür liegt darin, dass das Zeugniss Gottes nur erkannt werden könnte an der Wahrheit seines Inhalts. Ulrici, *Glauben und Wissen, Speculation und exacte Wissenschaft.* Leipzig, 1858, S. 324.

truth, the soul's freedom from moral error and from spiritual death, and became a sacrifice in the cause.

87. PRICE OF LIBERTY.

Eternal vigilance is the price of liberty, that liberty which else can have nor place nor name. For heaven is spiritual, and must be communed with spiritually. Every good thought, each blessed truthful affection, is a very effluence from paradise, leads to heaven away. Conscience, counterpart of the divine, is progressive, but the divine itself is unchanging and eternal. Belief, living for great ends, should also grow, the affections not drifting one way, the convictions another. For man's intelligence may not safely war with the feelings, but expand with them in unison and harmony for ever.

88. DESERT.

It ought to be blazoned in letters of adamant, graven in characters of light in the heart's chancery, that the best crowns in the divine gift, devolve not upon success but on desert. For desert is the very jewel and pearl of the soul, earnest and forecast of heaven.

89. A DIVINE ENVIRONMENT.

How adverse would it prove to every low mean thought and base unworthy impulse, were we only duly conscious of the divine environment. If even a revered human presence realise this precious efficacy, how much more the unseen spiritual presence which is with us of necessity and at all times. We should pause ere we ventured to sully the silken pinions, or the snow-white vesture, of a single angelic friend. For God, and spirits, of the infinite, are with us, and present always.

90. THE CURRENT OF EXISTENCE.

There is no delay in the great issues of existence. The divine business is transacted without delay. The vast current of being rushes onward without hesitancy or pause for ever. We are moving with the stream, whose swiftness we do not at once discover. For,

> Thou carriest us off as with a flood,
> We vanish hence like dreams.[1]

And in a little, our generation and our time will be swept into the illimitable ocean of infinity, to be replaced by fresh generations, new activities, yet more sufficing to God's glory and man's celestial destinies.

91. WORKING WITH GOD.

It is the mightiest aim to work with God. For religion is not a charm to win salvation by stealth, sudden illuminations, or sleight of hand withal, but the development of the soul in goodness, intelligence, and truth, the culture of every spiritual affection, nearness, in a word, to God. Only by self-knowledge can we attain to the knowledge of God.[2] Man comes to know the divine through knowing himself. The very wealth and excellence of humanity consist in our approximation to God. For this is the real election, correspondence with, and receptivity of, things divine. Spiritual safety, indeed, can only be compassed by faith coupled with charity, in thought and affection, habitual goodness in

[1] Psalm xc.   [2] Tholuck.

aspiration and in action, realising heaven in the soul. The soul happily is adapted to lay hold of celestial truth, and to become a progressive, conscious participator in the very life of God.[1] He speaks, it is the essence of his most divine revelation, through the voices of man's spiritualized motives and affections. For religion, as a living trust, is indeed reasonable, conformable with the divine, and with every truthful, sacred, holy thing.

92. PROVIDENCE.

Providence, divine Providence, seizes upon each several evil, disciplines, and eventually turns it to good. It is a wondrous, glorious process, but one which we do not always rightly fathom. To suppose, indeed, that He who is all power, all goodness, all knowledge, should tolerate perpetual evil, were an intolerable imputation on that power, that wisdom, and that goodness. For evil is suffered but for a time, permitted only to be eliminated from God's providence, and blotted out of His creation and His most holy empire for ever.

93. DIGNITY OF HUMAN NATURE.

To think meanly of human nature is a base, unworthy thing, at utter variance with man's inherent desert and dignity. For evil and imperfection are indeed earth-born and bounded, whereas purity and truth are inherent as they are boundless, susceptible of development and increase for ever.

Goodness and wickedness are unappeasable foes. One must necessarily overcome and devour the other. And

[1] Maurice.

therefore it is that elevation and advancement, as respects the knowledge of God and things invisible,[1] is the great and never-ceasing requirement of our souls.

94. YOUTH ETERNAL.

We shall again be young. The morning stars shall sing to us as in their prime. We shall love the flowers, smiles of God, very types and archetypes of paradise, with all the beautiful things of earth and heaven. Spiritual truth indeed is dependent, entirely dependent, on psychology.[2] For while nature conceals, man rises above her, and becomes to himself, the revelation of the divine. On psychology, then, for the testimony of consciousness is the criterion of all knowledge, depends wholly the proof of man's moral nature and the existence of God, as of every celestial, truthful, holy thing.

95. DIVINITY OF BENEFICENCE.

The beneficent influence of a single good man or woman on our species, it is impossible to exaggerate. For this, in its lower degree, is like unto the great Spiritual Presence itself, which frees, and one day shall entirely set free and transfigure, all mankind.

> 'Tis liberty of heart derived from heaven,
> The liberty that gives the flower
> Of fleeting life its lustre and perfume.[3]

A real effluence of holiness, and love, and truth pervades the moral atmosphere around, and, like a charmed

[1] Locke, *On Education.*
[2] Sir W. Hamilton. *Lectures on Metaphysics.* Edinburgh, 1858.
[3] Cowper.

circle, keeps every base, and wicked, and brutal thing at bay.

In a corner of Madely churchyard, now rifely beset with weeds and docken, is a tomb, on which is graven the name of one who shed this heavenly effluence. For his was a real existence of charity, and faith, and love. There was an Irish Dean, too, a man of such spiritual potency as to impress the most impassive. His, indeed, were tones that could evoke charity from hearts of stone. Fletcher's deeds and Kirwan's words should not lightly be forgotten. But infinite, almost, is the impress of beneficence on our kind. When once the angelic presence is felt, loved, and known, hearts bow gladly responsive to the precious influence.

96. TO SEEM AND TO BE.

Would we seem a thing, let us be it. Would we do a thing, let us do it. Would we aspire, let us realise that aspiration. For goodness can only be compassed by goodness, holy thoughts by deeds of holiness, and the glories of the inner life through the strenuous efforts of the living soul.[1]

97. DISINTERESTED AFFECTION.

Admirably illustrative of God's ineffable tenderness and goodness, is the production of the disinterested, the spiritual affections in the heart of man. For it is a canon most certain, most true, that if we love with deep affection, that affection comes finally to subsist inde-

---

[1] Das innere eines Menschen kann nicht das Werk des Andren sein. Schleiermacher to Eleonora. G. *Leben in Briefen.* B. 1. S. 368.

pendently of all return. And this result it is, given by the hand of God himself,[1] that realises or helps to realise, a heaven in the heart and eternity in time.[2]

98. THE CHURCH OF THE FUTURE.

Much has been said and written about the church of the future, but it is here present, it is also now. The church invisible has no distinction of sect or nation. Its members are everywhere. Unpaid, so far as material rewards are concerned, they work for the common weal. This church exists in the east, it exists in the west, it knows no distinction of north or south. It acknowledges all peoples, celebrates it services in every tongue. The orisons of the faithful ascend from every clime. Its members hear betimes of each other, sometimes by what they do, sometimes also by what they suffer. They perchance know each other when they meet. Worshippers of one true God, they do not malign opponents, or seek to consign them to moral perdition and social death. Members, too, abound in all the churches, but all the churches are not members. The church of the future, the invisible, the universal church, is increasing, must increase, for it comprises the right thinkers and well-doers at once of earth and heaven.

99. THE BRIDGE.

Love associates this world with the next by more than adamantine bonds, links that sunder never. The

---

[1] Die seltene Momente wo wirklich der Himmel im Herzen ist und die Ewigkeit in der Zeit. *Id.* to Henriette v. Willich. B. 2. S. 136.
[2] Maurice, *Lectures to Ladies*, 3rd ed. p. 8.

darlings who have left us, we shall meet again. We cannot cease to love them, and they, we are assured, do not cease to love us. And thus, O God, love bridges the abyss, and even here, unites those whom death and time have for some brief period severed.

100. SPIRITUAL INFLUENCES.

As material influences sustain our bodies, so do spiritual influences sustain our souls, ascending thus to higher realities, aspiration on aspiration, progress on progress, for ever. That only can be considered a real limitation which chokes the springs of spiritual life, severs us from God. For all self-imposed limitation, and every new duty is a limitation, which is a condition of a real exercise of the spiritual or higher life, is the reverse of a real limitation,[1] reconciles us in so far with God.

101. THE CHARITIES OF HEAVEN.

Through God's infinite charity, the pure, the spiritual affections are restricted to no class or condition of men. Sweetly, freely, do they spring up like flowers in the very gardens of heaven. One were, in truth, angelic, could one but maintain the holy frame which they so often induce. Behold the untiring constancy, the unspeakable generosity of women, the celestial confidingness of childhood, the countless beneficence of the poor. Love, through divinest intuition, proceeds to instant action, plays its angelic part, were it in the veriest depths of desolation and despair. For love,

[1] *National Review*, July, 1859.

with all the spiritual affections, is indeed the spiritual life of man. We cannot love enow.[1] Love it is, which frees us from the sin and stain else prone to mutilate the dear deep heart of man.[2] In virtue of the affections, angels dwell along with us in every strait and care, abandoning us never till they land us, and land with us, on the celestial shores. Thus, the divine is ceaselessly at hand, and providence for ever nigh.

102. GREAT THINKERS.

Great thinkers are the very salt and glory of the earth, rescue it from spiritual despotism, the tyranny of unreasoning, prescriptive thought, in a word, spiritual slavery and the idolatry of days and forms. According to their measure, they are a continual inculcation of goodness, and holiness, and truth, the very children of light and of the sun.[3] Regardless of material interests merely, they realise a higher life, the poetry of life, life and poetry together,

> Innumerous spirits who sun themselves
> Outside of time.[4]

For on them, and such as them, plays the very air of heaven, the divine afflatus which comes we know not whence, and goes we know not whither.[5]

103. THE CURATE OF MEUDON.

With all his faults, the Curate of Meudon was among the first of his time. Like Picus of Mirandola, ad-

---

[1] Tholuck, *Guido and Julius*, tr. Lond. 7th Ed. pp. 13, 107.
[2] M. Retsch, *Die Schachspieler*.
[3] Γένος τοῦ Θεοῦ. [4] *Aurora Leigh*.
[5] Τὸ πνεῦμα ὅπου θέλει πνεῖ, ἀλλ' οὐκ οἶδας πόθεν ἔρχεται καὶ ποῦ ὑπάγει.

mirable in literature and science alike, he might have sustained a concursus on all known things.[1] Rabelais received the commendation of De Thou, even Guinguené discusses his influence on the French Revolution. The author of Pantagruel, he says, attacked ignorance in the spirit of a true philosopher, casting down idols and removing prejudice. He assumed, indeed, for safety's sake, the cap and bells, uttering momentous truths as if in jest.[2] His precepts on education, or many of them, even now are admirable.[3] Lafontaine, Boccaccio, Bacon, Montaigne, and Montesquieu, with Molière, Sterne, and Swift, were all, I conceive, indebted to him. Of these, Montaigne, perhaps, was only less outspoken than himself.[4] Michel de L' Hopital, indeed, opposed the Cardinal de Lorraine, when the latter would have introduced the Inquisition into France. Yet, Rabelais did not scruple to ridicule that Francis the First, who cast human beings into the flames in Paris, butchered them at Merindol. Bartholomew's Day he did not see, though he witnessed its lurid aurora. But not the less in Paris than in Rome, all who were found to countenance such blood-stained doings, incurred the trenchant irony of his pen.

[1] De omni re scibili.

[2] Scriptum edidit ingeniosissimum, quo vitae regnique cunctos ordines, quasi in scoenam, sub fictis nominibus produxit, et populo deridendo propinavit.

[3] Comment Gargantua feut institué par Ponocrates en telle discipline qu'il ne perdoyt heuro de iour. *Oeuvres*, Chap. 23. Paris, 1835.

[4] C'est içi un livre de, bon foy lecteur. *Essuis*, Paris, An x.

104. THE DIVINE KINGDOM.

In the better life it is more blessed to give than to receive. And thus it is, that God sheds blessings on us ceaselessly, with love greatest of all. To some, indeed, the rising sun, the gushing streams, sea, sky, and air, the play of man's great powers, shall seem dull and drear, while to others they are as opening paradise, glimpses of that fair region where highest hopes shall be converted into angelic certainties. For sin, and disease, and death, with ignorance, and poverty, and care, are to be considered not so much mere heirlooms of past delinquency, as imperfections to be got rid of, means, in short, whereby to compass knowledge, goodness, holiness, and the better life to come.

It is the divine intention that each soul should dwell in duty, and through duty compass happiness and victory, proceeding from conquest to conquest, and into the celestial city at last. For each just, and true and pure aspiration is a possession for ever, yields fresh spiritual insight, conducts us in fine to heaven.

So long as we labour under the metaphysical illusion of treating sin and crime as entities produced by a personal evil genius, instead of looking upon them as a departure from God, the true good, but else transitional and eradicable, the influence of a sound theology, founded upon and united with a true psychology, on education and training, will remain nugatory. It is a contradiction, in terms, to speak of evil as innate, whereas it is goodness that is innate, as it is everlasting.

For evil, fortuitous indeed, and transitory, is inevitably eliminated in the soul's progress through time and eternity.

It is perilous to lose sight of moral distinctions in quest of things in themselves insoluble, or if solved, of no account. For the theology of God is simplicity itself, consists in approaching him, whereas the theology of the theologian too often is unintelligible even to himself.

Every thing essential to our spiritual safety has been made plain, were it to the heart and intelligence of the child. Evil is not infinite but good is infinite. Evil is not eternal, but good is eternal, even as love is eternal. Therefore, as contrasted with good, evil, were it never so great, never so oppressive, let us dare to hope and to believe, must become as nothing in the future of God and of time. For the seeds of holiness which subsist in all, shall one day overcome the evil that is in them. In innocence and purity do we enter on the stage of being, in innocence and purity, despite of every lapse and imperfection, through the infinite mercy, and goodness, and wisdom, and lovingness of God, shall we finally and for ever emerge upon it.

ASPIRATIONS

FROM

THE INNER, THE SPIRITUAL LIFE.

BOOK III.

Γλαύκων. Πῶς.

Σώκρατις. Τὸν ἥλιον τοῖς ὁρωμένοις οὐ μόνον, οἶμαι, τὴν τοῦ ὁρᾶσθαι δύναμιν παρέχειν φήσεις, ἀλλὰ καὶ τὴν γένεσιν καὶ αὔξην καὶ τροφήν, οὐ γένεσιν αὐτὸν ὄντα.

Γλαύκων. Πῶς γάρ.

Σώκρατις. Καὶ τοῖς γιγνωσκομένοις τοίνυν μὴ μόνον τὸ γιγνώσκεσθαι φάναι ὑπὸ τοῦ ἀγαθοῦ, παρεῖναι, ἀλλὰ καὶ τὸ εἶναί τε καὶ τὴν οὐσίαν ὑπ' ἐκείνου αὐτοῖς προσεῖναι, οὐκ οὐσίας ὄντος τοῦ ἀγαθοῦ, ἀλλ' ἔτι ἐπέκεινα τῆς οὐσίας πρεσβείᾳ καὶ δυνάμει ὑπερέχοντος. Plato.

Nos ne nunc quidem oculis cernimus ea quae vidimus, neque enim est ullus sensus in corpore, sed viae quasi quaedam sunt ad oculos, ad aures, ad nares, a sede animi perforatae. Itaque saepe aut cogitatione, aut aliqua vi morbi impediti, apertis atque integris et oculis et auribus, nec videmus, nec audimus, ut facile intelligi possit, animum et videre et audire, non eas partes quae quasi fenestrae sunt animi, quibus tamen sentire nihil queat mens, nisi id agat et adsit. Cicero.

ASPIRATIONS.

105. TRAINING SOULS FOR GOD.

Let us train souls heaven-ward, yet, so as to enhance the power of effort and self-mastery. For these, no formula, no precept, can replace. There is no other way to develop the individual man, to secure admission into the safe havens of God's eternal love, where every shortcoming, with all remorse, and guilt, and dread, must be put for ever away.[1] For no one can discharge the spiritual indebtedness of another. Each several soul, overcoming obstacles, repelling every slight and stain, must for itself aspire to heaven.

106. ONE PROVIDENCE, ONE INSPIRATION.

As there are not two divine providences but one divine providence, so there are not two divine inspirations, but one divine inspiration. For, well understood, a general and an individual providence, a general and a special inspiration, severally, as coming from God, are the same. In our weakness and inexperience we would crave continuous aid, would climb each steep ascent,

---

[1] Die vollendete Entwickelung der menschlichen Persönlichkeit muss wesentlich zugleich als das absolute Zugeeignetsein des Menschen an Gott gedacht werden. Rothe, *Theologische Ethik, Das vollendete Reich Gottes*, B. 2, S. 154. Wittenberg, 1844, 1848.

descend each rugged slope, with the assistance of another. But God imparts strength enough, his infinite oversight, his unutterable love and care, suffice for all. We have only to discharge, were it in our sorest need, the duty at hand. The sense of desert, the consciousness of a joyous, hopeful, striving, responsible existence, should be roused within our souls, and there fostered and sustained for ever.[1] For all true conversion is unison with God, approving itself in faith in Him, and faith in our fellows, as evinced and wrought out in the spiritual and moral life of man.

107. RELIGIOUS TRUTH.

Religious truth can never die. Its roots lie deeply bedded in the very heart and soul of man. But religious truth has been associated with religious error, and men, unwittingly, have cherished both. Science, however, for like faith and love science is eternal, science will eliminate the error, will unfold the truth. Then science and religion, sister seraphs, shall walk together, hand in hand, sustaining man in this life, as in the heaven which awaits him in the end.[2]

108. THE SPIRIT OF THE UNIVERSE.

As the soul of man is to the body, so is the Spirit of God to the universe. An African traveller it was,[3] who, sick, sorrowing, and alone, turned wistfully to the blue

---

[1] Γύμναζε δὲ σεαυτὸν πρὸς εὐσέβειαν.

[2] So mündet das Erdenleben mit seiner Vollendung in das Himmelsleben aus. Rothe, *Ethik*, *Das vollendete Reich Gottes*.

[3] Park.

flower which met his fevered gaze, comforted with the deep assurance that heaven was also with him, not less than with the tender flower. But the universe is a mighty epic, of which no philosophy, no poesy, ever yet has told the tale.[1]

109. MORAL DEATH.

The only death is moral death. The body, indeed, perishes, yet still are we God's children.

> There is no death, what seems so is transition.
> This life of mortal breath
> Is but a suburb of the life Elysian,
> Whose portal we call death.[2]

We leave nothing in the grave.[3] The change concerns the material only, and was attendant on life from the beginning. For man through it must realise the fulness of existence, and find his proper element in the ocean of immensity.[4]

110. LIVING DAY BY DAY.

To live each day as it were the last, is perhaps too much to expect of our humanity. Yet is it best to be

[1] Schelling.   [2] Longfellow.
[3] La mort ne nous ravit rien de notre être, rien de notre personalité, de notre esprit, de nos facultés, de notre amour, de nos affections. Tout en nous sera grand comme le ciel, grand comme l'immortalité. A. Coquerel, *La Mort Seconde*, Paris, 1850,
[4] In der unbeschränkten Communicationen mit aller Sphären der Schöpfung schleisst sich dem menschlichen Geschlecht eine unendliche Fulle von Gemeinschaft und Liebe auf. Alle Lebensquellen des Universums durchströmen nun die Menschheit, die ihr eignes Leben in den Ocean dieses allgemeinen Lebens hineinergeisst, und es aus ihm in unendlich gesteigerter Fülle wieder Zurückempfängt. Rothe, *Ethik, Die Letzte Dinge*, B. II. S. 159.

prepared when the end, the second life, the new birth indeed, arrives. The glory of it, however, is, that there is no end, but that the first day of our consciousness is also the first of eternity, and that for ever and yet for ever, must that consciousness endure.

111. A JUST APPRECIATION.

The manner and the form of our knowledge, as the Schoolmen were so well aware, depend exceedingly on the character and condition of the intelligence at the period of receiving it.[1] Were this important truth once duly appreciated, it would lead to a more reverent appreciation of man's great capacities and immortal nature, as well as to an infinitely increased forbearance in respect of his shortcomings and failings.

112. TRUE PRECISION.

A divine exactitude, so to speak, is required of us. The exquisite precision that obtains in the works of God, enchants the observant mind, testifies to his providential care, and prevision of things to come. In the sun's face we see his beauty, in the fire his fostering warmth, in the water his refreshing gentleness,[2] everywhere, in truth, his boundless exactitude and skill.

113. THE SERAPH WITHIN.

Mightiest possibilities lurk in every breast. We are, indeed, greater than we seem, greater than we know. The seraph that houses within, is ever there. So all

---
[1] Species cogniti est in cognoscente.
[2] Jeremy Taylor, *Guide to Eternal Happiness*.

excellence, every dormant virtue, should be roused into exultant development, nor is there a quality befitting us for earth, or commending us to heaven, which ought not to be elicited in every soul.

114. THE SOUL IN THE VOICE.

There are voices that bespeak the reality of generous culture or its opposite, the influence or the silence of elevated sentiment, those spiritual affections, which bring us nigh God, and realise community with celestial purity and truth. Love is among the sources of this, as of every great, and good, and generous thing, indeed life's very tree. At intervals, in truth, one hears tones that thrill the heart, utterances of passion-fraught emphasis, and voices that vibrate to the melodies of heaven.

115. THE TREE OF LIFE.

We are images of clay, of iron, or of gold. In some the clay predominates, in some the rugged iron, and in some, dear God, the red, red gold. But to all it is not given to mount amid the branches of the tree of life,[1] and straightway compass heaven.[2]

116. A NOBLE BOOK.

Each noble, excelling book does a portion of God's work. For, like a thing of beauty, a good book is in truth a possession for ever. A volume full of falsehood, malice, and invective, in short open or covert wicked-

[1] Rade volte risurge per le rámi
 L'umana probitate. Dante, *Del Purgatorio*, Canto vii.
[2] Beata l'alma che lassa tal pondo,
 E va nel ciel, dove e compita zoglia.

ness, wrings the heart, distresses the intelligence. And what a luxury is a good book. It becomes as it were a dear friend, revealing secrets from the invisible, realising not only the harmonies of nature,[1] but the very fragrance of heaven. Thus, a manual of devotion or philosophy, some old chronicle or volume of poor plays, speaking to the heart and from the heart, shall become indeed a treasure, snatching man from earth, bearing him to the empyrean, and realising satisfactions from the infinite.

117. LOOKING HEAVEN-WARD.

To look heaven-ward, is as a golden thread shot through purple tissue, interpenetrating every thought and action of our lives. For a divine providence is everywhere, now in some glorious deed or aspiration, the spiritual kingdom of odours, colours, and sound, the sheen of the yellow flower, strains of delicious harmony, surpassing work of art, or natural adaptation. How different indeed, are such teachings from the recital of formulas, once perchance replete with vitality and truth, but now grown old and sere. We require, indeed, fresh utterances from the heart, not the mere thoughts and words of those who worked and strove long years ago, but living, loving experiences, direct and flowing from heaven.

118. EFFORT.

The one word effort, symbolizes a universe of thought. For, well understood, everything, all the mighty crea-

---

[1] Einklang mit der ganzen Natur. Hoffmann.

tions of God, is effort visible or implied. If man had but true faith in it, he would be mightier, wiser, better than he is.[1] Unimaginable, in truth, is the virtue of persistent effort. Effort, indeed, is the exponent and the concrete of the law of progress, that progress without which there could be nor life, nor providence, nor movement. It is in truth, life, and happiness, and hope, whereas inertia is torpor, and listlessness, and doom.

119. SHADOWS.

I knew a dog with assuredly the strangest addiction, for a dog, that ever was. Its nightly passion was to pursue, with many an impatient cry and bound, its shadow on the wall. And thus do men themselves pursue shadows, nay, the shadows of shadows. A merchant, just deceased, died worth, was it a soul full of knowledge, affections human and divine. No, but three, or, as the blatant chronicle recorded it, it might be nearer four millions gold. Yet, this poor, rich man died, it seems, dreading poverty.

Do you not perceive, O wealth-seeker, that when you cultivate riches for riches' sake, you pursue a dream, the shadow of a dream.[2] Your houses, lands, hereditaments, cannot follow you to the tomb. And if they did, what would they avail in a land where a single affection is of greater moment than the untold wealth of the material universe.

---

[1] Fiendliche Prinzipe fallen dich an, und nur die innere Kraft, mit der, Du den Anfechtungen widerstehst, kann dich retten von Schmach und Verderben. Hoffmann.

[2] Σκιᾶς ὄναρ, Pind. Καπνοῦ σκιά, Soph. Traum eines Traumes, Hegel.

120. LIFE NO DREAM.

Quickly, quickly, doth life flit, even as a dream away. Thus wrote to me, citing the lovely words of the Sicilian poet, a soul now housed in paradise. He, the poet indeed, likened life to a dream,[1] the Spaniard called it sleep.[2] No, by the lofty heavens, it is not all sleep, nor yet a dream, quickly though it pass away, but a scene rich in noblest action, loftiest aspirings, the very forecourt and outpost of heaven, true arena of the multitudinous inspiration and providence of God.

121. THE FAITHFUL DEAD.

Forget them not the faithful dead.[3] Such is the legend, graven on tablets of stone, in one of the multitudinous battle sepulchres of Germany. No, forget them never, those who, faithful to their sacred trust, fought well life's fitful battle and perished in the act. For, were it not for these, and such as these, the world would become a sty and men mere rooting swine.

122. TO KNOW, TO BE, AND TO DO.

To know, to be, and to do, are all resumed in the conduct of the nobly good and wise. To such, to seem

---

[1] Ταχὺς γὰρ παρέρχεται ὡς ὄναρ ἢ βη. Theocritus, *Idyl* 27, line 8.

[2] Que es la vida. Un frenesé.
   Que es la vida. Una ilusion,
      Una sembra, una ficcion,
         . . . la vida es sueño,
      Y los sueños sueño son.
            Calderon, *La Vida es Sueño*. Jornada II.

[3] Vergiss die treuen Todten nicht.

and to be, to dare and to do, in very deed are one. For character and fate, oh golden truth, are only other names for one and the same conception.[1] An over-timid, meticulous conscience, straining at flies, slurs life's great aims in a fritter of needless anxieties, since in a life of real grandeur, as some great soul has said, petty cares are unknown.

123. A DIVINE IDEAL.

A divine ideal has been shed upon our souls, one that cannot die. From the same do we derive the mighty conception of the fatherhood of God, the brotherhood of Man. And thus does life assume an infinite significance, become associated with thoughts of eternity and of heaven.

124. IMPULSE AND PRINCIPLE.

Impulse and principle, intuition and judgment, should, if it were possible, be one. They can only, indeed, become so, through early training, as well as sustained effort, the tireless patience and unconquerable hope, which make duty, and inclination, and resolve, firmly and indissolubly one.[2] For only through belief comes love, and truth, and eternity.[3]

---

[1] Schicksal und Gemüth sind nur verchiedene Namen desselben Begriffs. Novalis, *Schriften*. Berlin, 1826.

[2] L'esprit juste, le coeur droit, enfin la grande route du sens commun et de la conscience universelle. Victor Cousin, *Oeuvres*, Quatrième Serie, Paris, 1849.

[3] Nur in dem Glauben ist die Liebe, und die Wahrheit, und die Ewigkeit. Hoffman, *Gesammelte Schriften*. Berlin, 1845.

125. WOMAN'S GRACE.

Grace was in her steps, heaven in her eye,
In every gesture dignity and love.

Such is the poet's unsurpassed, and indeed, unsurpassable delineation of the mother and parent of our kind. And such, did man but do his duty by them, might every woman become.[1] For what initiation, then, do we wait, is there not already divinest warrant for the task.

In a London print, a little girl, we find it said, some vagrant daughter of glorious Eve, was recently consigned to Wandsworth gaol, for pulling things, by means of hair-lines, off her parents' shelves, causing it to be imagined that the house was haunted. What neglect, what evil training, what vile antithesis, is here. Why did not the rector or the sitting magistrate, who it seems had to do with the affair, take the child to his home, or place her in some asylum where her poor heart might have been swayed by the invisible hair-lines of love, haunted, indeed, with things of heaven.

126. MORAL CONQUEST.

Each successful moral effort is a struggle, indeed, and victory. For there are no efforts more arduous than spiritual ones. It is, in truth, the mightiest

---

[1] Eclairer, instruire, perfectionner les femmes comme les hommes, les nations comme les individus, c'est encore le meilleur secret pour tous les buts raisonables, pour toutes les relations sociales et politiques auxquelles on veut assurer un fondament durable. De Stael, *De la Literature*, Tome II. p. 157. Paris, 1812.

achievement to place things in a just light, satisfying at once the intelligence and the heart, gaining, thus, far-off glimpses of the spiritual house and palaces of ecstasy.

127. A SOUL.

In veriest truth, we are spirits in the flesh. The body shields a soul, a living, loving, yet unseen, immortal soul. For the body is not the man, but the soul only,[1] whose purification and development should be life's mighty end and aim.

128. A CONFESSION.

Written in the beautiful round-hand of the period, in the fly-leaf of an old edition I possess of the Aphorisms of Hippocrates, is the confession of V. F. Christ is to me the way, the life, the truth.[2] Doubtless the confession was one not made in vain. To imitate, not merely profess, so mighty an Exemplar, the divine philosophy of him who bade the erring one sin no more, that so, sweetest of formulas, each trespass should be forgiven, his walk, his life, his truth, to relieve the morally sick and destitute, to comfort and enlighten, averting spiritual death,[3] in fine, to further, to the utmost, the eternal safety and moral well-being of our kind, is of all ambitions most holy, most just, most pure.

[1] Ἡ ψυχή σὺ, τὸ δὲ σῶμα σόν. *Hieroclis Commentarii in aurea Pythagorae Carmina.* Cantab. 1709.

[2] Christus est mihi via, vita, et veritas. A.D. 1687.

[3] Τοῦ θανάτου τοῦ δευτέρου.

129. KEPLER.

Man's soul is the counterpart of the universe, he himself a fellow-worker with God, and at one with the purposes of heaven. Thus was it with Kepler, a man of science indeed,[1] one steeped in goodness, intelligence, and truth. His was of the genius which elevates and regenerates our kind. As men, he says, enjoy dainties at the dessert, so do wise souls gain a relish for heaven. I thank thee, Lord and Master, he exclaims, in hymns of real praise, that thou hast ravished my soul with the work of thy hands, the light and life-giving sun, stars strewn through infinite space.[2]

All truth, all law, indeed, he named a thought of God,[3] and every outward thing a symbol of the divine. Philosophy and religion with him were as one. His candour,

---

[1] *Prodromus* 1597. *Harmonices Mundi*, 1697.

[2] Grosser Künstler der welt, Ich schaue wundernd die Werke
Deiner Hände, nach fünf künstlichen Formen erbauet
Und in der Mitte die Sonn'. Auspenderin Lichtes und Lebens,
Die nach heil'gem Gesetz zügelt die Erden und lenkt
In verschiedenem Lauf. Ich seh' die Mühen des Mondes,
Und dort Sterne zerstreut auf unermessener Flur—
Vater der Welt, was bewegte dich, ein armes, ein kleines
Schwaches Erdgeschöpf so zu erheben, so hoch,
Dass es inGlanz dasteht, ein weithin herrschender König,
Fast ein Gott, denn er denkt deine Gedanken dir nach
Herrscher der Welt. Du ewige Macht. Durch alle die Welten
Schwingt sich auf Flügeln des Lichts dein unermessener Glanz.
            Herder, nach Kepler, *Myst. Cosmograph.*

[3] La verité n'est que la pensée de Dieu. Quand l'homme y arrive il pense ce que Dieu pense, et la pensée de Dieu est toujours sainte et parfaite comme lui. Coquerel.

patience, and perseverance, were, indeed, unbounded. Rodolph II. his protector, tormented him to relinquish astronomy for astrology. The confessors of Rodolph plagued him to become a Roman-Catholic. The Lutherans, his co-religionists, persecuted him because he would not condemn the Calvinists. Tycho-Brahé besought him to abandon what he termed the reveries of Copernicus. The misfortunes of war drove his wife mad, while he himself was obliged to hurry off to protect his aged mother, accused of sorcery and condemned to the rack. Worn out with toil and sheer exhaustion, he died sweetly and greatly, as he had lived, after vainly riding to the Diet at Ratisbon in search of arrears of pay, leaving but some two-and-twenty rixdollars in his purse.[1] Yet was this ornament of humanity styled an atheist. But Kepler will be honoured while our race endures, or a tongue remains to proclaim that Being to whose glory he has erected a monument thrice sublime.

130. THE BODY.

The body, the rapidly-fleeting body, is not mere dust and corruption, but of the glorious works of God. Its chemical and vital changes are simply marvels of the divine. The ancients, perhaps, placed it on too high a platform, assuredly, we leave it on one too low. A body, indeed, maintained in health, and purity, and

[1] So hoch war noch kein Sterblicher gestiegen
Als Kepler gestieg—und starb in Hungersnoth,
Er wusste nur die Geister zu vergnügen,
Drum liessen ihn die Körper ohne Brod. Kästner.

well-being, subserving the purposes of God, is, in truth, a glorious tribute to the power which called it into being and sustains it as it is.

131. THE DIVINE EVERYWHERE.

God is in the storm not less than in the calm, in the waste as in the garden and the ploughed field. Nothing can subsist apart from Him. There is not a tyranny, whether of one or many, the cruelest fanaticism, atheism the most heartless, epidemies the most devastating, sins the most revolting, which have not their origin in conditions, which, however perverted and outraged, are not the less, when wisely ordered, sources of tranquillity and peace, results in all respects divine.[1]

> With steadfast faith that sin may be forgiven,
> And love like this to be renewed in heaven,
> Poor is the heart adversity can break
> And loss is gain for love and pity's sake.[2]

132. CELESTIAL LAW.

The celestial laws assert themselves.[3] Strength, honour, purity, lie folded up in them for ever. They are, indeed, a stern Nemesis or a law of love. But unlike some earthly laws, they ever welcome back the

---

[1] L'homme a beau s'agiter, il s'agite dans un circle inflexible. Ses appétits, ses besoins, ses exces, même, tout le ramène à un ordre contre lequel il ne peut rien. Au moral comme au physique, par ses vices comme par ses virtus, il obeit à des lois mysterieuses et inflexibles. Alphonse Karr.

[2] Mackay, *The Triumph of Love.*

[3] Wollaston, *Religion of Nature Delineated,* London, 1750, p. 265.

penitent offender, suggest, in truth, the peace and the trust which are of heaven.

133. SOUL-CULTURE.

After all, humanity's greatest hope and most precious healing, resides in the culture of the soul. As a mighty teacher has said, we are to ponder things truthful, and just, and pure, and lovely, and good.[1] For the spiritual fruits are love indeed, and peace, and goodness, and patience, and gentleness, and joy, with faith in the life to come.

134. DUTIES, OURS.

Duties, indeed, are ours, events are God's. The pursuit of truth is man's especial business, but the consequences of its discovery concern a higher power.[2] Niebuhr, whom Bunsen most justly characterises as a man of vast intellect, simplicity, and singleness of purpose, speaks of a city the women of which were deficient to that degree in mental culture, as not even to have a suspicion of its existence. But this city, alas, is also the world, its inhabitants are men.

135. TO CONFER HAPPINESS.

The most exalted happiness, indeed, is to confer happiness. God, we may not doubt it, enjoys the satisfactions of his creatures. And while in our measure we

---

[1] "Ὅσα ἐστὶν' ἀληθῆ, ὅσα σεμνὰ, ὅσα δίκαια, ὅσα ἁγνὰ, ὅσα προσφιλῆ, ὅσα εὔφημα—Ἀγάπη, χαρὰ, εἰρήνη, μακροθυμία, χρηστότης, ἀγαθωσύνη, πίστις.

[2] La verité est l'affaire de l'homme, les consequences sont l'affaire de Dieu. Athanase Coquerel.

benefit others, we imitate, in truth, while we also realise the divine.[2]

136. FAITH AND WORKS.

In our moral life, faith and works are mutually complementary, and co-essential. To him who has the constant purpose, the resolute will, must arrive the fitting occasion, the right season. Him, indolence, the great dragon, assuredly shall not devour.

137. TESTIMONY OF THE PLANTS.

The vegetable kingdom, with its treasures of fruit and flowers, is a mighty interpreter of the divine. Flowers, indeed, are of the smiles of God, the very wealth and opulence of heaven.

The resinous fragrance of Northern pinewoods, the spicy aroma from forests of the South, are of the tribute of creation to its Maker. I remember, as though it were yesterday, the music of a cocoa-palm which waved all day long, hard by the open casement of the chamber where, fever-stricken, I lay. Consumed by thirst, hardly conscious, it soothed my sufferings and lulled me to repose. Oh, blessings be on the Power which framed that palm, for ever.

138. THE SOUL'S PERMANENCE.

The soul is all too divine to depend on a little dust, the poor contingency of any material combination of atoms.

[2] La plupart des hommes construisent laboreusement l'édifice de leur malheur. Ils figurent que la vie leur doit des bonheurs infinis, et font consister le bonheur dans ce que ils n'ont pas, sans autre raison que ceci, qu'ils ne l'ont pas, et qu'un autre le possede.

It not merely transcends the body, its temporary vehicle, but, as Arago has said, even the planet, the grain of sand, on which, for a few short moments, it happens to us to appear. Since God is not, as some idly suppose, the world,[1] the merely visible things of this and other spheres, but an unseen, a pervading power, tenanting at once earth and heaven.

139. FAITH, OF HEAVEN.

God can only desire the happiness of his creatures, that in all desirable, excelling things, they should be at one with Him, great indeed as heaven, great as immortality.[2] If, indeed, we would keep faith with the divine, we must keep it with ourselves. If we believe in wisdom, goodness, truth, strain no principle, violate no law, surely we are on the road to the starry heavens.

140. THE INNER LIFE.

The outer envelop which cloaks human consciousness, the phenomenal world, the things of sense in fine, may perish, but the inner feeling, the soul's life, can never perish. Dogmatism deals in its own peremptory fashion with this great truth, of which love alone, yields truest assurance for ever.

[1] Das Atome oder der kleinste einfache Grundvestantheil der Materie ist der Gott. Von Ewigkeit her existirend und in Ewigkeit hin unvernichtbar, bleibt selbst in allen Wechsel der Erscheinungen doch immer dasselbe, unveränderliche. Buchner, *Natur und Geist.* Frankfurt, 1857. B. I. S. 7.

[2] Les puissances intimes de notre âme seront agrandies comme le sera notre horizon d'activité, notre sphère de bonheur, notre capacité d'adoration et de foi. Tout en nous sera grand comme le ciel, grand comme l'immortalité. A. Coquerel.

G

141. LOFTIEST AIMS.

There is a rational self-assertion which delivers us from the promptings of mean ambition and yet meaner acts. Without it, moral elevation seems impossible. Schleiermacher, assuredly among the greatest of modern theologians, relegated to the list of open questions, the ecclesiastical subtilties which would multiply the personality of God, imply the destruction of man's spiritual nature, assert, in short, any other than a spiritual reclamation, through God's favour, but apart from all vicarious or substitutive agency whatever.[1] The conception, indeed, which affirms man's natural and inevitable corruption, by a process here needless to trace, leads or tends to lead to spiritual arrogance and despotism, on one hand, or on the other to a self-humiliation hardly less pernicious. Whereas God, who commends us to our own self-respect and care, has imparted to us capacities almost boundless, with means adequate for their development.

142. RECIPROCAL DEVELOPMENT.

One virtue inclines to other virtues.[2] Like the graces, the spiritual affections, principles most elevated, most divine, sweetest gifts of an infinitely munificent God, very seed and corner-stones of heaven, by reason of

---

[1] *Sämmtliche Werke.* Berlin, 1842. *Glaubenslehre.*

[2] Ces divers sentimens, la pieté filiale, l'amitie, l'amour, et la tendresse paternelle peuvent exister à-la-fois dans nos coeurs. Loin de se nuire, chacun d'eux semble donner une vie nouvelle à tous les autres. Droz, *L'Art d'être Heureux.*

their common filiation, tend continually to reciprocal furtherance, and yet more and more to realise themselves.

143. FORCE OF CHARACTER.

More souls, perhaps, have gone to ruin from the absence of sufficient firmness, than owing to any particular proclivity to ill. Weakness, aggravating our shortcomings and those of others, is the especial malady of our moral nature. Force of character, indeed, is not always associated with excellence, but when it is, the results are admirable.

144. GENIUS, DIVINE.

Genius, safeguard and solace of humanity, truly patient and enduring, is of the mighty gifts of God. Intolerant of all that is base and low, its sympathies are attuned to every good, and true, and gracious thing. For genius, allied with a moral purpose, does battle with every hindrance, realises the ideal, in short aids to elevate and redeem the world.

145. THE CORRECTIVE OF EVIL.

Every evil has its corrective. When opposed by healthy moral natures, it is met by efforts only to be satisfied with success. The weak, indeed, may shrink, but no one duly impressed with man's celestial destinies, ever bated hope or trust under circumstances however disastrous or discouraging. The angels in human guise, their earthly labours closed, are sure to be appreciated at last. The good they have accomplished the glories they have won, must shed a light upon humanity for ever.

146. LOVE CASTS OUT FEAR.

To love God and man, and to cultivate the better affections, is the truest fidelity, while not to love God and man, and not to cultivate the better affections, is the saddest infidelity. I would not fray a single leaflet of the tree of eternal life, yet I feel, I know, that every superstitious, untruthful element does hurt to religion's holy cause, and that it should be eliminated, and cast aside for ever. For the life spiritual is begotten, not of terror, but of love, since perfect love excludes all fear.[1] So, perfect faith, God's spirit in unison with the inner life, casts out infidelity. There cannot be fear or unbelief, when the soul is steeped in the spiritual affections, and in the undying conviction of infinite goodness and love. For a godlike life is indeed divine.[2]

147. THE INTENT AND THE ACT.

In some, the interval between the intention and the act is as a fathomless abyss, while in others, intention and act go together, hand in hand. Thus, speaking of Schiller, some one said he did not fritter costly life away in the inconceivable infatuation of delay.[3] The relation between the intention and the act indeed, is a

---

[1] Ὁ Θεὸς ἀγάπη ἐστί. Φόβος οὐκ ἔστιν ἐν τῇ ἀγάπῃ, ἀλλ' ἡ τελεία ἀγάπη ἔξω βάλλει τὸν φόβον.

[2] Durch ein göttliches Leben wird man Gottes inne.

[3] Er vermeidete alle die leeren Zerstreungen wodurch andere das kostbare Leben vergeuden.

not to be questioned criterion of energy, not merely human but divine.

148. DEATH A SYMBOL.

From every death there issues the symbol of eternal life. The man has been, but is now become.[1] Time for him has lapsed into nothingness, and the divine purpose has advanced a step. Thou art mine, exclaims earth to the body. Thou art mine, exclaims the Lord to the soul. Never, in truth, were there more touching lessons of grace, spiritual aspiration, and resignation, than I have seen written, again and again, on the faces of the dead, the dead whom a living soul should animate and direct no more.

149. TESTIMONY OF CHRISTIANITY.

Christianity, religion, rightly interpreted, separating additions, legendary and temporary, from what is enduring and divine, elevating and developing every better principle, yields potent testimony to the truthfulness of the religious principle itself. How far merely figurative language has been actualised, how certain preternatural statements have found admission, in connexion with the Gospel narratives, it would now perhaps be fruitless to inquire. Suffice to say, they are not needed to enforce, nay, they often prove serious obstacles to, the sacred cause of holiness and truth. Instead of mysterious doctrines as to the origin of sin, a spiritual Christianity simply shows that sin severs us from God, and that through penitence and effort, making thus true atone-

[1] Fabri, *Briefe gegen den Materialismus*, Stuttgart, 1856.

ment, we are alone reunited to him, realising indeed here, the heaven which hereafter awaits us all.

The sublime Christian doctrine of the spirituality and permanence of man's soul, as distinct from, and independent of, the secondary phenomena we term matter, has, in its brightness and enduringness, become more and more firmly rooted with the advance of time. Yet, still are there numbers unable to conceive existence apart from a frame, which, however fitted for purposes local and transient, is unsuited as a permanent adjunct to a spiritual nature and a more permanent home.

150. THE MIGHTY REVERSION.

All sin is irreligion, and there is no irreligion except sin. For purity, and sweetness, and truth, are of the essence of religion, which without them cannot be. The loftiest, holiest ideal that ever throned it in the saint's breast, or in the poet's soul, does not perhaps excel the living reality subsisting in many a heart, much more the great, the mighty reversion, which, through favour of the Infinite, awaits us all,

151. A DIVINE INITIATION.

As dealing with spiritual facts and a most divine initiation, religion yields mightiest intuitions. But inasmuch as it has to do with humanity, it also has to do with imperfection, shortcomings, error, and gets mixed up with them. In time, however, our insight becomes clearer, what is erroneous and imperfect falls away, while that which is excellent is laid hold of, and perchance retained for ever.

152. UNITY WITH GOD.

Philosophy and jurisprudence alike, disclaim retributive dealings on the part of God and man. And religion, too, which, rightly interpreted, is but a loftier philosophy, disclaims them. The only suffering, the only retribution, since there is and can be no other, is not to be at one with God.

Like Böhme, Swedenborg, his fantasies and follies apart, had frequent glimpses, indeed sweetest insight, into divine truth. The true church, he says, is within.[1] Love to God and charity, he adds, make heaven. For love, of a verity, is the fire of life, the very life of man, that which seeks, and one day shall secure, the spiritual safety of our kind.[2] We are, indeed, to live with God, not through dread of punishment, or the hope of reward merely, but because it is good to be with Him.[3] For this is its own reward, in this resides the simplicity and the grandeur of true religion, from which every illusory, artificial, insufficient, and conventional sanction must one day for ever disappear.

153. THE PROCESS OF ASSENT.

It is with religious, as with all truth, that when the heart is open to its reception, it must needs be taken

[1] *Heaven and Hell, passim.*   [2] 'Αγάπην δὲ μὴ ἔχω, οὐθέν εἰμι.
[3] Lasst uns auch erkennen dass es ein heroischer Gehorsam ist, die Gesetze Gottes zu beobachten, bloss weil es Göttes Gesetze sind, und nicht weil er die Beobachter hier und dort zu belohnen verheissen hat, sie beobachten ob man schon an der künftigen Belohnung ganz verzweifelt, und der Zeitlichen auch nicht so ganz gewiss ist. Lessing, *Erziehung des Menschengeschlecht,* § 32.

in. The consent which conscience yields, alone is necessary. By no other conceivable process, can the mind arrive at conclusions that concern the spiritual life. Thus, then, there is a stage in progress when the light can no longer be excluded. When there are eyes to see it, the light must be seen, when there are ears to hear it, the truth must be heard. And every error, along with every misconception, at variance with the light and with the truth, must some time fall away and cease to affect the soul, just as if it had never been.

154. HARMONY OF DIVINE TRUTH.

The great and singular characteristic of religious, of divine truth, is its universality, its joint approval by the heart and intellect, its harmony with all other truth, with philosophy, the highest ideal, the best and holiest literature, the loftiest poesy, all science and art, in fine, every thing that constitutes the crown and glory of humanity, the very flower and peace of heaven.

155. THE SAFE ROAD.

Spiritual truth is the ceaseless aspiration of every earnest, striving soul.[1] Of this I am assured, that no mere spiritual nostrum, no empirical formula or play of words, can save man's soul, whether in the seen or the unseen life, but goodness only, and purity, and truth, in conformity with the divine. For what is spiritual safety but goodness, the cultivation of sentiments which impel the soul to God and a world beyond our own.[2] And what

---

[1] Τί με δεῖ ποιεῖν ἵνα σωθω.
[2] Bishop Hampden, *Lectures on Moral Philosophy*, p. 96.

is goodness, itself, but nearness to the divine, the realisation of heaven within the breast, that heaven which lies by every hearth and at every door.

The theory of the good, the beautiful, the true, is very simple and very intelligible, as well as in perfect consonance with the moral, spiritual law, and the fundamental convictions of our kind. No shedding of innocent blood is implied here, no sacrifice except self-sacrifice, in order to find acceptance with God. For unless we become as little children, we cannot, indeed we cannot, enter heaven.[1] Unless we be actuated by the pure, the celestial affections so largely diffused into the hearts of the young, we cannot partake of the sweet realities imaged forth by the terms, kingdom of God, the blessed life, the happy, the divine estate of childhood.

150. TRUE AFFECTION UNSELFISH.

The affections, in themselves, are so very, very beautiful, that we are slow to discern that they may lapse into little better than a more refined selfishness. For there is a selfishness of the heart as well as of the intelligence,[2] quite at variance with the spiritual harmony and perfection essential to developed humanity. Sentiment, indeed, is the harmonious and living relation between reason and sensibility itself.[3] For there must not be any divorce between intellect and affection. Their objects are alike divine, in veriest truth are one.

---

[1] Εαν μὴ γενηθε ὡς τὰ παιδία, ου μὴ εἰσιλθητε εἰς τὴν βασιλείαν των οὐρανῶν.
[2] *Evening Thoughts, by a Physician.* London, 1850.
[3] Cousin, *On the True, the Beautiful, and the Good.* Lecture V. *On Mysticism.* Wight's tr.

Cherub and seraph, things of beauty and of grace, they walk hand in hand, home-ward and heaven-ward together. Even the body, itself, as transfigured by intelligence, and grace, and love, becomes an emblem of spiritual things. And genius and love, with every sacrament, and each spiritual and holy evangel, proceed in closest association, without hesitancy or pause, for ever. For the heart has aspirations that precede any thought, as thought itself, goes farthest when guided by the heart.

If, indeed, in the spiritual life, there be a thing truer, more ravishing than another, it is that genius, and duty, and holiness, and love, are in closest dependence on each other. For the noble and the beautiful are not a dream, and never, never, shall be wanting in this thrice wondrous and exquisite world. The affections, indeed, are essential to all excellence, all true greatness. It is only what the soul drinks in with eagerness, that becomes thoroughly and perfectly its own. So, affection and refinement, with all the graces, should be wedded to goodness, as to every just, and sacred, and beautiful thing. For thus, and only thus, can humanity become united with its better self, and the inner life, and with heaven.

157. COMPASSIONS, DIVINE.

Being of beings, exclaims Sheffield from his Westminster Abbey tomb, have compassion on me.[1] And wherefore should not the Infinite Heart, founder and fountain of the celestial affections, have compassion on

---
[1] Ens entium miserere mei.

him and on all men. For religion is not a thing of drear and gloom, but one of joy, and hope, and fruitions present and to come. Mere words too often, a fictitious instead of a real morality, a supposititious instead of a real theology, have, in a degree, estranged men's souls from that full reliance on the unlimited mercies of God, so much needed by the often sorely-tried, dependent heart of man.

None of the modern systems of doctrinal theology, it has been remarked, subsisted in Christ's day, or in those of his immediate followers. In Christ's conversations, observes Jean Paul, we do not find a single word of souls falling with Adam, or of satisfaction for sin.[1] How slender, indeed, is the foundation in the New Testament, two passages of Paul and those of uncertain interpretation, for the doctrine of Adam's sin being imputed to his posterity.[2] All, says Niebuhr,[3] acquainted with church history, know that a system of doctrines respecting redemption, hereditary sin, grace, did not exist for at least two centuries after Christ, or, indeed, find any sufficing countenance in the Christian Scriptures at all.

Whatever may be said in respect of these critical utterances, certain it is that any coercion that does not imply the coercion of truth, a spiritual religion instead of a spiritual despotism, a religion of hope and love and joy, instead of one of sorrow and menace and gloom, is rife with misery and ill. For a true theology, in a

---
[1] Letter to his son Max. *Life*, London, Chapman, 1845.
[2] *Jowett's Epistles of St. Paul*, vol. i. p. 162.
[3] *Life and Letters*, 2nd ed. vol. i. p. 217, vol. ii. p. 119.

word God in the heart, is alone in accordance with his light and with his love, the simple intelligible dictates of universal spiritual truth, man's spiritual safety, the changeless and unchangeable convictions of the best and wisest of our kind.

158. CHILDREN OF GOD.

To be named the children, sons and daughters of God, is surely the loftiest designation that human beings can receive, or to which they can aspire. As in the beautiful words of Aratus,[1] cited by St. Paul, we are, in truth, the offspring of the divine. For it involves a mighty fact, one that comes with peculiar emphasis on the soul, yields loftiest incentives to imitate the divine. That we are, indeed, God's children and his creatures, is of those angelic truths, consonant with every right affection, the very marrow of goodness and intelligence, the loftiest and most consolatory that it is possible for us to imagine or conceive.

159. THE BUSINESS OF AGE.

There is, at least there need be, no mental or moral decrepitude. For every sweet affection, the entire intelligence in fine, grows, or ought to grow, brighter with time and sustained effort. The body, in truth, decays, but the soul need never decay. The business of age, then, is to nourish our powers, discipline our perceptions, multiply the loftier influences that spring at once from the sensuous and spiritual worlds.

Does age, indeed, shut out the secret paths along

[1] Ὡς καί τινες τῶν καθ' ὑμᾶς ποιητῶν εἰρήκασι, Τοῦ γὰρ καὶ γένος ἐσμέν.

which souls are led to the goals of perfection, the very gates of heaven. Is the spirit which forgets itself in the joys and sorrows of another, of necessity less radiant in advanced than earlier years. Angels of purity and intelligence haunt the chambers of the soul in age as in sunny infancy, if we will. And their spiritual solace shall attend and wait upon us, along the fields of time, to our celestial happy home.

160. THE INNER VOICE.

He, in truth, begins a new life, who determines to act up to the best dictates of his inner nature. Christ enlarged not so much on the soul's immortality, as on inward purity, best and only real preparative for it.[1] There is not a requirement of the loftiest truth, the most sterling manliness, the soundest philosophy, the noblest patriotism, the broadest philanthropy, that will not be found in unison, if we only obey the inward voice that tells us to go on, and not to palter with the great requirements of our position and our time. Since life is so short, so short,[2] that we may not pause till the morrow, but in what is to be said, and done, and felt, and thought, to say, and act, and feel, and think it now.

161. THE VEILED LIFE.

In each of those who pass, there may be veiled the sweetest spirit-life, probity, thoughtfulness, courage, gentleness, and patience under difficulties. There is,

[1] Eine innere Reinigkeit des Herzens in Hinsicht auf ein anderes Leben. Lessing, *Erziehung des Menschengeschlecht*, § 61.
[2] Das Leben ist kurz und die Zeit ist edel.

indeed, nothing amid the wide-spread marvels of existence more wondrous than are the hidden powers, hidden from all save the soul's deep discernment, in fine the phenomena of the inner life. For man is a mystery to himself, a mystery only to be fitly appreciated by the mighty Originator of all things.

152. ACTION AND REACTION.

Action and reaction subsist not less in the moral, than in the physical world. Do good and you shall be done good by, respect others and you shall be respected, love and you shall be loved. For God will do this by you and more, through the medium of your own soul, in which he dwells potentially and for ever. On the other hand, hate and you shall be hated, despise and you shall experience despite. Life, liberty, and the just pursuit of happiness are the rightful inheritance of all men. The legend, indeed, is blazoned on the American declaration of independence, with the living context and correlative of four millions of slaves.

163. EVIL OF FEAR.

Fear inflicts even larger evils than do violence and crime, since it saps the masculine energy by which alone they are to be combated. Had the conservators of truth been less faithful to their sacred trust, what were our position now. Great thoughts animate the soul to deeds of heroism, best preparative for a heroic eternity. And there are perhaps few things more heroic than to state the truth, the entire truth, and the truth only, to our kind.

A little leaven, were it of truth and goodness, impels wholesome thought into appropriate channels of utterance and action. The slave of selfishness will never conquer earth, much more the holier, lovelier realms of heaven. The great and adorable marvel, in respect of the eternal principles of the moral law, is this, that they work, not by signs and symbols merely, any inversion or invasion of natural, that is to say divine, law and order, but only through the regeneration and spiritualisation of the dear, deep heart of man. When this mighty truth is felt and known, sects shall vanish and controversy be no more. There shall be no church except God's church, and no contention except to do His will.

Societies and individuals, alike, can only purchase advantages, not by owing them to others, but by personal effort and sacrifice of their own.[1] A divine energy should animate us, whether in sustaining the responsibilities of life or in furthering the interests of truth, greatly to dare and to do.[2] For heaven has yielded us the kingly boon of self-control, the heroic power of the spirit over itself, the heavenly union and unison of goodness, and moderation, and energy, the genius which vivifies, while our turn of duty lasts and ere we hand it to another,[3] lighting up as with a torch, a diviner life within. Would we, indeed, touch other hearts, we must speak like angels from our own. An infinite

[1] *Guizot's Democracy*, 5th ed. 1849.
[2] Certare ingenio, contendere nobilitate, noctes atque dies niti praestante labore, ad summas emergere opes rerumque potiri.
[3] Λαμπάδια ἔχοντες διαδώσουσιν ἀλλήλοις.

courage combined with cheerfulness as infinite, venturing to be great and true, should animate each single soul. It is the instinct and destiny of genius, since true genius is virtue, ceaseless effort, indeed the very marrow and divine energy of the soul, to do battle with every prejudice, all ignorance, folly, vice, and sin. Since genius may not scathless evade its celestial obligations, forfeit its holy mission, sell itself for gold.

The world needs all its labourers. For God, who loves us, and to whom, as to everything that is spiritual, and truthful, and good, we are for ever nigh, yields his devoted servants and children his utmost sympathy, and the crown of victory at last, requires all the truth that is in us, our most strenuous efforts, our best resolves. We are, indeed, to aim at perfection, even as God is perfect, and never for a single instant to doubt our final success, and the success of the mighty principles for which we are to contend. The seeming defects of the moral world argue, let us be persuaded, nothing against the moral government of God. For all torpor and decay, and even spiritual death, itself, with every doubt and difficulty, must sometime be got rid of in the soul's progress towards that spiritual perfection, at which, assuredly, it is the divine intention we should steadfastly and ceaselessly aim.

ASPIRATIONS

FROM

THE INNER, THE SPIRITUAL LIFE.

BOOK IV.

I REVERENCE physical science, more as the source of utmost human practical power, and a means by which the far-distant races of the world, who now sit in darkness and the shadow of death, are to be reached and regenerated. At home or far away, the call is equally instant. Here, for want of more extended physical science, there is plague in our streets, famine in our fields. The pest, we know not why, strikes root and fruit over a hemisphere of the earth. The voices of our children fade away into the silence of venomous death. The population resists every effort to lead it into purity of habit and habitation, to give it genuineness of nourishment, and wholesomeness of air. Frightful superstitions still hold their own over two-thirds of the inhabited globe. The phenomena of nature, those legends of God's daily dealing with his creatures, which were intended by the Creator to enforce his eternal laws of love, remain unread, or are read backwards into blind hundred-armed horror of ideal cosmogony. How strange it seems that physical science should ever have been thought adverse to religion. The pride of physical science, indeed, is adverse to religion and truth. But sincerity of science, so far from being hostile, is the pathmaker among the mountains for the feet of those who publish peace. Ruskin.

ASPIRATIONS.

164. INSISTENCE OF PURPOSE.

As power imparts grandeur only to the grand, so opportunity is fitly embraced but by the good. Each elevated conviction is in unison with power over, not bondage to self, ingredient of all virtue, root of all progress. Insanity and vice, however different the direction, are one, as collectedness and firmness of purpose rightly to dare and to do, are the other, of two extremes of which every soul is capable.

165. THE DIVINE WANT.

Without compromise, as without reserve, are the ever-expansive revelations of divine truth, and such, too, should be our avowal and appreciation of them.[1] For knowledge, and philosophy, and science, and religion, are at one with each other, as with God.[2] Indeed we need the divine. The good need it because they are good, the wicked because they are wicked, and all because they are human. Therefore it is, that God con-

[1] Erziehung ist Offenbarung, und Offenbarung ist Erziehung, die dem Menschengeschlecte geschehen ist und noch geschieht. Lessing, *Die Erziehung des Menschengeschlechts*, § 2.
[2] Und warum wird jene Rüge so häufig gegen die Philosophie ausgesprochen. Aus keinen andern Grunde als weil es noch immer Gelehrte giebt, die Philosophie und Wissenschaft trennen. Moleschott, *Kreislauf des Lebens, Zweite Briefe*.

tinually reveals himself in the soul's deep affections, the voices of outward nature, the confidences of our kind. Here, the wise and the ignorant, by a sort of moral parallax, look up alike through the infinite interval that separates divine perfection from human imperfection.

166. HEAVEN AT OUR DOORS.

The birds that carol in the lofty ether, the flowers that enamel the mead, or blossom in the parterre, are as angels proclaiming that paradise is within, heaven at our doors, and the divine everywhere. For each day regeneration, unity with celestial things, begins, or ought to begin anew.

Alas, exclaims a thoughtful writer,[1] the really good and wise but too deeply feel how terrible is the struggle, how incessant, how determined, to emancipate the soul from low desires, grovelling thoughts, and earth-born impulses, to make their being truly beautiful and truly free.

This, indeed, is a struggle which can never cease, till, as Sir Thomas Browne has styled it, we reach our jubilee-day, and compass the spiritual life which is life indeed, flee the spiritual death which is death indeed. For else the soul is as a fallen angel which finds no peace in heaven.[2]

167. THE PARADISE OF CHILDHOOD.

Some time or other, if not now, we shall renew the heaven of our childhood, the heaven of the moment

[1] *Atlas*, Jan. 13, 1844. [2] *Newman's Theism, The Hardened Politician.*

that is passing by. And why should we not realise enjoyments which circumscribe no duty, are at variance with no spiritual law. For a just faith and morals pure, in action, are of necessity divine, assure the satisfactions of heaven, not less in the life of the instant than in that which is to come.

168. DIVINE UNITIES.

Knowledge, and trust, and truth, proceed ever hand and hand. This mysterious, wondrous, and in part incomprehensible existence, hastens on to another yet more wondrous, mysterious, and incomprehensible. We are surrounded by a boundless world of sense, as by an unseen world not less boundless.[1] It is impossible with all our insight, to appreciate spiritual truth through the medium of the intelligence only. It is the rock on which intellect has been shattered from immemorial time. For the divine is not mere knowledge, but love also. And religion, too, is love, true exponent of God's unutterable tenderness, man's boundless obligation and conformity.

169. MAN AND GOD.

Nothing can extinguish the spiritual sympathies of man with man, and of man with God. One who knows our requirements and infirmities, some husband, wife, mother, sister, child, friend, shall oft-times rescue us from spiritual defeat, save, or help to save, the soul from death. And thus would He who knows our weaknesses and infirmities do by us all, did we only suffi-

[1] Atticus in the *Critic*, Oct. 9, 1858.

ciently aspire to and love him. For every aspiration brings the soul to God, helps to realise heaven.

170. MEDISANCE.

Of all the addictions adverse to the soul's weal, there are few, perhaps, so injurious as that which the French term *medisance*. The literary assassin revels in misstatements to which he dare not append a name. To bear false witness against our neighbour, to gloat over his shortcomings, real or imaginary, is odious alike to God and man. For not less important even than faith in* God, is faith in humanity. We need to believe in God, yet we also need to believe in man. No one who is void of the one, can be truly actuated by the other.[1] The gentleman will not sully his soul with falsity, were his name never so much concealed and unknown. Medisance, in respect of individuals, whether open or cloaked, is evil indeed, but doubly evil is it when directed against nations and peoples, against that which is of God, and in truth divine. Religious, or rather irreligious medisance, is surely not less serious, not less sinful than social. To be lenient to others, inexorable to ourselves, cauterising the ulcers which eat into our better nature, is alone obligatory on all.

[1] Der Mensch, Gipfel der Natur, Basis der Geschichte, in der Mitte zwischen einem von Körpern erfüllten Raum und einer von Thaten erfüllten Zeit, zwischen einer unermesslichen Leibwelt und einem unabsehbaren Geisterreiche. Karl Fortlage, *System der Psychologie als empirischer Wissenschaft aus der Beobachten des Innern Sinnes.* Leipzig, 1855, Einleitung.

171. ASSOCIATION OF IDEAS.

The property which an idea or an emotion has of calling up another idea or emotion, and reciprocally, termed the principle of association, is of deepest interest in our mental and moral constitution. It builds, or aids in building, up the intelligence and heart in infancy, fortifies them in adult age.

Association discharges in psychology much the same function which affinity does in chemistry. As respects our moral nature, it enables us to confront evil with good, to make the latter the very basis and groundwork of our being. Habit, with its iron or its golden rule, is no other than association. For as the sandheap is added to or degraded, grain by grain, so is character formed by imperceptible degrees, till passion's mighty pulses overthrow the frail structure, or confirm it, perchance, in endurance and solidity for ever.

172. ASPIRATION.

It is the necessity, the very hunger and thirst of the spirit, to rely upon God, in a word, to aspire. There is not a spiritual longing whose object we have not the means to compass, a perfection which it is not within our power to achieve. For our human nature, with its various and almost divine capacities, is founded by God. He subjects us to laws which we did not originate, imparts to us our wondrous powers, and, through culture and ceaseless effort, amplest means for their development.

173. INTROSPECTION.

The human soul, as we learn by introspection and the observation of others, is subject to most precise and positive laws.[1] Consciousness, in truth, is the great teacher.[2] Philosophy and religion, though intimately related, and both from God, are nevertheless in certain respects distinct. Those divine emotions, the anxieties of thought, aspirations after liberty,[3] which bring us nigh high heaven, and reason itself, reflection of the silent influence of the image of God, are alike sacred and needful to each other. If we give ourselves wholly up to sentiment, we lapse into mysticism and sacrifice reason. For sentiment has the pretention to elevate man directly to God, without the intermediary of the visible world, and the still surer intermediary of intelligence and truth.[4] But reason without the affectious, in matters which concern both, will not alone conduct us to heaven.

174. DIVINE ADJUSTMENTS.

Exquisite, in truth, are the divine adjustments to our several wants and weaknesses. Yet, their highest usefulness, assuredly, is to lead us to their mighty

---

[1] Dans la construction de nos systèmes philosophiques, nous devons toujours tendre à concevoir la nature sous le plus simple aspect possible, mais à condition fondamentale de subordonner toutes nos conceptions à la réalité des phènoménes. Comte, *Philosophie Positive*, Tome iii. p. 83. Paris, 1833.

[2] Das psychologische Messer ist die Schärfe der den innern Sinn beobachten den Aufmerksamkeit selbst. Alle wirkliche Wissenschaft geht diesen Weg. Fortlage, *Psychologie, Gegenstand und Methode*.

[3] M. de Montalembert.

[4] Cousin, *On Mysticism, On the True, the Beautiful, and the Good*.

Originator, to generate lovely thoughts which conquer death, make us at one with the empire of eternal life. For man needs a living, loving, commerce with God, fresh revealings, renewed aspirings, rescuing him from ritualism, dulness, and spiritual decay.

175. UNITY WITH THE DIVINE.

A well-known theological empiric, once addressing his hearers, rightly enough observed. If you were in heaven without a new heart and a right spirit, you would be glad enough to get out of it. But paradise is not a place merely, as is here imagined, but unity with the divine, the well of sweet waters in the heart.[1] It is wherever the divine is acknowledged, believed in, loved.[2] For celestial thoughts and celestial things, indeed, convert the else lowliest soul, the humblest precincts, into a very hostelry of heaven.

176. PARTINGS.

Touching, in truth, was that passage in the great reformer's life, when he was required to give up his little Magdalen, his child. My little daughter, my beloved Magdalen, he said, you would remain with your earthly father, but if God call you, you will also willingly go to him. Yes, dear father, it is as God pleases. Then he took the Book and read from Isaiah. Thy dead men shall live, and thus to the end. Again, he said, my daughter, my Magdalen, enter thou into thy rest. And she turned her dying eyes upon him, and with angelic innocence replied, yes, father.

[1] *Newman's Theism.*   [2] Swedenborg, *Heaven and Hell.*

Another daughter and another father abode in a lone log-hut far towards the western sun. And he too was called on to part with his treasure, his darling, his child. Father, she said, I am cold, cold. And twining her fever-spent arms around him, she murmured, father, dear father. My daughter, he whispered, does the flood seem deep to you. Nay, father, for my soul is strong. I see the further shore, and its banks are green with immortal verdure. I hear voices, too, as the voices of angels calling from afar. But there is a mist in the room, father. You will be lonely, lonely. Father, dear father, farewell.[1]

When Olympia Morata, worthy compeer of Vittoria Colonna and Lady Jane Grey, was breathing her angelic life away, at Schweinfurt, October 26, 1555, but barely twenty-nine, she said to her husband and little brother Emilio. I can no longer see you, my best beloved, but all around me seems adorned with the fairest flowers.[2] Death, then, was not terrible to these children of heaven. Why should it be so to any of us.

177. THE HIGHEST WISDOM.

Suspended from a soldier's neck, one slain at Sebastopol, was found a leaden tablet, a mother's gift, on which were traced characters in the Russian tongue.

---

[1] Liebend blickte die sterbende Tochter den stummen Vater
An und drückt' ihm die Hand. "Vater, ich bin nicht mehr!"
Sprach sie, zarte Thränen bedeckten ihr brechendes Auge
Und den weinenden Blick schloss die verhüllende Nacht.
                      Herder, *Die Sterbende Tochter*.

[2] Jules Bonnet, *Vie d'Olympia Morata*, Paris, 1856. Wildermuth, *Olympia Morata, ein Lebensbild*, Stuttgart, 1854.

The highest wisdom is to serve the Lord. And what better could this poor mother have written, had an angel guided her hand. What angel could surpass a mother's self-sacrificing tenderness. For the good mother, joint head of the family tie, very precursor of heaven, is indeed an angel, one of whom surely none in heaven's loftiest hierarchy may take precedence.

178. SIN AND SUFFERING.

It was once supposed that there was a material hell, some sulphurous region where men were tortured for deeds wrought in the flesh. But we know better now, know that the sinner's suffering is a moral suffering, sorrowing over sin and severance from God. This, however, is a state of grace contrasted with that lower hell, the apathy which no sense of error, no awakening of contrition, serves to chasten. For goodness is unison with God, while its opposite is disunion at once with God and with heaven.

179. CONTENDING WITH EVIL.

It is incumbent on us to contend with evil whenever and wheresoever we meet with it. As tyrants tread out the life, the beautiful life, of the free, so do evil thoughts, foul indeed, and dreary,[1] creep with sufferance into each neglected soul, and enslave it. Spiritual quixotism is not necessary, though spiritual quixotism be indeed rare. Yet, to assimilate what is beautiful, to make the faulty good, the good better, is like inhaling the fragrance of celestial flowers. For the beauty of

[1] Αἰσχρὰ μὲν δὴ πάντα τὰ ψυχῆς νοσήματα καὶ πάθη. Plutarch.

the spirit, that beauty which likens it to God, grows, in truth, in each happy environment, as the flowers. And every deed of self-sacrifice and spiritual endurance, in its measure, raises the soul for the time to paradise, bears it, indeed, aloft as in a chariot of fire.

180. PHYSICAL NEGLECT.

What with incessant wars and social neglect, half the French conscripts, it seems, are found physically unfitted to serve. And thus is it, more or less, everywhere. The very idea, in truth, of effectively providing for the bodily conservancy and material elevation of the people, seems practically unknown.

181. NEEDFULNESS OF THE AFFECTIONS.

The understanding is more slowly developed than the affections, which, in early life, are needful as a mother's milk or a mother's fostering care. The mother, indeed, loses in a measure, her identity in offices of self-sacrifice and love. Without the affections, the infant could not so much as live, could neither evince nor evoke the exceeding joyousness which likens him, and the mother who bore him, to the heavenly inmates, realises, in truth, for the affections of the very ecstasies of heaven.

182. SEEDS OF HOLINESS.

A holy life is of greater moment than what is termed a sound theology, a spiritual revelation than any verbal creed.[1] For religion is of those certainties which are

---

[1] Τὸ γὰρ γράμμα ἀποκτείνει, τὸ δὲ πνεῦμα ζωοποιεῖ.

to be entertained without any doubt or hesitancy whatever.[1] Fanaticism and atheism, twin sisters, are in unison in this, that they deride philosophy, decry every appeal to the eternal standards of divine truth and human excellence.[2] In short, superstition is the one unhappy extreme, of which atheistic unbelief is the other, that clamours continually at the portals of the spiritual life, and would fain compass their overthrow. Alas, that we can deny the Being who loves us as his children, Him who created the father's heart, the mother's tears and smiles. Yet, each wind speaks of Him, and the heaving deep, the green earth, and the sunny flowers declare his purposes and assure us of their fulfilment, suggest aspirations which foster seeds of holiness and truth, rescue us from the dust of corruption and spiritual death, and approximate us, however immense the interval, to the immaculate and unseen.

183. FELLOWSHIP WITH GOD.

The great aim of man's existence is fellowship with God and the life invisible. Yet, to imagine any direct or immediate intuition of the unseen, or of its ineffable Head, is of the essence of mysticism, opens the door to

[1] *Carlyle's Life of Sterling*, Part I. p. 128.

[2] Ich habe kein Hehl es auszusprechen, die Angel um welche die heutige Weltweisheit dreht, ist die Lehre vom Stoffwechsel. Moleschott, *Kreislauf des Lebens*, Mainz, 1852, p. 363.

Gedanke ist eine Bewegung des Stoffs, *id*. p. 401.

Keine Kraft ohne Stoff, kein Stoff ohne Kraft. Buchner, *Kraft und Stoff*. Frankfurt, 1855.

Alle jene Fahigkeiten die wir unter dem Namen der Seelenthatigkeiten begreifen, nur Functionen der Gehirnsubstanz sind. Vogt, *Physiologische Briefe*, Stuttgart, 1847, p. 206.

extravagance and error. For sentiment, though it elevate and vivify, can never prove a substitute for thought. Modern quietists but reproduce the conceptions of a bygone time. Musselman Sufis in the East, Tauler and his associates in the West, erroneously pronounced for the renunciation of earthly things, the potential, if not the actual union of the soul with God. Yet Tauler, it was, that good soul, who, in 1340, formed among the Waldenses the mystical association of the Friends of God. His boundless charity, indeed, was shown in his devotion to the victims of the Black Plague, in Hamburgh, in 1348. The great Alexandrian Neo-Platonists, among whom, as Vacherot states,[1] Greek philosophy found its final utterance, declared for absolute unification with God. With Plotinus, as with Plato, to die was in a sense to live. In more recent times, Servetus, then Spinoza, and, long after, Hegel, held that everything was God, and the soul but a thought of God. But man and God, at least in the sense of the Mystics, are not one.[2] Enough for us, then, to imitate the divine, and with Simplicius,[3]

[1] Toutes les écoles grecques y coexistaient et y travaillaient chacune dans le sens de ses principes et de ses traditions. *Histoire Critique de l'Ecole d'Alexandrie*, par E. Vacherot, Paris, 1846, Preface.

[2] Pour vivre d'une vie supérieure, l'humanité n'a pas besoin de changer de nature. Pour entrer dans la vie, pour posséder Dieu, comme dit Plotin, il n'est pas necessaire qu'elle devienne elle-même un Dieu. Elle trouve dans sa propre nature tous les éléments d'une vie supérieure. *Id.* Tome iii. p. 450.

[3] Ἱκετεύω σε Δέσποτα, ὁ πατηρ καὶ ἡγεμὼν τοῦ ἐν ἡμῖν λόγου. *Commentarius in Enchiridion Epicteti, cum versione Wolfii et Salmasii.* Lugduni Batavorum, 1640.

himself a follower of Proclus and Plotinus, to await the better life to come.

184. SPIRITUAL TREASURES.

The power of thought is a possession most divine, likens us to God. Genius, which is lofty thought and parent of heroic desires, sacrifices itself for its generation and for all time.[1] What is philosophy, what religion, even, except a purified ideal, the sublime of genius and of thought. But knowledge is the result of two factors, our experience, namely, and its reception as governed by the laws of thought. Consciousness is the great arena, the especial point of union between man and God, where, amid the spirit's priceless treasures, we realise the divine.

185. A TRUE FAITH.

The religious sentiment is infinitely desirable, but that yields no grounds for combining it with error, since faith should ever be coupled with the exercise of reason and love of the divine. Whatever, observes Jacobi, be the insufficiency of philosophy, we must still philosophise, else deny the supremacy of reason itself. The existence of a living personal God, the absolute worth of virtue, the divine origin of man's soul, the reality of feeling, and the sovereignty of conscience, were by this great thinker incessantly instilled. Philo-

[1] Nichts ist bezeichnender für das Genie, als dass seine Aeusserungen oder Erfindungen der Ausdruck der Zeit, das ausgesprochene Wort, die hingestellete Erfüllung für den dunkeln Drang für das Sehnen und Bedürfen einer ganzen Generation sind. Haym, *Hegel und seine Zeit*, Berlin, 1857, p. 201.

sophy, indeed, exercises the right of verification and interpretation, while the religious sentiment, by declaring that love is the basis of the moral law, implies its own celestial sanction, yields prescriptive proof of immortality.

186. OUR REAL BIRTHPLACE.

Preserved from all mean and vulgar contact, nourished by lofty example, to what might humanity not aspire. The Pitcairn, now the Norfolk Islanders, had no uncommon origin to boast of, yet in conduct and character they awaken deepest interest. Children, indeed, very hostages of heaven, are of divinest mintage, born each several instant in the paradise of God, wherein it is the eternal problem of education and of civilisation to retain them.[1]

187. TRUE SCIENCE, DIVINE.

All true science is sacred, all true science is divine, the earth is alike holy, we are all the children of God. For a true theology and a true astronomy, a true morality and a true physics, come alike from Him, reveal themselves from heaven.[2]

188. CONSCIENCE.

It is Herbart's position that there is no original legislative moral principle.[3] Without a doubt our sense

[1] Speaking of Jeanne D'Arc, Michelet observes. Elle eut d'ame et de corps ce don divin de rester infant. *Histoire de la France*, Tome Cinquième.

[2] Πάντα μέτρῳ, καὶ ἀριθμῷ, καὶ σταθμῷ διέταξας.

[3] Herbart, *Lehrbuch zur Psychologie*, Konigsberg, 1834.

of obligation is gradually built up, results from many factors. Cumulative experience is transmitted from generation to generation, furnishes a basis for acquisitions ever true, ever new. This, the philosophy of religion establishes without appeal.[1] Thus, as Butler remarks, humanity is adapted to virtue, and man by nature becomes a law unto himself.[2]

189. THE GREAT REALITIES.

Visibly and invisibly, we are placed in ceaseless relation with spiritual things. The unseen, the eternal world is ever nigh, and the divine, with all goodness, and spiritual beings of every degree, are at hand. Everywhere the unseen subsists beneath the seen, a moral and immaterial behind a material reality.

190. LOOKING INWARD.

Some, alas too many, close their eyes to the spiritual life within. Yet not to look inward, to abdicate the faculty of introspection, is in its degree to put ourselves on a level with the unreasoning brute. The intellect alone does not originate our highest thoughts or acts, since these derive their sanction from the heart.[3] For religion is not only reason, and knowledge, and philoso-

---

[1] La philosophie est immortelle comme son principe, la pensée, révélation progressive de l'immuable vérité, elle se fait chaque jour et ne sera jamais faite. Vacherot, *Histoire Critique*, T. iii. p. 511.

[2] *Sermons on the Love of God.*

[3] La raison et le sentiment se conseillent et se suppléent tour à tour. La force est dans le coeur. C'est le sentiment, l'instinct moral. Les grandes pensées viennent du coeur. Vauvenargues, *Reflexions et Maximes*. Paris, 1821.

I

phy, it is also emotion, and gratitude, and conformity, and submission. These aid the soul in its strife with self, as in its combats with what Herbart terms the great enemies of religion, and I will add of man's soul, blind submission namely, to received dogmas, ignorance, fanaticism, and hypocrisy.

191. EARTH A PARADISE.

There is a happy harmony pervading all things, at once of earth and heaven, which is as the voice of God. Faith in the divine, founded on the contemplation of nature and the intelligent appreciation of final causes, of distinct means to distinct ends,[1] is, if not the most perfect, at least among the more perfect of earthly witnesses to the being and perfections of God,[2] and if not actual knowledge is all but knowledge.[3] For in the divine empire there is no real evil.[4] What we so term, is simply negation, limitation, transition, opposition. Death itself is but a transformation, a getting rid of the material, a spiritual necessity. In nature there is no repose. Action and reaction, birth, development, and becoming, conspire with divinest energy for the good of the whole. With all its shortcomings, the earth is a paradise. With every breath we inhale an ethereal lethe-stream, so that joys are only moderately, and pains hardly at all remembered.[5]

[1] Bishop Hampden's *Moral Philosophy*, p. 111.
[2] Dr. Wilson, *Edinburgh Essays*, p. 349.   [3] Herbart.   [4] Herder.
[5] Mit jedem Athemzug ein ätherischer Lethestrom unser ganzes Wesen durchdringt, so dass wir uns der Freuden nur mässig, der Leiden kaum erinnern. *Briefwechsel Zwischen Göthe und Zelter*, Berlin, 1834.

192. GOLDSMITH.

It has been said of Goldsmith by competent judges,[1] as it has been admitted by the world, that his writings were characterised by the good, the natural, the gentle, the pure. Like those of Burns, they are revealings of the poetry of life, the divine sweetness of the heart of man. What then of his faults, to us his goodness, to cynics, if they choose, his carelessness, heedless of the morn. Johnson, his great cotemporary, went through life bravely enduring many a buffet, tortured by melancholy and disease, but he had not the angelic temperament which has caused Goldsmith's words to compass earth and sea, and which will render them a comfort and a joy to generations and generations to come.

193. ART, DIVINE.

If we can, let us render art natural, reconcile nature with art, and if it be possible, imbue man also with this manifestation of the divine. But without self-forgetfulness and lofty culture, high art, with all its fulness of grace and of truth, is impossible. The statue of Love, by Edmee Bouchardon, in the lower hall of the Louvre, displays celestial truth and beauty. As with many of the works of Geefs, Mac Dowell, Marshall, Fraikin, and others, souls imbued with the divine fire, one only wonders that heart can conceive or hand embody such marvels of excellence in the stone. For art of a verity is precious, raises souls towards the Infinite, inoculates them with things of heaven.

[1] Forster, De Quincy, Goethe.

194. THE ROMAN AND THE GREEK.

Nothing can well exceed the perfect naturalness and absence of vulgarity displayed in Greek, and commonly in Roman literature. In spirit and in heart, indeed, the Greek was a gentleman, but the Roman, though most assuredly not all Romans, was plebeian. In civil and social polity, however, they made, it must be conceded, many advances on the Greek. With the Greeks, women were a cipher in the body-politic, with the Romans the wife was at least a portion of the social, the civic circle, that circle in which even yet she does not fully hold her place. The Greek, indeed, had the exquisite wild grace of the hind and the roe, the poppy in the corn, but the Roman combined the strength and wilfulness of the half-tamed brute. The Greeks, in truth, had the poetry and the grace of life, and, as was once said in their exquisite tongue, they shall be loved and remembered so long as there is beauty, or eyes to see it.[1]

195. THE REVELATION OF POESY.

Oh ye in whose souls the pulses of the spiritual life beat faint and low, come listen to the poets' lays, to some Hood, Barrett Browning, or Tennyson, to strains breathing divinest inspiration, thoughts glowing with celestial fire. They shall unlock the hidden fountains for you, perchance rouse you from deathly slumbers, waken you up to perceptions that never die.

[1] Μέχρις ἄν κάλλος ᾖ καὶ ὀφθαλμοί βλέπωσι. Longus.

196. UHLAND'S DREAM.

There are things, as it seems to me, quite heavenly in certain of Uhland's ballad lyrics. The Angel's Serenade in the dying girl to her mother, raises one as on the wings of hope and love to heaven. The Graf von Greiers, the wild grace and surpassing melody of the Dream, with the bitter-sweet accents of the joys that are never to return, echo in the heart, and thrill the very soul.

Dream.[1]

I dreamed not long ago
I lay on a lofty hill.
It was nigh the ocean strand,
And I saw far into the land,
And far, far o'er the sea.

Hard by the shore below
A dainty bark there lay,
With streamers brightly flowing,
For the pilot he was going,
Would brook no more delay.

There came from distant mountains
A joyous company.
Like angels glancing fair,
Flowers wreathed amid their hair,
They journeyed towards the sea.

They swept in long array,
This troop so fair and gay,
Some their bright cups swaying
Others dancing, playing,
With song and minstrelsy.

[1] Traum.

They said unto the skipper,
Wilt thou take us on our way.
Earth's hopes and joys we be,
Here no longer tarry we,
Must far from earth away.

Into the ship they hied them,
The joys both great and small.
And then he said, each dear one,
Behind remaineth none,
By dell or mountain wall.

They said, we are here together,
Now haste, we may not stay.[1]
And the swift winds freshly blew,
As on their way they flew,
Earth's hopes and joys that day.

197. THE MOUNTAIN SIDE.

It is glorious to rest by the mountain side, some lone Highland strath or long hill of Mourne, where the tall heather waves, and the clouds course along the sky, list to the lark's carol, the plover's call, and dream of heaven. For although we must work most times, we need to dream also, ponder things invisible, the coming time when life with all its marvels for us shall be no more.

The mountain's slope stretches with all its greenery to the sun, the brook bounds from shelf to shelf of its rocky bed, the breeze fans the passive hair, and everything bespeaks peace and quietude, the deep, the holy serenity of heaven.

But, now, the hill is clothed with grey, the winds rise as the evening falls. They wail, they almost sob,

[1] Fahr zu wir haben Eil.

and the heart is filled with care. Nature, the bountiful mother, has altered her mood, and the recipient soul, faithfully responsive, reflects it back again.

198. A TWOFOLD LIFE.

When we lose a being whom we love, observe William von Humboldt,[1] and Zschokke after him, we exist in two worlds. For love unlocks the gate, admits us to communion with the lost associates, whom once and for ever we shall join again. Fortitude to bear, with discernment to look beyond, has been imparted to us by heaven. To us, also, is the fair heritage, the silent realms of thought and love, embellished with every bright reality, all the affections that shed grace or glory on our kind.

199. ESOTERIC, EXOTERIC.

There are believers, esoteric and exoteric, those who believe in the spirit, and those who believe in the letter merely. Yet what were the letter except as a spiritual declaration, nothing, less than nothing, an unrecorded dream. Nature and man's soul are the very texts and sacred manuscripts of God, yield the only clue to the science of the universe. That there is a ceaseless inspiration made continually manifest in the heart of man, is among the most certain of spiritual truths.[2] Our convictions need incessant revision. The theology that is stationary is lost, nay, is already numbered with the

[1] Briefe an eine Freundinn.
[2] John Hancock's Address to the People called Quakers, Lisburn and Belfast, 1801.

past. Revelation and development are one. Where there is no development, there can be no revealing. Where there is no revealing, neither is there development. We must descend into the soul's depths, as we would refer to the green-robed trees, the golden stars. When we examine nature's developments, we discern the revealings of nature. When we ponder the developments of the soul, we discern the revealings of God in humanity. For the letter avails only as the symbol of progressive truth, genesis on genesis, development on development, for ever.

Progress is to be measured not by the coming or going of comets merely, the revolutions of the sun, but by the stirrings and the strivings, the workings and the winnings of those who are no more. Instead of only looking up through nature to nature's God, we shall find witness to him who moulded us, in the depths of our souls, looking out on nature from him, rising to nature on the wings of faith and love.[1] Let us build religion on science, indeed, but also on the heart, let us found it on the affections, but also on truth.

The religious teacher should combine an Aristotle and a Paul. The image of the Great Reformer beckons to us through the mists of eighteen hundred years. The swinging waves, the gushing fountains, the wind-chased clouds, the sighing breeze, the perfume-laden flowers, with men's fair thoughts and deeds, invite us to continue and perfect his work. To set forth mere formulas from the past without acting, loving, thinking for the present, will not, cannot suffice. We must

[1] *Talfourd's Vacation Rambles.*

elevate women, free the proletary and the slave, train and educate the ignorant, reform the vicious, rescue the famine-stricken and the insane, raise the downtrodden and the oppressed, set aside beliefs which degrade humanity, do not honour God, ere religion can avail us as it might and as it ought. For religion is a thing of freedom and of joy, of trust and of truth, of grace and of hope, of confidingness and of love, which yields no colour to baseness or degradation, and which can only subsist in its fulness and its grandeur in the hearts and in the practice of happy, regenerate man.

200. MATERIALISM.

Materialism is an hypothesis so much the more hazardous, since neither philosophy nor experience yields any proof, direct or indirect, of the existence, as vulgarly conceived, of matter.[1] The materialists not only affirm the exclusive existence of what they term matter, but they also reject interior observation,[2] affirm the identity of brain and mind. Yet the brain is not mind, exercises no one function of mind.[3] Like all matter, what we so term, is but a perception, the resultant of certain outward forces indeed, operating on the soul.

[1] *Ferrier's Institutes*, Prop. xii. § 3.
[2] Der Phrenologe theilt mit dem speculativen Psychologen den Irrthum sichere innere Beobachtung für unmöglich zu halten. Fortlage, *Psychologie*, Band i. S. 11.
[3] Es giebt gewisse Irrthümer im Menschengeist welche, obwohl an sich selbst nicht werth dass man sich mit ihnen beschäftigt, doch ein unleugbares Interesse bekommen. Zu ihnen gehört der Irrthum vom Sitz der Seele im Gehirn, Fortlage, *Id.* Band I. S. 108.

Man, in truth, has no mental instincts, whereas the brute has many, available for the various acts of life.[1] The problem of the brute, however, is one of singular difficulty, but one, also, which, happily, we are not required to solve. In man, himself, the thinking principle comprises the whole soul. Exclusive, indeed, of errors of observation and inference, the materialist commits the capital solecism of confounding the phenomena of the moral and material worlds.[2]

201. MUSIC CULTURE.

It seems incredible, almost, that the few elementary sounds supplied by nature, should constitute the foundation of the divine, the joyous thing which men term music. Yet, in nature, as in art, like laws prevail. In one as in the other, a half note must succeed three whole ones, major keys and minor must alternate. In the sensuous, as in the higher life, the law of needful change, the great law which pervades all nature, and on which all life and the joy of life depend, obtains.[3] Musical culture, and the culture of the feelings and affections, which rule or ought to rule it, should run together. For true culture is full of grace, flings a robe of loveliness over commonest things.

[1] *Holland's Mental Physiology*, p. 203.

[2] Wenn Feuerbach die Gedankenbildung eine Phosphorescenz des Gehirnes nennt, so hat er damit in trefflicher Weise die Impotenz der materialistischen Grundgedanken, die weder Licht noch Wärme zu erzeugen vermögen, sondern nur Schein-und-Irrlicht geben, characterisirt. Fabri, *Briefe gegen den Materialismus*, Stuttgart, 1856, p. 130.

[3] Gesetz des geforderten Wechsels, Göthe, *Gespräche mit Eckermann*, Feb. 1, 1827.

The solace of art, like other gifts divine, is addressed to the affections and intelligence of all. True sentiment imparts delicacy and refinement to music, which, as a science, an art, is indissolubly bound up with the spiritual and the unseen. Nothing, it has been said, more strongly proves the angelic tendency of music than the very tender age, as in the case of a Handel, a Haydn, a Mendelssohn, or a Mozart, at which the mind declares for it. For music in itself is heavenly, incites to celestial purity and truth.[1] In its chaste simplicity, it is replete with faith and nobleness, aspirations for the great, the generous, the good, yet with all its enchanting loveliness and simplicity, is not too fastidious or refined for the common uses and behoof of man. Allied as it is with heaven, it should be wedded to our aspirings and our affections, brought beside every hearth, and into every home.

202. A DIVINE TRANSFIGURATION.

As we grow older, wiser, better, a divine transfiguration, so to speak, should animate every countenance, inspiring at once nations and men. Yet, alas, it is often far otherwise. The revolting doctrine of demoniacal possession, has led to the destruction of whole hecatombs of men. Rose Cullender and Amy Duny once lived in happy, careless childhood, at Lowestoft. By and by, they grew up, grew old, and, in 1665, were attainted as witches, at Bury St. Edmonds,[2] before Sir

---

[1] Unter den Künsten ist die Music die religiöseste. Sie ist ganz Andacht, Sehnsucht, Demuth, Liebe. Tieck.
[2] *State Trials*, Volume VI.

Matthew Hale, who, pious Christian and humane man as he otherwise was, sentenced these poor creatures, not quite two centuries ago, to be charred alive. The excesses of the New-England Puritans, their weird and dreary laws, the juridical murder of Mary Dyer and others, show how utterly the principle of fanaticism can trample out every spark of pity in the breasts of otherwise sincere, and earnest, and pious men.

The trial of Urbain Grandier, a good and gentle priest, for the imputed crime of bewitching the Ursuline nuns, at Loudun,[1] is amongst the most singular of its kind.[2] A certain Père Lactance, under the inspection of an unjust magistrate, one Laubordemont, subjected Grandier, who had been previously stuck all over with pins to detect the badge of the fiend, to the accursed torture of the boot. They would also have torn out the nails of his feet and hands, but this the surgeons refused to perform. After his poor limbs, bone and flesh, had been crushed to a jelly, Grandier was fastened by a circle of iron to the stake, and consumed quick. May all such foul beliefs and evil dealings pass away, and men, chastened by the blessed conviction of God's felt though unseen presence, dwell as one family in his holy city for ever.

203. LIFE'S HEALING.

Duties, that usefulness which no crosses, no vexations, should interrupt, are, with the affections, life's great healing and reality. When we know that this planet is but a speck amid the profusion of immensity,

---
[1] Michelet, *Histoire de la France.*   [2] *Histoire des Diables de Loudun.*

how can any one cringing here, engaged in tortuous policy there, longing for that which only brings him nearer the end, not hesitate ere he sully his soul.[1] Why fear we to stand alone. The dread of blame, a morbid deference to opinion, is the secret weakness of many a soul, applies the axe to those great principles which lie at the root of all right action and generous enterprise.

Consider the divine instruction, how the highest teaching, the very treasures of the spiritual life, are addressed to all. A strenuous sense of duty, as it seems to me, must accrue from even a partial apprehension of these truths. On the other hand, the slightest impairment of moral tone is replete with injury to nations and men. For every effort should be made to commend all just and holy things to the great true heart of living, loving humanity, taking them out of the range of mere ritualism and barren profession, incorporating them with the actions, the affections, and convictions of our kind.

204. THE STARS OF SPIRITUAL TRUTH.

The stars of spiritual truth are brighter, clearer, because of the efforts and the insight of that genius, very instinct and effluence of heaven, which has removed from our eyes full many a film of clay. No, were principalities, and powers, and distinctions numerous as are the grains on the wave-washed strand, never could they sufficiently endow those great spirits to whom, coupled with insight and faith, we owe it, that

[1] *Claims of Labour*, 2nd ed. p. 42.

we are enabled to think, and act, and love, as beseems those who are to think, and act, and love for ever. Here is the spot indeed, now is the very time for devoted service to the spiritual and the unseen.

Human nature, in fact, is a hierarchy of powers, each, when it knows and holds its rightful place, destroying the usurpation of mean errors, restoring the sway of lordly truth, the right aim of morals in philosophy and action.[1] A noble life must spring from pure intention and sunny hope. What the soul's light pronounces incredible, that, in God's name, let us leave uncredited.[2] Truth alone, lives for ever, and we may not steal, were it into paradise, with falsehood in our mouths. We cannot hope to inherit heaven by fallacies on earth. For belief in human brotherhood and in the divine reversion which awaits us all, is the very salt and spiritual life of man. Through insight we discern that death is a new birth, that else, death is an impossibility, since once conscious we are so for ever, and that here we live in a twofold world.

The multitude must be educated, women trained to highest excellence, women, whose finer intuitions and loftier capabilities, we, nay they, have yet in a degree to learn.

How sweetly and equably might we glide along the stream of time, were the earth, through some newer, more spiritual crusade, awakened to the great realities, the lofty ideal, which, in consonance with God's eternal gospel, never for one moment cease to subsist around. Until we have moral and spiritual unity, the same

---

[1] *Westminster Review.* [2] Carlyle, *Life of Sterling.*

unity that obtains in the canons of lofty art and material science, there can be no effective or permanent progress. For belief and action, thought and affection, should extend to our daily life, shedding sanctity and security on the world. The very anticipation lends colour to the belief, while the love of everything great, and good, and beautiful, and true,[1] yields hope that one day we shall effectively abate the sin and evil, the error and the ignorance, that incrust the priceless gem we style the soul of man.

205. FREEDOM IN OBEDIENCE.

God knows each desire of our hearts, each thought and aspiration of our souls. Never can we enough appreciate his tender care. Yet, while we commune with and praise him, let us not put up mere begging petitions, ask him to stay the order of his providence, or to perform our special work for us, for this He will not do, however much we entreat him. Then let us look infinity in the face, and, bravely subduing selfishness, compass regeneration for ourselves. For where the spirit of God is felt, there also is liberty.[2] This conviction alone, subduing self indeed,[3] yields release from slavery, confers absolute freedom within the wide range of spiritual law. For there neither is nor can be, safety irrespective of incessant self-development, unconditional conformity with the divine.

---

[1] *Guizot's Corneille.*

[2] Ὁ δὲ Κύριος τὸ πνεῦμά ἐστιν, οὗ δὲ τὸ πνεῦμα κυρίου, ἐκεῖ ἐλευθερία.

[3] Οὐδεὶς ἐλεύθερος ἑαυτοῦ μὴ κρατῶν.

206. HEART'S CULTURE.

The longer I live, the more intimately am I persuaded of the urgent need of culture. Spasmodic utterances are here of no avail. The heart must be revived, there must, as thus, be a change of soul.[1] This it is, which can alone enable us to appreciate God's miracles, the marvels of man's skill. It is culture that imparts perception of the beautiful and the good, yields truest insight into literature, religion, science, art.[2] The education of the heart makes us cognizant of God's love, the treasures of goodness that subsist among our kind. Training supplements the divine providence, while the absence of training fills this our magnificent dwelling-place with lazar-houses for the helpless, the incompetent, and the insane, soaks the earth with blood, ravages it with crime. Without culture, man is a contradiction and a nonentity, as with it he becomes a creature but a little lower than the angels,[3] very counterpart and impress of heaven.

[1] Μετάνοια.

[2] Vous soulevez, mon ami, une grande question, celle de savoir mêler la poésie à la raison, l'imagination au positivisme, la tendresse à la discipline, dans la conduite chaque jour plus difficile de la vie. Pierre Bernard, *Confession du numéro* 13, *L' Union Médicale*, Paris, 25 Aout, 1859.

[3] Ἠλάττωσας αὐτὸν βραχῦ τι παρ ἀγγέλους.

ASPIRATIONS

FROM

THE INNER, THE SPIRITUAL LIFE.

BOOK V.

No knowledge of things, indeed, will supply the place of the early study of letters, *litterae humaniores*. Yet, it is not other than remarkable and humiliating, that some of those who taught the mental science of Aristotle or the speculative dogmas of the Schoolmen, should have wholly forgotten the successful energy which Aristotle and Galen, in the very dawn of literature, had expended in investigating the laws of organic life. Oxford, ancient seat of learning, was not exempt from this intellectual one-sidedness. It cultivated chiefly classic lore, and pursued the metaphysical notions of the Schoolmen, not always in the far-seeing spirit of true philosophy. It has taken some centuries from the epoch of Roger Bacon, followed here by Boyle, Harvey, Linacre, Sydenham, besides nearly two hundred years unbroken publication of the Royal Society's Transactions, to persuade this great English University to engraft on the education of her youth, any substantive knowledge of the great material design, the astonishing unwritten revelation, of which the supreme Master-worker has made us a constituent part. Acland.

Repandre dans le public des notions saines et precises. Chaque découverte est un coup de force qui absorbe, qui concentre, qui résume une multitude de petits essais, de petits faits antérieurs depourvus jusque-là de netteté, de cohérence, et de grandeur. Arago.

K

ASPIRATIONS.

207. ANGELIC COMMUNION.

COMMUNITY with angelic natures helps to make us participators with them. Breathing the same spiritual atmosphere, we come to share the divine effluence. The world, observes Fichte, is a moral arrangement, the very law of reason. For the kingdom of God, as Oersted so often says, is a kingdom of reason. We witness the divine, and call its author God. There cannot be a doubt that the ministry of the wise and good, both in the visible and invisible worlds, for the kingdom of reason and love, which is the kingdom of God, can never be at variance with itself, proves of precious efficacy in exalting and redeeming the priceless soul of man.

208. THE PURPOSE OF NATURE.

Nature, at once in the general and the detail, is choicely regulated in respect of the purposes of God. There is in it the immanent, as well as the outward adaptation which teleology, indeed, propounds. In this sense, only, can we agree with Schelling, that nature acts rationally, yet without consciousness, evoking the observer's sympathy, the poet's inspiration. Here, the philosophy of man's soul and of objective nature approximates, since the ethics of religion and of philosophy are one. Humanity, as Cousin well observes, is greater than nature. Humanity, however, comes from God, as well as nature. But while humanity recognises, nature is ignorant of Him.

209. MAN AND BRUTE.

The lower animals are born, rejoice, and die. Man they know, but the Divine they never know. Though conscious, they do not rise as man rises, to the perception of their consciousness.[1] They are not, although man in virtue of his spiritual nature be so, created in the image of God. He, indeed, sublime distinction, as Aristotle words it, is conscious that he is conscious,[2] and thus, by a privilege thrice exalted, arrives at the knowledge of heaven.

210. SPECULATION.

The speculations of German philosophers, like those of the Eleatics of old, are most interesting so long as they confine themselves to the actual phenomena of consciousness, with Hegel conjoining subject and object, if they please, but not, with Kant and Fichte, extinguishing the objective in the subjective, or with Schelling, and in a degree Oersted, sacrificing subjectiveness to objectiveness. Thus, when in words they would depicture the mysteries of the infinite, the unconditioned, the Absolute, in short the irrecognisable essences

---

[1] Der grösste Theil der Welt in welcher er lebt ist für das Thier so gut als nicht vorhanden, muss eine Art von Traumbild bleiben. Fortlage, *Psychologie, Erweckung durch Triebe*, § 50.

[2] Νοησις της νοησεως.

of nature, our own being, and of God, they become alike unintelligible to others and themselves.[1]

211. THE INNER POWER.

The power which by degrees we build up in the soul, can alone rescue us, when evil principles would cut us off from unity with our better selves and with the divine, the one thing which shall sustain, and finally realise the glories of the higher life, a loftier heaven, and unspeakable felicities to come.

212. THE MAGICAL IN NATURE.

There is a magical, a so to speak enchanted, side of our inner, spiritual nature, which, were it not rooted in the very depths of our being, would long since have been crushed out of us. We love the old narrations of our childhood, the wondrous English, Scottish, and Irish tales, the queer, delightful recitals of a Grimm, a Tieck, or a Musaeus, the glorious Arabic Nights. Of all moderns however, leaving aside what we find in him of the too fantastic and appallingly grotesque, Hoffmann has perhaps most forcibly appreciated nature's enchanted utterances. An admirable artist and musician, he rejoiced in the play of colours,

---

[1] Ainsi que l'ont si bien dit Plotin et Proclus, ainsi que l'a répété Fenelon avec tous les grands docteurs de l'Eglise, retrancher de la Divinité tous les attributs qui lui répugnent, ce n'est pas la diminuer, c'est au contraire l'enrichir. Mais du moment qu'on essaie de l'élèver au-dessus même de la catégorie de l'être, qu'on en fait un je ne sais quoi que échappe à la pensée, et qui ne peut être saisi que par un acte tout aussi chimérique que son objet, n'abuse-t-on pas étrangement de la methode rationelle. Vacherot, *Ecole d'Alexandrie*, iii. 465.

every harmony, the mysteries of sound and of sweet perfume, the ravishing incense of flowers, the melody of birds. For him, indeed, they realised, in their degree, the ecstasies of heaven. Believe, he said, only believe, for belief is love, and truth, and eternity. All this he sets forth in his narratives, unsurpassed perhaps in any tongue. List to him, were it but for a moment, as he sings.[1] Glowing tulips, and hyacinths, and roses, raise their fair heads. Our perfumes, they said, are the longings, the joys, the ecstasies of love. We are thine, thine, beloved one, they cry, thou who dost understand us, thine for ever more.

213. EVOLUTION OF THE DIVINE.

There is not a station, a position, which does not afford scope for usefulness, the evolution of the divine. For, let us only try to realise it, we are in the very paradise of God, environed by his presence and his love, if we will. The seeds of error and wrong-doing should be continually burnt out of us, by a divine contrition and regret. For God, indeed, pays us, step by step, for each duty accomplished, and word uttered in his name.[2] Every effort develops our moral strength, since to the conquering energy of firm resolve, in truth, does heaven commit the liberty and progress of our race.

In the culture of the individual, resides the true

---

[1] Glühende Hyazinthen, und Tulipanen und Rosen erheben ihre schönen Häupter, und ihre Düfte rufen in gar lieblichen Lauten dem Glücklichen zu. Unser Duft ist die Sehnsucht der Liebe. Wir lieben Dich Geliebter der Du uns versteht, und sind Dein immerdar. *Der Goldne Topf, Zwölfte Vigilie.*

[2] Bungener. *The Priest and the Huguenot,* tr. Lond. 1854.

nobility of man, very temple and representative of the Infinite and the Unseen.[1] For let us only reflect, not one man but all men are born in paradise, mighty, sanctifying truth that seems but now to flash upon the convictions of our kind.

214. SEEDS OF PARADISE.

From our common capacities drop the seed, from which, if ever, the bloom of paradise must expand and blossom in the soul. Without culture, some fostering for the heart, raising the rejoicing spirit on wings of hope and love to heaven, divinest energies remain frozen and inert. Spiritual life and progress are incompatible with grovelling ignorance and sordid cares. The mighty principles which, at the cost of so much suffering and sacrifice, have been born into the world, should not be suffered to lapse through indifference and neglect, but giving issue to an evangel of deeds and affections, and not of words merely, interpenetrate every emotion and action of our lives.

215. EVIL TO BE OVERCOME.

Evil, or rather the potentiality of evil, is not instituted for evil's sake, but for the development of our fortitude, our forbearance, and our strength. Smooth seas, it has been said, do not make a mariner, nor uninterrupted prosperity a man. It is better far to incur the ache of spiritual pain, than the consciousness of moral defeat. Were it rendered impossible to err, how should we imitate the spiritual, the divine beauty, the

[1] Ναος και εικὼν του Θιου του ἀορατου.

infinite perfection, in short, which is the source of all truth, all excellence, in a word, the holy, the infinite Intelligence which men term God.

216. THE ANGEL ON GUARD.

The belief in a guardian angel, solacing and elevating as, in a degree, it undoubtedly is, also serves to flatter our indolence and our self-repose. Fain, indeed, would we lean upon another, rather than on ourselves. But each several soul must prove its own angel, must mount guard for itself. And any belief that turns attention from this, frustrates the divine intention, is fraught with ill. For God requires our best individual development, in goodness, intelligence, and strength. Would we realise the bliss, avoid the bane, we must watch well. Eternal vigilance is the price of liberty. And, after all, we have angels to guard and to save, beneath our roof and at our very doors. Man, in truth, with all his sympathy and love, is responsible to man. The great spiritual republic, householders, angels and archangels of God, with the moral law, urging us to progress, and self-discipline, is on guard for us ceaselessly.

217. PRAYER AND PRAISE.

I have heard the Africans, poor children of the night, pray openly, audibly for things most material. Yet, prayer is also testimony to an unseen power, the soul's devotion to the Author of our days. And, therefore, should prayer be unselfish, simple, holy, pure, the expression of our deepest thankfulness, the avowal of error, the confession of a better resolve, and ceaseless, tireless, heartfelt praise.

218. EFFORT AND DEVELOPMENT.

Conduct and character are a mean at least of two factors, the training we receive, with the efforts we make and the attention we bestow. Consciousness, in truth, is the spot in which each instant we build up our heaven or our hell, the soil in which the seeds of goodness are blighted or experience development divine, that development short of which, we cannot exercise our trust with advantage to others or profit to ourselves.

219. THE OBJECT AND THE PURSUIT.

The pursuit is often of vastly greater moment than the thing pursued. Love, a lofty ambition, all the celestial affections, become more or less disinterested, realise in a degree the object aimed at. The love of God, the earnest desire to reach the higher mansions, the hidden, the better life, proves its own reward. For a continual aiming, is likewise a ceaseless becoming, and realisation as well.

220. PROGRESSION.

Individuals, sects, may err, but truth is ever progressive. Fain would we bind convictions to our confessions, but we might as well bind space, or light, or time. The formula, indeed, remains, but man is borne along the river of life to the ocean of eternal truth. The fundamental, the vital, retains its significance, but the form is cast aside, cumbers the stream, or drifting shoreward, like other waifs, marks the advances of opinion and the progress of the centuries.

221. THE MORNING STARS.

I have but reached my quiet fireside. It is still the early morn, and, save the stirrings of those who tend the sick, no sound is heard, no moving light is seen. The moon, indeed, with gentle radiance, holds her sweet regency aloft, and stars innumerable begem the sky. The poor wanderers have betaken them to their dreary rest, and, except the guardians of the night, and the tenants of the grave, the once animated envelops of those we loved, none remain abroad. But God is with us, he is with all. He is everywhere, and the chastened soul looks out upon the mighty universe, where all is perfection, all is divine.

222. THE SPIRIT IN THE FLESH.

We are spiritual beings indeed, but with the accompaniment of the material by which our souls are nursed, made free as it were of the celestial republic,[1] cognizant of the adorable harmonies which pervade the world, and the thrice-admirable affections of our kind.

223. NIL DESPERANDUM.

The saddest day is sure to pass, the weariest night to close. Grim difficulty, it may be, is stared out of countenance, and common-sense and self-control assume

---

[1] Luce intellettual piena d'amore,
Amor di vero, ben pien de letizia,
Letizia che trascende ogni dolzore.   Dante.

their lofty sway. The wise and good, those who would realise truth divine, have earned at least the right to scan the future with courage and with hope.

224. OUR VERY BEST.

What we do, each according to his measure, we should do well, even as God does each thing well. His medals have no reverse. The flowers that flourish in the desert, are lovely as those that blossom in the parterre. Bright rubies and red gold lie buried in the drift, where human skill and endurance shall one day perchance unearth them. The utterest savage that bears the name and wears the lineaments of man, however decried by the arrogance of an imperfect civilisation, has yet within his soul the loftiest capabilities, a receptivity, indeed his birthright, for the most ennobling culture. In every infant house capacities, powers which never yet have been all unfolded. Yet, were they only roused, life even here, might become a continued series of heaven-ward enterprise,[1] and as the poet hymns it,

> A fair still house well kept,
> Which humble prayers had swept,
> And holy thoughts made clean.

225. THE AFFECTIONS.

The affections are the ecstasy of existence, key of paradise, very life and glory of the soul. With divinest

[1] Prima creatura Dei fuit lux sensus, postremo lux rationis. Et hoc ipsum est, coelo in terris frui, quando mens humana in caritate movetur, in providentia quiescit, et supra polos veritatis circumfertur. Bacon.

discernment they spring instant to the mark, ere reason, tardy leader, finds time to bring up the rear. And thus it is that sentiment partakes of the divine grace, aids us in the discharge of duty, the inspiration indeed of God, the very voice of heaven.

226. FAITH AND FACT.

Some formulas are the embodiment of celestial truth, as others are of hideous error. Yet were a formula never so beautiful, never so true, one should prefer to embrace it with heart and understanding, rather than with blind zeal or unreasoning constraint. Alas, if this be so, when truth is the issue, how intolerable must prove the spiritual arrogance which seeks to impose what is revolting and untrue. For when the soul is prepared, nothing can stay the reception of truth, but when it is unprepared, so neither will it entertain truths the most precious, and clear to others as the day.

227. THE FORMULA AND THE TRUTH.

The ill-constituted mind merges the natural in the supernatural and unintelligible. The savage looks upon the hurricane and the eclipse as symbols of some divine Nemesis, while we who boast our civilisation, would detect the immediate intention of providence in conditions so eminently artificial and modifiable as a famine, the productiveness or the unproductiveness of a tract of soil, the ravages of disease. This, however, is far outdone in the pretention to direct religious illumination,[1] when this, as it has so often done, going

---

[1] *The Lord's Doings with George Müller*, 5th Ed.

the length of every extravagance, outrages reason at once human and divine.

The mingling, observes the Canon of St. Paul's, of human error with religious truth, has given birth to fanaticism in all ages.[1] To purge popular convictions, to educate the people, to reconcile faith, and truth, and love, and hope, is a task that yet awaits the intelligence of our kind.

228. DIVINE CONSIDERATION.

With what divine consideration and courtesy, so to speak, does God treat us every one. By day he lights our path with the genial sun, by night with the radiant stars. He recreates our nostrils with sweetest odours, with ravishing harmonies our ears. By treating men as better than they are, indeed, we oftentimes develop their higher qualities, surprise them, as it were, into goodness. There was not a boy whom Arnold could not lead by the magic touch of kindness, a sailor's granite heart whom Ball did not mould as if it were very wax. And thus are men impelled to goodness by a fascination which they find it impossible to resist.

229. PERFECT LOVE.

Perfect love casteth out fear.[2] Denunciation and hatred, in truth, would expire, were only sympathy and intelligence the measure of our souls.[3] The worst blindness is spiritual blindness, but love guided by in-

---
[1] Sydney Smith, *Essay on Methodism.*
[2] Ἡ τελεία ἀγάπη ἔξωβάλλει τον φόβον.
[3] Qui vult habere notitiam Dei, amet. Hugo de St. Victor.

telligence casts out this blindness. For these, completed and perfected, coupled with the ever-growing consciousness of the divine presence, must one day subdue and get the better of all guilt, and sin, and despair. And when this adorable consummation ensues, spiritual blindness and hardness of heart shall be no more.

230. CULTURE AND SELF-CULTURE.

All education, all bringing-up, all training, are but as preparatives to that self-culture without which we cannot reach the higher life, in fine, realise the kingdom of heaven.

No philosopher, perhaps, appreciated better than did Bruno, God's universal presence.[1] Those, he says,[2] who realise it, need apprehend no suffering, nor sorrow nor vicissitude can touch them any more. They feel the divine laws in their hearts and obey them. For this is the true endowment which elevates and purifies the intelligence, leads us to real happiness, teaches the impossibility of death.

231. HEART'S INFLUENCE.

In commenting on the great issues of human life and man's fortunes, the heart too often is left out. Yet it is precisely by and through the heart, as supplemented by the understanding, that such things can be understood and explained. In short, without moral sympathy, in firmest unison with the affections, our best intelligence is at fault. This, which is so true of elevated humanity, culminates in the Godhead. And this

---

[1] Vacherot, T. iii. p. 108.   [2] *Dell' Infinito Universo et Mondi.*

is the true, the only Theodicea, that conception of infinite goodness and perfection which alone befits the divine Author of love, and wisdom, and beauty, and all excellence.

232. CONFIDING IN THE DIVINE.

Let us cast aside all fear and apprehension, and cherish a boundless confidingness in the divine, for the soul can never die. We speak of death as awful, whereas the real awfulness is to dread death at all. It is a great and wondrous, nay, most solemn change, but tempered with the sweetest affections, truest hope, and tenderness divine. For the death which we behold, and of which we too much speak and think, is but of the material,[1] whereas the real death is translation to heaven, and God's presence, with every glorious fruition to come.

233. PHILOSOPHY AND FAITH.

Philosophy demonstrates what faith takes for granted. Theology, rightly understood, is the application of philosophy to religion, involves the same care, patience, and study, as any other branch of science.[2] Faith never doubts, never questions, whereas philosophy doubts, questions, and, where it can, resolves. Religion involves the union of philosophy with faith, blessed nuptials which realise the true ideal, and the deep conviction of a happy, an active, and ever-conscious eternity.

[1] Vom Tode als Freiwerden des innern Sinnes. Fortlage, *Das Selbst oder die Person*, § 39.
[2] Preface by a Mother to *Greave's Maxims on Education*, Lond. 1841.

234. REVELATION OF THE BEAUTIFUL.

Beauty, the great Artist's gift, in its ineffable sweetness, is indeed a revelation of the divine. The sense of beauty, which sometimes steals over the human soul through avenues of sense, gives promise of heavens, worlds, realities, transcending far our own. A surpassing excellence, in truth, dwells around, scenes which tell of paradise to the heart, nay, are a paradise bespeaking love and hope divine. The lily, the carnation, and the rose, fair sisters of the family of flowers, with their enchanting loveliness and grace, are as gifts from the very treasuries of heaven. Since, as the poet, with truest, sweetest insight, says,

> Not a natural flower can grow on earth
> Without a flower upon the spiritual side.[1]

Thus, too, some fair young child shall evince a radiance of loveliness, inferior to the beauty of holiness, and purity, and truth, alone. For there is an instinctive perception of beauty, in perfect conformity with divine reason, as there is an instinctive perception of goodness, in man. But in one case, as in the other, it needs culture for its preservation and development, else it declines and is seen no more.

235. GENIUS.

Genius, in a sense, is the glorification of humanity, the culmination of the spiritual in man. It is, indeed, a moral struggle, and patience, and crowning victory.

[1] E. Barrett Browning.

Without it, never should we conceive, much more achieve, the great ideal which resides in man. Every one, indeed, has seeds of excellence within him, yet are they realised to the full but in the few, since to the few, only, is it given to approach the fairy palace, aided, since genius must needs thus be aided, by the lamp.[1]

An exquisite feature in true genius is its spontaneity. It perceives relations which else escape observation, compasses results, which, to dulled perceptions, seem impossible, and indeed, until realised, unimaginable. For genius imparts divinest breadth and fulness to the soul, girds it with a glory as of gold. Misery, and poverty, and misappreciation,[2] have assailed, while on earth, many a child of paradise, though now transfigured, and like some Castor or Pollux, transferred to the stars.[3] Yet, since genius itself is angelic, it were better if united ever with prudence, serenity under difficulties,[4] the noblest temper and self-control, in fine the young child's heart, the genial wisdom of the man.

236. POETRY.

Poetry exists but to interpret life. It is indeed a revealing from heaven, although not all revealing. It deals with our joys, loves, affections, clothes with fresh

[1] Bulwer, *Address to the Students of Glasgow University*.
[2] Barbarus hic sum, quia non intelligor ulli. Ovid.
[3] Tröstet euch, ihr Unerkannten, ihr von dem Leichtsinn, von der Unbill des Zeitgeistes gebeugten. Euch ist gewisser Sieg verheissen, und der ist ewig, da Euer ermüdender Kampf nur vorübergehend war. Hoffmann, *Schriften, Höchst Zerstreute Gedanken*, Berlin, 1845, p. 73.
[4] Sursum corda.

life and beauty, each grand, and just, and generous thing. It is the utterance of a golden hope, an infinite longing, aspirations only quenchable in the waters of eternity. It imparts form and substance to what else were shadowy and void, yields visible, audible reality to the lovely secrets of earth and heaven. It is not music, yet its whispers are most musical. Poetry, in short, reveals the mysteries of the invisible, deals with the language of angels, pourtrays the celestial union of goodness and refinement in the human soul. It is, indeed, the very waywiser to heaven, to which it points as with a smile, and says, there, there is your home for ever.[1]

237. SPIRITUAL SAFETY.

Salvation is realised by every creed, not in virtue of its errors, but of its truths. We must deal tenderly with human illusions, not from fear, indeed, but a motive far more generous. It is not doctrine only, but purity of soul, reconciliation with God, that yields spiritual safety. For to be good is to be saved, is to be at one with God and with heaven. The moral law, in truth, is not less certain and immutable now, than it was in the remotest past. For religion is made for man, not merely man, essence and record of the divine, for religion. Moral truth and practice, coupled with

---

[1] Verzweifelt nicht und hofft und traut,
   Die Welt sieht immer Schein,
   Was hin ihr in die ew'ge baut,
     Scheint nimmer und wird seyn.

Johanna Gray, Zu ihrem Bildniss. Herder, *Werke*, Stuttgart, 1852, Band xiii. S. 188.

the religious affections, lie at its root. Love of truth, with the conviction of its vital necessity, is the piety of the intelligence, love of God and of humanity is the piety of the heart.

It is better, in respect of any great and good thing, to be worthy of success rather than to obtain it, to be, in short, rather than to seem, or were it even to know. If we can but find the golden key, we have paradise at hand. For this, this is the mighty truth which the centuries have revealed, that heaven is everywhere, and God is ever nigh.

In religion, indeed, as in other things, we aim many times ere we hit the mark. Religious un-truth has hurt a multitude of souls, yet the divine signature is written in the skies, is impressed on faithful souls. Piety strengthens the moral sentiments, while they in turn impart a right direction to the affections, the spiritual beauty which it is a heaven to realise and to behold. For there is freedom in obedience, the freedom that springs from within, freedom as in God's presence, the freedom that yields the utmost scope of action, since it compasses at once the visible and the invisible kingdoms of heaven.

238. THE PITCHER OF TEARS.

Things of beauty and of grace abound in the tales of old, and thus it is with the Pitcher of Tears, which goes very near the heart. It was of a mother who dearly loved her child, and could not live or be without it. But a sickness came upon the children, and the little one lay upon its couch and was ready to die.

Three days and nights the mother wept, and watched, and prayed, ere her darling was taken away. Then was she seized with a nameless sorrow, for she was alone on God's earth, and wept day and night, calling on her child. And on the third night, as full of sadness and weary with tears, she sat on the spot where the young child died, the door gently opened, and lo, there stood her child. It had become a happy angel, and smiled sweetly as innocence, and beautiful as one transfigured. In its hand it bore a pitcher, full to the brim. Mother, said the child, weep no more. For see, this pitcher holds the tears which thou hast shed, and which the angel of grief has gathered therein. And if thou dost shed but another tear, then must the pitcher overflow, and I shall no longer have peace in my grave or joy in heaven. Therefore, O mother, weep no more, for thy child is well above, is happy, and has angels for its mates. And so strong and mighty is a mother's love, that she stilled her soul's deep pain, and wept no other tear.[1]

239. SPIRITUAL RECLAMATION.

The progress of souls from darkness to light, from ignorance to knowledge, is among the more beautiful spectacles of our spiritual life. And, soon or late, this is a consummation which awaits us all. Yet, spiritual reclamation, whether on the large scale or the small, demands concentration of purpose, energy, and intelligence.

[1] So stark und mächtig ist Mutterliebe, Bechstein, *Deutsches Märchenbuch, Das Thränenkrüglein.*

Would we realise heaven, let us begin now. The paradise of our aspirations has its foundations here, and the capacities of the future are grounded on those of the present life.

> A twofold cosmos, natural things and spiritual,
> Must go to a perfect world.
> For whoso separates those two,
> In arts, in morals, or the social drift,
> Tears up the bond of nature and brings death.[1]

As we love here, we shall love in a degree hereafter, as we feel and think now, so must we in somewise feel and think for ever. The unseen world, with all its momentous transactions, let us be assured, is simple and natural as that in which we dwell.[2] Ascetic horrors and ascetic gloom, travestying and deforming with frightful, yet vain imaginings, the beautiful city of God, are sorry preparatives for heaven. How, indeed, should sourness and formality, convictions on which no ray of imagination or feeling seems to shine, consort with the angelic amenities, the transporting assurances of the life to come. For this, let us be well assured, is not as some inquisition torture-chamber,[3] reformatory hulk, or condemned cell. In the celestial life, as here, so surely as God is light, and truth, and love, goal shall succeed goal, and quest follow quest, for ever. A new iris shall spring up, not to foil past efforts, but to allure us on to new, a constant becoming of which the perfect realisation is never. There, indeed, the great-

---
[1] Elizabeth Barrett Browning.
[2] *Physical Theory of Another Life.*
[3] Folterkammer.

souled patriot shall freedom find at last, there each self-denying saint the sanctities which lie folded within the inner life, and of which the perfect home is heaven.

240. PROVIDENCE, OF HEAVEN.

All men, but through conviction, through love, shall yet be of one mind, one soul. The worst, the only heresy is an unworthy life, tenets that torture the affections, suffocate the heart. Nothing, long can live that love condemns. Every view that is not in strictest accordance with the moral spiritual law, must yield. Every sectarian church must be included in God's church. It is the prime commendation and peculiar feature of Christianity, that it inculcates the infinite significance of man's soul, not of one man but all men, not of a select few but of the whole. The most levelling of doctrines, it is nevertheless one which levels upwards, makes as much account of the peasant, as of the prince's soul. The unbought mercies of God are set at no other price than renunciation and purity. For as the poet greatly sings,

> Not even God himself,
> Can save man else, than as he holds his soul.

Let us have a lofty conception as to the aims and objects of the spiritual life, that eternal, that ceaseless aspiration, which is not the tissue of negations to which some would fain condemn it.[1] For they err, indeed, who conceive that God has fallen through in the economy of the world, since the designs of heaven never

[1] Pectus est quod facit theologum.

fall through. Divine providence was perfect in all its parts on the first day, as it is now, and so shall remain to the end.

241. THE QUEEN OF NATURE.

With all her errors, shortcomings, and imperfections, woman is the queen of nature, cynosure of excellence, guardian, in truth, and preserver of our kind. Genius, indeed, exerts a like conservancy, but genius is partial and occasional, whereas woman's influence is everywhere and at all times. Woman represents the unselfish affections, affections most angelic, most divine, God's tender mercies, his directest handiwork. Without her ceaseless conservative influence, our race would lapse into remediless barbarism. For woman dwells nigh the springs of life, and close by the very gates of heaven. The character of every human being depends, of necessity, on some one woman.[1] And, therefore, whatever redeems and elevates woman, at large, yields scope to her angelic nature, also tends to the preservation and elevation of our kind.

[1] Wie ein nüchtern Vögelchen, das höret,
Siehet seiner Mutter Flügel schlagen
Ueberm Neste, wenn sie Speis ihm bringet,
Und es neu belebt mit Blick und Speise—
* * * *
Ungeduldig reg' ich meine Flügel
Voll von innrer Liebe, dass ich selbst mich
Wie vergessend, nur bei ihm, bei ihm bin,
Ihn zu loben, ihm zu danken.
Herder, Nach Vittoria Colonna, *Sehnsucht nach Gott.* *Werke*, B. xiii. S. 363.

242. THE LOWER ANIMALS.

The principal sympathies of the lower animals, the mutual sympathies of like species of course excepted, are with man. Fable, indeed, has long adumbrated a closer relation between man and brute than fact has sufficed to realise. Occurrences there are, from time to time, however, which touch the heart. Nor are the examples few in which the lower animals, those grateful creatures of God, have evinced their sympathy and attachment in the very article of death.

243. PALACES, DIVINE.

This world and the worlds we do not see are cities, palaces of God, sustained in beauty and perfection by his unflagging wisdom and power.[1] The day, indeed, must come when man shall adorn this fair earth as he never yet has adorned it, when he shall cover it with creations of loveliness and grace, and when, like the inner life itself, our material existence shall receive accessions, experience developments,[2] compared with which the past shall seem very faint and poor.

244. THE VOICES OF THE TELEGRAPH.

Music has received quite a new development in the telegraph. This we come to discern, when, the winds

---

[1] Der Anblick giebt den Engeln Stärke
Da keiner Dich ergründen mag,
Und alle Deine hohen Werke
Sind herrlich wie am ersten Tag. Faust, *Prolog im Himmel.*

[2] Sobald man die Trägweite der Gesetze des innern Sinnes ermessen lernt, sobald der Quell sprudelt wird man trinken. Fortlage.

blowing fitfully, we apply the ear to the standards which sustain the wires. Aeolian harps of surpassing richness and expression, abound by the highways. Some, in truth, are discords, but others are as the ravishing voices of chorusing angels. They have the beauty, too, which the music of Palestrina so peculiarly possesses,[1] of sustaining almost without interruption, a body of sound of unspeakable sweetness and power. A single one of the invisible vocalists may cease his song, but others take up the strain, and so, on and on, as if for ever. The ocean, indeed, as it booms on the Causeway of the Giants or some western Irish strand, alone may match the telegraphic wires. For here, too, swell succeeds swell, and utterance utterance, with fitful peal, as each gigantic wave rolls with unspeakable majesty to its bourne, hymning the praises of the mighty God and sweeping the soul to heaven.

245. TRANSFIGURATION OF LOVE.

As the man beholds the woman
As the woman sees the man,
Curiously they note each other,
As each other only can.

Never can the man divest her
Of that wondrous charm of sex,
Ever must she dreaming of him,
The same mystic charm annex.[2]

There is in all nature nothing comparable to love's glamourie, for seeing the lover sees not, hearing he does

---
[1] Palestrina rufft in unserer Seele das Bild der Ewigkeit. *Tieck.*
[2] B. W. Procter.

not understand. What he sees, indeed, in a measure is not, what he hears was never said. The lover and the loved one are transfigured alike, seem different, and in effect are so. And thus it is with all true passion. Anything or nothing suffices for its staple. For passion can gild the veriest dross, make the pebble seem a glittering gem, impart to lead the sheen of yellow gold.

Love elevates the little, holds yet more aloft the mighty. The meanest of souls, if happily entrapped into this sweet delirium, has tasted of real heaven. After all, there is no deceit in love, which shows our divine capacities, yields loftiest token of man's immortal destiny. Strange, yet sweet enchantment, that can make those subjected to it, if only for the passing instant, so renounce all base, and low, and wicked things, converting man and woman alike, into angels of light. The lover, then, is not all deceived, for the being who has fixed his gaze, if she reciprocate his preference, becomes in a sense divine. The image which the soul cherishes, is real enough for the time. The intention of Providence is carried out, and humanity, if but for the moment, has supped on ecstasy.

246. THE HEAVEN IN OUR PATH.

The commonest utterances of feeling, provided they be genuine, spring from the heart and find their way there. Raphael discovered his divinest madonnas by some wayside cottage, or beneath a vine. Heaven, in truth, crops out everywhere, since it is everywhere. For oft God imparts glimpses of the celestial land, many a gleam of purple and golden light. Often, too, you shall hear voices, witness a gaze, in which all the blessed affections stand revealed. For,

> Earth indeed, is crammed with heaven,
> And every common bush afire with God.[1]

I am not afraid to die, murmured a poor woman to whom I had shown some little kindness, kissing my hand with her fevered lips, and bedewing it with her tears, as she spoke. A peasant woman recounting to me her humble fortunes, told me, with many a sob, of those whom she had loved and lost, how her dying child took from beneath his pillow a fragment of slate, it was all he had, and handing it to his father, feebly faltered, take it father, it will cleanse your spade. Once, too, I beheld a poor son of toil trying, with hands welked and horny, to attire his motherless babes. Dust and moulder lay thick around, but the sun shone through the cobwebbed panes, and seemed to bless the work.

247. TRUE REFORM.

All true reform, repentance and restitution alike, comes from within. There, freedom is seated or nowhere. There, indeed, do we rise or fall, since there only is the man. This great truth the Stoics urged with all their souls. Their philosophy was a ceaseless exhortation to cultivate that freedom and moral self-assertion, which can no more be given, than they can be taken away. For self-restraint and moral earnestness are the very life and sinews of the soul, bring

[1] E. B. B.

victory and dominion over self, the divine purity which bows only to the verdicts of conscience and of heaven.

248. TURNING TO GOD.

In moments of great joy or extreme despondency, the soul turns spontaneously to God, Author of the sweet affections and of every joy, rock indeed and founder of the universe, man's mighty sustainer and stay.[1] And the higher the soul aspires, the more continually do angel voices, do hope, and truth, and trust, and love, cry out to their Author and source, the more ceaseless become the longings for the things of the unseen life and realities to come.

249. GENESIS OF SOULS.

Where there is no genius, no inventiveness, no love of knowledge, in fine no moral or spiritual freedom, there will be no great men. For moral death borders closely on spiritual. The soul is handed over to materialism, chained to formulas, which fail utterly to bespeak the infinite, the inviolate tenderness of the great Father and Parent of our kind.

250. A MIND DISEASED.

Insanity, whether as regards the mind or the heart, is simply the last result of impaired control over one's soul. Indolence, hypochondriasis, imbecility, spleen, in their several degrees, are forms of the same drear malady. But insanity evinces as many varieties as does the sound mind itself. It is still mind, indeed,

[1] Ein' feste Burg ist unser Gott. Martin Luther's Hymn.

but mind in ruin, perversion, and decay. Partial insanity, the tyranny of false ideas and emotions, or of emotions or ideas wrongly placed, is the minimum of which confirmed insanity, dementia, in short mental ruin, is the maximum. Multitudes, wanting power over their own minds, are continually lapsing into insanity, or living on its very verge. For, let us repeat it, there is no exact line of demarcation between the sane and the insane. The defects and perversions of the insane mind, are simply, in a more or less exaggerated form indeed, the deficiencies and perversions of the sane mind itself.

The more decided our self-mastery, the greater, so to speak, is the impossibility of becoming insane. But the feebler our self-jurisdiction, the more the soul is given up to a perverted will, is wanting in development, the greater becomes the proclivity to spiritual decay. Illdirected culture alone, lies at the root of this monstrous evil, and not mere disorganization of the brain and nerves, as an illogical, and, in itself, in truth, insane hypothesis, would have us to imagine.

251. TO-PAN.

Among the earlier declarations of Pantheism is the sublime inscription at Saïs. All that was, and is, and shall be, am I, and mortal yet has never raised my veil.[1] Hardly less peremptory is the affirmation of Spinoza. There neither is, nor is it possible to conceive, any substance save the Divine.[2] For, indeed, we

---

[1] Εγώ ἐιμι πᾶν το γεγονὰς, καὶ ὄν καὶ ἐσόμενον, καὶ τὸν ἐμὸν πέπλον οὐδείς πω θνητὸς ἀπεκάλυψε.

[2] Praeter Deum nulla dare neque concepi potest substantia.

only reach truth, each object of moral interest, every natural conclusion concerning God, the soul, and future destiny of man, approximately.[1] Yet, the cultivators of spiritual science shall one day join hand in hand, while a loftier goddess than that at Saïs, with smiles shall raise her veil.

252. SWIFT.

Swift, with his subtle irony, bore resemblance to him who aided to rehabilitate the memory of Calas. He was a great-souled man too, of inflexible honesty, iron energy, and vast attainments. But his soul seemed cased in steel, and his character, as a whole, is of painful interest. Devoted hearts there were too, which beat but for him, and bled as well as beat. Alas and alas, for he was very unhappy. All his peculiarities seem referable to his consuming ambition and personal wretchedness. He might, apparently, form no wedded tie, and his ambition was a blight. For him, indeed, there was no peace, could not well be any till he reached the bourne, where, as is graven on his chancel tomb, fierce indignation no longer lacerates the poor troubled heart of man.[2]

253. THE SOUL'S HEALING.

It was the remark, though only conditionally true, of a keen thinker,[3] that the mind's health is not more certain than that of the body. That the mind, the

---

[1] Hamilton's *Discussions on Philosophy and Literature*, Lond. 1852.
[2] Ubi saeva indignatio ulterius cor laceraro nequit.
[3] La Rochefaucauld.

thought-mind and the heart-mind, may become diseased, and so undergo a sort of living death, is most true. Spiritual health must be upheld by strenuous effort. Would you sustain the soul's health, act wisely. Would you sustain the heart's health, do good. By doing good, in truth, you become good. But there must be the constancy and purity of purpose that can suffer no weakness, tolerate no stain. For life is too short, the stake too great, to squander on secondary aims, to the prejudice of the holier sentiments and affections.

Foolish pretension, mock greatness, are a sorry exchange for the lofty purposes of a temporal, an eternal existence. No, nothing should be suffered to override our sense of self-respect and usefulness. We forfeit very treasures of wisdom, and tenderness, and goodness, owing to our poverty of conception and spiritual inability to appreciate them.

God, the infinitely pitiful and merciful, sanctifies our efforts, blesses the results. For to him, in truth, as the poet sweetly words it,

<blockquote>Each wish is as a prayer.</blockquote>

Life is a combat in the face of difficulties, with heaven and all the angels as spectators. It is an inexpugnable truth that man will obtain what he deserves, will find what is really good for him, exactly as he seeks for it.[1] Like the Titans of old, we must scale the heavenly heights by efforts of our own. But it is needful to cherish nothing at variance with the soul's

[1] *Westminster Review*, Oct. 1853.

weal, with purity and truth.[1] Now, science can accomplish this for us, at least in part, that science within whose sacred precincts no grovelling error or revolting superstition can survive. To overcome evil with good, to have no paltering with sin, and, hand in hand with the divine, to compass purity and truth, is indeed to win the life celestial on earth, and secure its reversion in heaven.

254. PROGRESSIVE PURITY.

The real riches comprise every expansion of the heart and intellect, everything that tends to render man not merely happier, but wiser, better, more faithful, and more true. We are born very poor, but with boundless capacities for goodness and excellence, a receptivity for every angelic, celestial thing. The very salvation of men and nations depends on the supremacy of the generous affections. It is the soil from which the flowers of life, the soul's best harvests, spring. Trust and truth, the sentiment of progressive purity, would render life a living prayer. For between truth and truth, excellence and excellence, variance there cannot be.

Man must not lose heart, never for an instant cease to look upon art, and poetry, and nature, and heaven itself, as things divine. Let science advance as it may, the revelations of the soul in things that concern their common weal, precede it ever. Spiritual truth, let us be assured, is just as determinate as any other. Nay,

---

[1] Wenn Zeit ist wie Ewigkeit,
Und Ewigkeit wie Zeit,
Der ist befreit in allem Streit.

it is the science of sciences, the great certainty, which one day shall overwhelm doctrines that rack the heart, offend the understanding, and impair our unity with heaven.

The angels that stand beside us, urge ceaseless progress, a holy intentness, an ever-growing confidingness in the declarations of conscience and of God. Resolvedly to will, and then as resolutely to do, will bring us nigher Him, free the face from many a cloud, the heart from many a care. Death, indeed, reveals the spiritual life, as night reveals the stars. No principle of duty acted on, no habit of self-sacrifice enforced, is ever lost, and surely not those great, sweet, rich, and pure affections, the love that brings reversion of eternal life, the patient practising that yields costliest fruits, in fine, the soul's insatiate craving for a more congenial, an eternal home.

255. HE LIVETH BEST WHO LOVETH BEST.

We need not only the development of the moral faculty, but also its healthy development. Truth and excellence are to be cultivated as in the presence of God, beneath the umbrageous foliage of the tree of life, and not as if dwelling in some evil environment, in a region of darkness, and sin, and death. For man must be brought to feel and to know that he is created in the very image of God, the all-present God who is constantly near him, present in all creatures and in all things.[1] When the moral faculty is unhealthy, it becomes weak, deficient in depth, in earnestness, in

[1] Jacob Böhme, *Aurora*.

beauty, and in truth. A healthy moral development leads to a healthy moral life, with the cheerful discharge of all its requirements. Man must be instructed as with a mother's love, a father's unfaltering care, and, adding self-culture, led to individual and collective excellence,[1] to knowledge at once secular and religious, being and becoming together, union of all the powers with all the affections, crown of the spiritual arch, and, so far as may be, perfect intuition with perfect faith, abating spiritual destitution, indeed, and sustaining his elevation, for ever.

256. ANGELIC LINEAMENTS.

There are those whose faces are as the faces of angels. Goodness and truth are stamped on their lineaments for ever. Goodness realises heaven in him who has it, awakens it perchance in the beholder's soul. Since the highest culture, seeks excellence for itself, confers a yet loftier expression than what mere happiness can bestow.

257. SYMPATHY, DIVINE.

We cannot entertain a doubt as to God's entire sympathy with his creatures. In death as in life, we are alike sure to find him. But He has confided us to our own care, shews us the end, while he also imparts the means. An infinite capacity, in truth, subsists in man. Each soul is endowed with endless powers. But our efforts must be made with all our strength. Our whole

---

[1] La vie de l'homme n'est en réalité qu'une grande education dont le perfectionnement est le but. Degerando, *Perfectionement Moral, et de l'Education de Soi-même*, Paris, 1825.

soul must be poured into the work. Else we cannot compass the sweet will of God. For He is, indeed, our Redeemer. He will cleanse our souls from every soil, and raise us to purity and truth at last.

258. FREEDOM THROUGH GENIUS.

The sin, and folly, and ignorance, that incrust that wonder of wonders, and miracle of miracles, the human soul,[1] must one day disappear, yield to the incentives furnished by God and the sweet spirit life. Face to face with infinity and the divine, we may not dare, without impiety, to sully our souls with untruth. The marriage of perfect wisdom with perfect goodness, cannot be perfected without liberty. We cannot, indeed, arrive at right conclusions, short of the fullest approval of the intelligence and the heart. How, indeed, are men to rise to lofty conceptions if they never lift their thoughts above constraint. For the ideal and spiritual are not less real than the visible and tangible. Nay, there is greatness in the very conception of an infinite growth in wisdom, and purity, and truth.

To the genius which in all times and places has laboured in the service of humanity, has providence assigned the task of educating the great family of our kind. For genius with its magical gifts, sits as if on some Galileo or Brahé's tower, beholds clearly in the spiritual horizon, things dim and misty on the common soil. To genius, indeed, are heavenly patience and sacred aspirings, the knowledge of the mysterious

[1] Mens est quaedam vis animae, qua inherimus Deo et fruimur. St. Bernard, *De Amore Dei*, Cap. 10.

beauty with which heaven endows the soul when chastened by lofty intelligence and hallowed by the affections. From Syria, it has been said, we derive our religion, from Greece our literature, from Rome our laws, not indeed to degrade, but to improve upon them, not to follow with servile submission, but with spiritual insight and extremest care. And genius steeped in celestial truth, with angel utterance is ever prepared to declare the exquisite analogies, lift the veil behind which resides the inner, the divine life, very atmosphere of wisdom, and gentleness, and love.

Nothing, indeed, can affect the issues that await us on the further shore. The roses may wither, but not the aspirations which are lighted by an unsetting sun, fed by sources that never can run dry. As children of one God, we cannot imagine a joy which shall not be ours, for the change which snatches us from an earthly, also introduces us to a more sufficing home. Even here, now, there are flutterings as of seraph's wings, winds which whisper things divine, holy thoughts which render all things holy, in fine the celestial world with all the ineffable amenities of heaven.

ASPIRATIONS

FROM

THE INNER, THE SPIRITUAL LIFE.

BOOK VI.

Denn alle Kraft dringt vorwärts in die Weite,
   Zu leben und zu wirken hier und dort,
Dagegen engt und hemmt von jeder Seite
   Der Strom der Welt und reisst uns mit sich fort.
In diesem innern Sturm und aüssern Streite
   Vernimmt der Mensch ein schwer verstanden Wort,
Von der Gewalt die alle Wesen bindet,
Befreit der Mensch sich der sich überwindet.
                                      Göthe.

   Gar klar die Hülle sich vor dir erhebet,
Dein Ich ist sie. Es sterbe was vernichtbar,
Und fortan lebt nur Gott in deinem Streben.

   Durchschaue was dies Streben überlebet,
So wird die Hülle dir als Hülle sichtbar,
Und unverschleiert siehst du göttlich Streben.
                                      Fichte.

ASPIRATIONS.

259. THE WORLD'S LOVELINESS.

How beautiful is the world. To see the sun rise in the tropics, the ocean flashing with phosphoric light, each starry constellation, as it sets and rises beside the line, the great and grand aurora, like some banner of eternity waved by angelic hands, spanning the sky with rosy arch or dropping like a curtain, frosted with silver and gemmed with stars. To inhale the aroma of the pine, the ravishing fragrance of southern flowers. To watch the western humming-birds, the red birds and the blue, the gorgeous serpent, the many-tinted creatures of sea, and earth, and sky, gay blossoms, fishes, and the ceaseless insect whirl. To gaze, face to face, and eye to eye, upon the mighty whale, the arrowy shark, the swift sea-fowl, the multitudinous denizens of earth and sea, the inhabitants of many lands, the people by many shores. In fine, to witness the ceaseless action of animate and inanimate creation, ascending in one mighty diapason to heaven. Ah, how beautiful is the world.

260. THE GRAVE NO RESTING-PLACE.

We are so to live, observes Arnold, in one of his school sermons, that death should prove an infinite blessing. For death is not the pit, as by a dreary metaphor it is too often named, but peace, and activity, and love, and hope, and joy. It will conduct us to a double life, expanding in action and enjoyment, along with those we hold most dear, those who, even here, are with us, as God is with us, in affection and in love. There could not indeed be a future without sharing it with our kind. For, undoubtedly, if he will but listen to God's word in the centre of his soul,[1] man will arrive at insight into the divine economy of his life and being. Let us then confide in goodness, though aware of evil, foster pity though versed in pain. Since, as has been said, the water of life is faith, its bread love, its salt work, its sweetness poesy, the grave but a passage to the higher, the better, the unending life to come.

261. A CHARTER OF FREEDOM.

Christianity tolerates no slavery, whether physical or moral, holds out a charter of freedom to all our kind. But religion, itself, must be freed from the errors with which sectaries have encumbered it, errors which they discern in each other, but ignore in themselves. The allegory, as Coleridge terms it, the grisly conception, of an unholy evil being, antagonistic to God, taken literally, has been productive of an infinity of ill. There cannot be permanent evil in a universe, where God and nature have enveloped goodness with eternal sanctions. Let us then discard every low conception, unworthy at once of heaven and ourselves, harmonising our actual life with our aspirations, our aspirations with

[1] Jacob Böhme, *Aurora*.

our conduct. We are bound by obligations nothing less than divine, to abide by the dictates of our intelligence, the impulses of our hearts, not passively either, but with all our bravery, our utmost strength. For the great interests of truth and of the soul, brook nothing short of our firmest action and our best resolves.

262. NO CONCESSION TO EVIL.

No one ever yet made concession to the principle of evil, in men or things, who did not in the end regret it, for to listen to evil is to be lost. But evil differs from barbarism and ignorance, with which, however, it may be allied, in that it is essentially insidious and aggressive. It is not the less, however, weakness or moral cowardice to submit to it. When the healer of souls, in whatever walk he may ply his task, is guided by goodness, intelligence, and truth, he may approve himself a real miracle of energy and usefulness. But whenever he is led by mere motives of gain, pays grovelling submission to error and ignorance, what is it but the worship of the principle of evil.

263. NO ONTOLOGY.

Things can only be known as they present themselves. Ontology, then, reposes on no solid basis, does but discredit the science with which we conjoin it. No mortal, says the inscription at Saïs,[1] has ever raised my veil.

[1] Und wenn kein Sterblicher nach jener Innschrift dort dein Schleier hebt, so müssen wir Unsterbliche zu werden suchen. Wer ihn nicht heben will ist kein achter Lehrling zu Saïs. Novalis, *Schriften*, Berlin, 1826, B. i. S. 47.

Novalis, however, makes one of his mystical characters, exclaim. If no mortal have raised the veil of the goddess, let us ourselves become immortal, else are we no true disciples. We cannot, indeed, have an ontology, but we may have a psychology or soul-lore, by which we register the soul's acts, its aspirations, and its powers. We can have the positivism of truth, the cherished certainties of nature, God, and immortality.

264. A NATION'S GREATNESS.

A nation's greatness consists in its great men. For without great men there can be no greatness, hardly even the conditions by which it is fostered and appreciated. Great men, indeed, are the earth's salt, very seed and leaven of heaven. Material greatness is very small beside moral greatness. Emerson, after paying a graceful tribute to English greatness, proceeds to let us know that England is not larger than the Georgia of the Americas. Yet Greece, and Athens, which is smaller still, contained at a given period more great men than England and America, with its Georgia inclusive, perhaps do now. Were size the criterion of spiritual greatness, certain countries should be rich indeed. But the fine aroma, the blossoming of humanity, cannot subsist under low spiritual conditions. For oppression brutalises the oppressed, and by an inevitable Nemesis, the oppressor also. Humanity, itself, can alone become truly great, when, through the happy progress of liberty and enlightenment, the nations become as one nation, and the oppressors and the oppressed, alike, shall be no more.

265. UNIVERSAL INSPIRATION.

Great spiritual truths should be brought home to the convictions and moral exigencies of mankind. The heart and understanding must be appealed to, and doctrines which wage war with the affections and intellect, replaced by others more accordant with universal spiritual truth, the general inspiration, potentially, and very often actually, subsisting in every breast, the convictions of the good and wise of every age and time. For spiritual truth is the common heritage of earth and heaven. The wise and good, the apostles of God, in whatever age or time, realised the divine by the very same inspiration which reaches us now. It is, indeed, of God, the very same, according to their several measures, which rejoices the heart of poor troubled humanity and the exultant angels, who, mighty in their spiritual possessions, rejoice unceasingly beside God's throne.

266. THE PETREL OF THE DEEP.

There is a bird, the least of those that haunt the green sea-wave. In the wildest weather, when the winds most fiercely blow, and sea and air seem mingled in the drift, this little creature hovers fearlessly mid rack and spray, now advancing, now receding, or swooping down behind the combing wave, finds rest and shelter on the white floor of the seething deep. Thus, too, like the petrel, man betimes realises safety amid the tempests of life,[1] and skill and courage are begotten of the storm.

---

[1] Παθήματα μαθήματα.

267. THE PURE AFFECTIONS.

Each pure affection, the father's tireless fondness, the mother's unfaltering love, bespeaks itself from God. Children bring down fresh revelations, the very aroma of paradise, from the infinite. The mother, herself, experiences emotions unfelt before.[1] For the babe, as the poet says,

> Was given to sanctify
> A woman.

Fain, indeed, would she exhaust life's capacities for her child. No wonder, then, that children are beloved, very corner-stones and exponents of heaven.

268. CIRCUMSTANCES.

If an infant be reared with the wise and good, amid a pure environment, or, on the other hand, among the unwise and wicked, in a word, amid an evil environment, who can doubt that its future will be commensurate. And this is the doctrine, so named, of circumstances. But circumstances are the means only, and not the end, serve but to sow the seeds of goodness, which man, through strenuous effort, and despite of every obstacle, must bring to happy harmony and excellence at last.

269. FRUITFUL INTUITIONS.

Whatever the developed heart and cultivated intelligence approve, we have, so far, the crowning assurance

[1] Mutter treu wird taglich neu.

must be true, and whatever the developed heart and cultivated intelligence reject, for to these and through these are the divine revealings addressed, we have the equal assurance must be untrue. It is, indeed, the heavenly privilege, the blessed prescription of aspiration and holiness to realise themselves. For that which we earnestly and conscientiously desire, in the best sense do we eventually and certainly become.

270. THE EVIL AND THE GOOD SEED.

As the sting of the little tsetse fly, which travellers tell us of, destroys the powerful horse, the brawny ox, so the unchecked infusion of a single malignant passion or base addiction, shall perchance destroy and pervert the whole soul. On the other hand, by a blessed necessity, some generous principle, when once we are happily imbued with it, shall transfigure the entire man, approach him to the angels, bring God and heaven in its train.

271. SAFETY FOR ALL.

Oak and triple brass, the poet says, swathed his breast who first tempted the fickle main, but surely ten-fold iron encircled his, who, in an unhappy moment, ventured, even in speculation, to consign his brother to destruction beyond the tomb.

We do not urge the favour or disfavour of heaven in respect of propositions in natural science, yet religious and moral truth is not less self-sufficing, demands in its behalf no extrinsic favour or disfavour whatever.

The common ground, in regard of the higher truths, is becoming more and more extended, the delusions of a darker time are passing away, and the sectaries, despite their strained unnatural pretensions and mutual antipathies, are approximating, to merge their differences one day in the glorious unity of the truths of God.

272. SELF-RESPECT.

Any prescription or prerogative, whatever, that tends to crush the principle of self-respect, partakes of evil. It is imprescriptible truth that we have a right to stand firmly on the privileges and immunities of our better nature. He, observes Paracelsus, who would know the courses of the heavens, let him first know what is heavenly in man,[1] sublime and beautiful saying, perhaps only to be surpassed when he adds that from the knowledge of ourselves we rise to that of the divine.

273. THE RELIGION OF THE SOUL.

We need not more, but fewer religions. We need not less, but more religion. The religion of the affections, indeed, tends to reach all hearts, purify all souls. But it needs the religion of the intelligence, also, that intelligence whose deep recesses no one yet has fathomed, to regulate its outpourings. If the understanding do not rule the heart, the heart the understanding, we are liable to lapse into the error, not less selfish than unnatural, of supposing that we alone can be saved. Yet, goodness is salvation, and wisdom is salvation, and love

[1] *Opera*, Geneva, 1658.

is salvation, safety, indeed, and joy for the soul which harbours them.

Would sectaries but meet on this common ground, what good might they not accomplish, what neglected households might be lighted up, what souls incited to the moral effort which is of heaven. Else, how can the great example of the men, the women, saints indeed and martyrs of our race, avail, if the delinquent spirit make no effort to rescue itself. To this it must come at last. The battle must be fought in the very soul of man. For God, who sees the inner, the true life, wills that we should be holy, even with the holiness of childhood. He loves purity and truth, the humblest service, the very first steps on the long ladder of progress which is to conduct us to the celestial land. Enough at first to know that God is love, that obedience to the divine is happiness, till earthly transition, at length, yield place to the permanence of heaven.

274. THE INNER MANSIONS.

Santa Teresa,[1] desirous to image forth the perfection, the beauty, and the dignity of a soul in grace, compares it to a palace of diamonds in which there are many mansions. Catherine of Siena,[2] speaking of ecstasy, exclaims, much as St. Paul did before her. I know myself no longer, but only the divine that is within me. How great is the contrast between either of these, and Edwards, for example, author of the treatise on the

[1] *Castillo Interior o las Moradas.*
[2] *Opere della diva e Seraphica Catherina da Siena, Venetia,* 1505, *De la Divina Providentia.*

Will. The Roman Catholic mother makes no appeal to the understanding, with the Protestant divine the heart is as naught. Yet, in matters of religion, assuredly, we are bound to realise all the truth which the heart and the intelligence, guided and supported by each other, yield.

Nothing can well be more detrimental than faulty conceptions as to the goodness and mercy of God. The penitential psalms Niebuhr esteemed it a perfect horror to teach to children. How, indeed, can we find it in our hearts to inflict upon them rituals, confessions, which shadow forth the possible spiritual destruction of any portion of our kind. Let us rather dwell on the beautiful things of God, whose spirit is everywhere, and in whom, in very deed, we move and live for ever,[1] his mercy, his holiness, his truth, and the heaven which consists in wisely loving and doing well.

275. TRUE GREATNESS.

No people can be great, unless they feel and act greatly. For meanness of soul is destruction, opposed to all moral and spiritual elevation. To obey inferior impulses, only, however disguised and decorated, is to sacrifice the bloom of the soul. To obey the intellect, merely, is but a degree higher. There are sects, indeed, as there are individuals, in which a trace of gentle culture is hardly to be found. Yet, to secure the loftiest results, the highest aims, sects must be united on the broad platform of intelligence and faith, noblest action conjoined with truest love.

[1] Ἐν αὐτῷ γαρ ζῶμεν, καὶ κινούμεθα, καί ἐσμεν.

276. THE VIRTUES OF NO SEX.

The loftier virtues, spirituality, gentleness, unselfishness, by a law of the inner, the higher life, appertain to men and women, to our common humanity, alike. For God has made no distinction between the highest and holiest manhood, the highest and holiest womanhood. The inward light, the masculine independence, necessary to the formation of character, are evinced alike, regardless of sex, by the best and wisest of our kind.

277. A JUST ASCETICISM.

We must not make our bed too soft. Some degree of asceticism, not, however, the asceticism which courts infliction for infliction's sake, is needful for the soul's weal. Stoicism, indeed, enjoined unflinching endurance. But thanks to the better spiritual culture of our times, we know that endurance, though a great, is not the only virtue, and that the object of our hopes and our aspirations, may be a present reality as well as a joy to come.

278. THE CARRIAGE OF OUR SOULS.

We are like soldiers on guard, have the charge of mighty truths, in short, the carriage of our own souls. Most certain it is, that we are called on for ceaseless effort, not only in the moral, but the intellectual and physical worlds. Were it possible, then, it should be blazoned in characters of light, proclaimed as with the thunder's roll, that our powers must be exercised and developed to be retained.

279. ASPIRATION AND REALISATION.

There is not a faculty of which the just exercise does not insure gratification. A happy frame of mind is, in itself, happiness, and happiness springs up here, as I am persuaded it will spring up in heaven, from appropriate moral, intellectual, and affectionate activity.

280. FLOWERS OF PARADISE.

It is pleasant to reflect that the Maker of the primroses can adorn the mansions of heaven with yet other flowers. We do not, indeed, live sufficiently in our emotional life,[1] our sympathies, and our affections, in devotion to nature and to art. If we did, it would bring us into closer relations with the celestial world.

> The hungry beggar-boy
> Who stares unseen against our absent eyes,
> Bears yet a breastful of a fellow-world,
> Contains himself both flowers and firmaments
> And surging seas and aspectable stars.[2]

The paradise which is at hand, we do not see, the angels which house beside us, we do not know. In these respects, children have advantages over us which it almost needs to be born again to appreciate. For they live in the very forecourts of the higher life, compass, in their degree, the divine ideal, and are already communicants of heaven. I still remember my childhood's ecstasy while inhaling the rich perfume of the red wallflower and the rose, gazing in some leafy arbour

---

[1] *Slack's Ministry of the Beautiful*, Lond. 1850.
[2] Aurora Leigh.

at the emerald hues which strained through the beechen leaves,[1] or handling the spray torn from some verdurous tree. But children, themselves, are gems of paradise, at one with the flowers and with heaven.

281. KEEPERS OF THE GATES.

How sweetly shall a real saint, some man or woman aiming at the divine, dilate on the truths of the better life, truths which yield rest to those who toil indeed, and are laden heavily.[2] The friends of God are also friends of man. Theirs is the courtesy which shrinks from the infliction of pain. For they who invite others to the celestial mansions, keepers of the gates of heaven, should surely approve their mission by deeds of gentleness and love. Enough for them, faithful to their sacred trust, to rescue sinners from their soil, and fellow-workers, perchance fellow-sufferers, so to lead them as to arrive at the safe havens of eternal peace at last.

282. ASSOCIATE ANGELS.

Sin is the only stain, and with ignorance the one great evil and destroyer of our race. Knowledge, to be sure, is not virtue, but it is a stepping-stone to virtue, its firmest ally and associate. For love and science, twain angels, approximate ever more and more, as they ascend the celestial scale, till they merge, at last, in the harmony of heaven.

[1] Die dicht verflochtenen Buchengänge in denen das Licht zu Schmaragden verwandelt wird. *Tieck's Phantasus.*
[2] Δεῦτε πρός με πάντες οἱ κοπιῶντες καὶ πεφορτισμένοι, κἀγὼ ἀναπαύσω ὑμᾶς.

283. A REAL FAITH.

A sincere faith can ill brook the imputation of error. Each cherished conviction we would, indeed, share with those we love, would pause with and hold by them for ever. Yet, who does not feel and know that an unworthy life is the greatest impiety,[1] and that love and heavenlymindedness alone can take us by the starry path that leads to paradise away.

284. SPIRITUAL INFLUENCE.

Celestial influences are everywhere, heaven trifles not with the spiritual, any more than with the material law. For God sustains in holy earnestness the world. The conditions of the inner, are fixed and immutable as those of the outer life, the laws of mind as those of matter. True philosophy and religion bear the strictest tests, court alike the light of day. Yet, truths half appreciated, are capable of being turned into deadly errors, not the less serious for being conjoined with an affection or even a vital certainty.

In the spiritual, as in the material life, God, so to speak, puts forth no greater, yet no less an effort than what is needful to the end. In like manner, the goods which we desire, must be sought for through and by means which are adequate to the end. Belief in an incessant intervention in our spiritual states, is just as great a moral solecism as the belief in the suspension of material law. Never, for an instant, in either case, is the divine order suspended or interfered with. Let

[1] Vita indegna, l'immenza impieta.

us only have faith, for this is the keystone of the spiritual arch, that God acts ever for the best. For the greatest goods, the very loftiest truths lie indeed in common ways. They pervade our homes as they pervade infinity.

285. DIVINE EFFICACY.

The many admirable instructors notwithstanding, there is incessant need of culture to develop the powers pent up in every breast. Unworthy convictions degrade those who entertain them, impair the spiritual efficacy of culture itself. On the other hand, just conceptions dispel doubt, give birth to thoughts and feelings which ring like strains from paradise through the heart. For every truth is consistent with itself and with every other truth, never yet has contravened the handwriting and Scriptures of God within the soul. In a life of love, a life lighted by a holy light, the heart is as a welling spring, in which fresh truths continually rise, while truths already felt, experience new and ravishing developments.

As Christ himself has taught, the divine oversight extends to all men, for all are children of the divine. He insisted, indeed, on moral accountability, on gentleness, for he was gentle, and on truth, the brotherhood of humanity, the final extension of one spiritual rule over the earth. The teacher's duty, indeed, includes not merely the appreciation of vital truth, but its spiritual utterance. Brutality, vulgarity, and ineptitude, are at utter variance with the divine. But earnestness, too, is needful to those revealings which conduct us to the heaven beyond this life, nay, render life itself a heaven while we stay.

286. HEAVENLY EARNEST.

God, by making us susceptible of affections pure and holy, and thoughts divine, has yielded unassailable earnest of the safety and redemption of our kind. For as night admits us to the glories of the visible heavens, so, what men term grief and care,[1] with death itself, afford yet further access to the paradise of God. There cannot, indeed, be rational life without effort, or successful life without a struggle. Passiveness and inertia are the soul's bane, as a life bright with heavenly faith and holy earnestness, sweetly and evenly passing on to the Great Communion, is replete with satisfactions divine. The oftener the spirit bathes in the serene waters of the river of life, the greater becomes its enjoyments. Like buds of immortal promise, replaced for ever, the fountains of eternal truth flow on the more freely the oftener we draw from them.[2]

287. ROAD TO PARADISE.

As prayer and praise purify and solace the heart, so each spiritual effort leads us nigher to God. What happiness, then, to aid were it but a single soul on the road to heaven. But commerce with the celestial, the unseen, needs ceaseless patience and perseverance. I

---

[1] Πονοι τριφοντες βροτους. Euripides.

[2] Con immortales rosas,
  Con flor que siempre nace,
  Y quanto mas se goza mas renace.

know not always what they mean who speak of taking heaven by storm. Hers surely was the better lore who in words of unfaltering sweetness has declared,

> It was the soul of love and faith
> That planned the gentle words.
> Whose music woke like summer's breath
> My young heart's hidden chords.[1]

288. TRUTH, TRUST, LOVE.

The human race are continually educating each other for good. Men, conscious of an unseen God, aiming at the hidden life, are to strive for something higher than mere personal felicity. There are appointed relations between intellectual power and moral goodness which nothing can set aside. Moral pravity arrests the soul's development, as goodness quickens and directs its flight. This great truth, practically derided and set at nought by all fanatics, from Omar down, Coleridge clearly saw and appreciated. He, himself, was an illustration of the divine union between goodness and intelligence. Casaubon was not less so, as witness his daily morning prayer, his self-denying toil, his touching Diary, his converse with his friends, Joseph Scaliger and Herbert Lord of Cherbury, his grief for the loss of his Philippa, his life, his child, his all.

289. FAITH AND REASON.

Some have imagined that superstition was allied to faith, where it is the antinomy of a just faith, wars alike with reason and with the divine. Now, as in the darkest ages, superstition, wherever subsisting, rejects

[1] Frances Brown.

a spiritual God, substituting some immoral figment of its own. For truth perverted or deformed, is not truth at all. The degeneracy, on the other hand, named infidelity, thrusts aside everything not founded on the senses and the logic of the intellect. But further, infidelity, like fanaticism, ignores the law of love. Conjoined, they form that combination of the horrible and grotesque, which too often has thrust true religion aside, and shed as if it were water, the blood of the intelligent and the good.

290. MASCULINE DEVELOPMENT.

A state, like an individual, owes its development to its relations with the world of thought and the world of action. The masculine intellect needs the sustentation of public affairs.[1] Man in truth, is formed for heaven through the medium of earth. The insane desire for concentration, for centralism, uncorrected by adequate local municipal development and federal union, ruined Rome, and threatens to injure, nay has injured, the British, as it has injured the Gallic commonweal. Let us indeed have union, concentration, strength, but so as not to militate against the moral life and material wellbeing of the parts. Social science, the *politiké* of the Greeks, deals with the great questions which concern man's living welfare,[1] questions which it imports each striving intelligence to resolve.

[1] Crescit enim cum amplitudine rerum vis ingenii, nec quisquam claram et illustrem orationem efficere potest nisi qui causam parem invenit. Tacitus, *Dialogus de Oratoribus*, Cap. 37.

[1] *Arnold's Life and Correspondence*, vol. i. p. 216.

291. PROGRESSIVE OPINION.

In law as in philosophy and religion, in philosophy and religion as in law, what is incongruous and inept is continually eliminated through the illumination furnished by progressive goodness and intelligence. The great college of thinkers, the universal, the invisible church of the present and future, emits its judgments, which then become law, any opposing record or statute to the contrary notwithstanding. But presently, opinion shoots ahead, and the process is repeated, and shall continue to be repeated, so long as man remains free, which we trust shall be for ever, to decide upon the infinite problems of the present, the future, and the past.

292. INTROSPECTION.

As we never actually behold our material selves, so some, so to speak, never behold their own souls. Yet, introspection is a great duty, one of the various processes which benignant heaven, through the medium of reason and the heart, has enjoined for the development of man's soul and the education of our kind.

293. NO PARTIAL CULTURE.

The better affections, the very necessity of acting and loving, yield infinite proofs of celestial wisdom, and goodness, and love. Such, in effect, is their resistless sway, that they tend to self-development even when the object is merely personal. From the intimate connexion of the three leading principles of our nature, sentiment namely, affection, and material activity, all partial culture proves eventually ruinous and absurd, replete, indeed, with elements of disruption and decay. Civilization is indissolubly bound up with the recognition of spiritual law.[1] The persistent denial of the rights of thought, as many an example shows, is only productive of social ruin and political decay.

The ideal of Christianity, as of all religion, presupposes a creed which shall satisfy at once the intelligence and the affections, in a word, the intellect and the heart. The Roman Catholic does not dare to think enough, the Protestant does not venture to love enough, and so they remain apart. Yet, the filmy veil of ancient misconceptions must one day fall away, and become as if they had never been. Led hand in hand by religion's loftiest ideal, love's tenderest aspirations, men's prayers and praise shall some time ascend in blended incense to heaven. Guided by a truer and not less loving appreciation, faith shall yield its glad assent, and the wounds of suffering humanity shall be healed.

294. UNITY OF NATIONS.

Concurrently with the amalgamation of creeds, there is a tendency in the nations to form one immense family. The unity of nations is surely not a dream. Yes, a time may come when nation shall no longer oppress nation, when our wretched differences shall cease, when the earth-products shall be as a usufruct to all, and when the world, as it ought to be and would

[1] Buckle, *On Civilization*, p. 206.

be, if we only suffered it, shall become as a garden, the very paradise of God.

295. MENTAL SOUNDNESS.

One of the earliest evidences of recovery in insanity is a returning sense of self-respect.[1] And thus, indeed, is it in every rally from folly, vice, and crime. The saving, the angelic principles of self-respect and self-mastery resume their blessed sway. The individual begins to hold commerce with his better self, with heaven above, and man around. The heart regains its influence, lofty reason its sway, and the demons of folly, impurity, and sin, retain their drear ascendancy no more.

296. LOVE A FACULTY.

What we have learned we must sometimes unlearn, and what we have once respected we must perchance respect no more. Man's celestial faculties, introspection and love, sink into inaction from disuse, become impaired, and, finally, even lost. There must, indeed, be the violation of no divinely-appointed law. It is through the culture of the whole man only, not passively, but with every energy of the soul, as moral and sentient beings, that the dire results accruing from the mismanagement or neglect of our God-awarded powers, can be brought to a close.

297. UTTERANCES OF LITERATURE.

To many French writers, would it were to all, we owe deepest obligation and gratitude. In his Attic

[1] *Hood's Report on Bethlehem Hospital*, Jan. 1853.

Philosopher,[1] Emile Souvestre speaks oftentimes like an angel from heaven. Only listen to this prayer by Alphonse Karr, one of the great hierarchy of thinkers, writing perchance, for daily bread, yet uttering between whiles, things worthy to be remembered for ever.

Thanks, he says, O Lord, for the beautiful things thou hast created in common. Thanks for the blue heaven, the sun, the stars, the murmuring waters, the shade of embowering trees. Thanks for the poppy in the corn, the flower upon the wall. Thanks for the linnet's song, the nightingale's hymn. Thanks for the perfumed air, the music of the winds. Thanks for the clouds, gilded by the rising and setting sun. And thanks, too, for love, the most common sentiment of all.

298. THE ANGEL IN HUMANITY.

Everywhere among the men and women of our kind, are angels of charity and disinterestedness, men and women whose desires are as the perfume of paradise, whose hearts glow with celestial fire, whose eyes are lighted with the very light of heaven, doing what is right with self-denial and cheerfulness, tongue of gentleness, soul of wisdom, and heart of love.

Don Manuel de Montesinos, of Valencia in Spain, holds charge of a sort of penitentiary for the morally sick and infirm. The penitentiary receives the man, indeed, but his crime remains at the gate.[1] Don Manuel is ever present. He finds no fault publicly, but

---

[1] *Philosophe sous les Toits.*
[1] La penitenciaria solo recibe el hombre, el delito queda à la puerta.

with persuasive, gentle words takes the culprit aside, never wounding his self-respect, insulting his consciousness, or provoking hatred.

At Palermo, lunatics are or were treated by a Sicilian baron with extraordinary assiduity and success. The whole secret of his method, would that it were universal, was ceaseless occupation and kindness. The name of Florence Nightingale is one no Englishman shall soon forget. But now here, now there, men, women, whose names are written in the Book of Life, pursue the task of reclaiming the outcast, relieving the destitute. And thus, through the infinite clemency of God, the extremes of humanity meet, misery and crime are remedied, and it may be set aside for ever.

299. DIVINE TRUTHFULNESS.

Untruthfulness is the vice of inferior natures. There are in fact, numbers who have the very loosest notions on the subject of veracity. Yet, should man be truthful even as God is truthful, in each and every transaction of his soul.

300. THE HIGHER LIFE.

It may be quite right to say that morality, as a body of truth, a science, was elaborated long ago, nevertheless, spiritual verities are in ceaseless process of development, at once in the individual and the race. The affections, too, render duty ever true, ever new. We can only escape from our defects by rising into a higher region of life, and thought, and action. How true is it that sin dims the spiritual eye, dulls the fine perceptions of the soul, impairs the infinite, the bitter-sweet longings, the eager gaze, which hoping, straining, it may be, by night and by day, to burst our chains, we direct towards heaven.[1]

Progress is the result of an endless series of small advances, since no one yet reached perfection at a bound. The road to the higher life, in this, our earthly existence, which flits, so swiftly flits away, often leads over broken, precarious ground. And he who, in any degree, has succeeded in acting up to his ideal, will often have occasion to survey the past with a regret not unmingled with admiration and dread. For oft, in the soul's strivings, there is that which causes the heart to thrill, and the voice to falter, in those who are worthy to know and to behold them. It is not, indeed, so much what we have believed, as what we have loved, observes Bernard, which is of moment, words, in truth, deserving eternal memory. For love is the one twin angel, as of knowledge is the other, which stands by the throne and before God's face for ever.

[1] 'Εγενήθη τα δακρύα μου ἐμοί γ' ἄρτος ἡμέρας καὶ νυκτος. Sept.

ASPIRATIONS

FROM

THE INNER, THE SPIRITUAL LIFE.

BOOK VII.

THE redeeming influence of sorrow, leaving no poisoned, incurable wound, needs very much to be insisted on. Men cultivate remorse as a virtue, to atone for past sin by aggravating the sting of regret. They are scared by the ghosts of their past misdeeds. What a man does, be it good or bad, is so much less than what he is, that it is weak and miserable slavery to be in subjection to the past. A man may not tarry with his past acts. He must not allow his life to be hindered by either the reproaches or the applause of his conscience. To change evil into good, to perfect that which is imperfect, is the problem assigned to each to work out on his entrance into the world. Nature, indeed, has no reprobates. Nothing is finally or irretrievably bad. Mistakes and even crimes, are not dead inorganic results, to remain in stern unchangeable evil. They may be transmuted into good, for they spring from living human nature. They are to serve as experiences, for the purpose of helping us onward, not dragging us back. Since experience, as Göthe says, is knowledge gained at the expense of something we would not willingly have done. For those who use it aright, experience leaves no brand. There is strength and regeneration in life, even in the life of the moment that is passing away. Anon.

"Αφες τοὺς νεκροὺς θάψαι τοὺς ἑαυτῶν νεκρούς. Matthew.

ASPIRATIONS.

301. SELF-SACRIFICE.

A LIFE of sacrifice is a life of liberty, since it is a life of love, the liberty of imitating that Being who loves continually and cannot err. Self-sacrifice is among the highest requirements of the mighty Taskmaster, puts us in possession of the very law of God, charges it with our everlasting weal. It is the final issue of the reverent faith which lifts a man out of himself, instils the loftiest principles, the conviction of a higher life. It imparts vitality and reality to the deep matters of the soul, faith in the divine future, faith in goodness, faith in the unseen ear, the all-pervasive presence, begets thoughts which are as portals to heaven, angels to guide and to warn. It suggests, and likewise helps to realise, aims which exalt a nation and an age. It confirms the virtue which outshines circumstances and defies temptation. It is associated with the poetry which floats through the universe, with the genius which allies itself with all goodness and all truth. It is indeed no other than the house of God, the very gate of heaven.[1]

302. THE NIRVANA.

Some controversy has arisen in respect of the Buddhist word *nirvana*, as to whether a conscious, or an un-

[1] Swedenborg, *A Biography*, by J. Wilkinson. London, 1857.

conscious absorption into the Divinity, were meant by it. Bournouf and Colebrooke both state that a condition of eternal felicity is spoken of, which, if mystics in regard of the reason did not continually contradict themselves, would at least imply a conscious absorption, since consciousness must be the correlative of all felicity.

We may not, cannot deny our own individuality, the reality and individuality of a providential God.[1] And whatever wonders the soul shall behold, or whatever initiation it may have to undergo, let us firmly believe, leaving Buddhist and Pantheist to decide as they please, that our intelligence and our love shall experience augmentation and development for ever.

303. A NATION'S HOPE.

It is a fearful, a crying ill to extinguish a nation's life, a nation's hopes and liberties. A Pole whom I had befriended, used sometimes to repeat for me his national airs. But ah, the lost hope, the dying pathos, that spoke beneath his hand. Another Pole, I heard exclaim over and over from his dying couch. Ah, were I only not sick, not sick.[2] Hungary, too, is fallen, while Dembinski's son has perished, dying, it is said, of starvation, at Melbourne.[3]

Who has not wept to think of Athens, glorious even in her fall, of Saxon Harold, despoiled of life and reign

[1] Mens humana adaequatam habet cognitionem aeternae et infinitae essentiae Dei. Benedicti de Spinoza, *Opera, Ethices, Pars Secunda*, Prop. 47. Lipsiae, 1843.

[2] Wenn ich nicht nur krank wäre.

[3] *Manchester Guardian*, June 24, 1858.

through impious trickery, of Kosciusko, when he cried that Poland was no more.[1] Too often, alas, has despotism's fell hoof stamped out the fires of human liberty. Thus, when Monti sings of Italy,[2] his exquisite lines ring through the heart, and evoke, as the poet has hymned it,

> Tears from the depths of some divine despair.

For alas, when a nation's aspirations are trampled in the mire, the very ecstasy of life and hope is blotted out, for millions, for ever.

304. THE WORLD A PARADISE.

The world is yet an Eden, hues golden and purple are still seen, ravishing melodies are yet heard. All nature, indeed, is a revealing, a ceaseless declaration of the else unutterable excellencies of God.[3] And each man is an Adam, undergoing apprenticeship in the garden of life. Sin as erst, is still the only fall, its destruction our paradise regained.

[1] Finis Poloniae.

[2] Bella Italia, amate sponde,
Pur vi torno à riveder.
Trema in petto e si confonde,
L'alma oppressa dal piacer.

[3] Die Natur ist auch eine Offenbarung. In seinem, reinen Glanze hell voranleuchtet, die innere Süssigkeit, die geistige Blume, als der verborgene Lichtkern der in ihr immer noch paradiesischen Lieblichkeit, jene heilige Schönheit von welcher die ganze Seele des wahren Künstlers erfüllt ist, und für welche der begeisterte Denker vergebens den Ausdruck sucht, besonders so lange er jenes Geheimniss der Liebe noch nicht in seiner Wirklichkeit begriffen hat. F. V. Schlegel, *Philosophische Vorlesungen*, 8te Vorlesung, Wien, 1830.

Life is an Aladdin's cave, whose jewels are all the virtues, conscience the enchanted lamp, lighting up the soul. Man is a Prometheus scaling the heavenly heights, happily not suffering the vultures of moral pravity, ignorance, and despair, lacerating his poor heart, to turn him from his purposes. He is a pilgrim, too, whom honest, downright Bunyan, honest and downright though he did not originate his wondrous allegory,[1] shall take by the hand, lead past Doubting Castle and the pit, all the demons that would prey on his unguarded soul. For ours is a merciful and compassionate God, and wills not that a single one should sink or perish by the way.

305. CONVERSION.

Conversions, missions, revivals, must go hand in hand with the advance of civilisation, the age's progress, and form a part of it. What does it avail though individuals, whole nations even, like the Indians of Paraguay, should put on the outer garnish and livery, the profession, if the living, loving, hopeful reality, that alone constitutes a pure religious faith, be wanting. For were religion only shown to be the sweet and gentle, albeit serious, solemn thing it really is, man would fly to its embrace. Some teachers, are as very angels, while others surely have mistaken their vocation. Instil fewer dogmas indeed, or rather leave dogmas aside, but instil with heart and soul, faith, and hope, and charity, then divinest influxes follow as

[1] Guillaume de Guileville, *Pelerinage de l'homme*, Hill, Pickering, Lond. 1858.

things of course. In short, religion, knowing God but as a parent, is the great correlative of the soul's progress in goodness, intelligence, and truth, and love, and cannot so much as be conceived or imagined apart.

306. HUMAN NATURE.

Nor writer, nor painter, nor poet, nor sculptor, has ever yet realised the at-times unapproachable majesty and dignity of human nature. Let those who, under colour of religion, would degrade that nature, look to it. Some, indeed, have reached a pitch of excellence, that refreshes the soul to contemplate, an excellence which not the very angels perchance may surpass, and which yields celestial forecast of a time when the material interests that loom so largely here, must give way to the lofty aspirations, the pure affections, which link our earth with heaven.

307. PURPOSE.

As Coleridge keenly observes, the wise possess ideas, whereas the rest of mankind are possessed by them. What, indeed, is infirmity of purpose, what incapacity for spiritual or moral progress, what insanity even, that departure from sound reason and sound feeling, but the being given up to an idea or ideas, from which, since the individual does not or cannot assert his freedom, there is no release. But the man of moral energy will not submit to the tyranny of an idea. He will employ his imagination to ameliorate and refine, he will live in the future somewhat, because embodying his ideal of life, and because, as Niebuhr says, in working out life's problems for himself, he works them out for others also, in short, he will remain exempt from the bondage to self, with which no soul is free. For as it has been said, the

> Man who would be man,
> Must rule the empire of himself—
> In it must reign supreme,
> Establishing his reign on vanquished will.

309. SWEDENBORG.

Swedenborg's visions were true or they were otherwise. Certainly they were not objectively true, and very often they are subjectively false. All his interlocutors, as Herder has shrewdly remarked,[1] deliver themselves alike. Many of his conceptions, placing the false, as has been said, under the aegis of the holy, are dreary enough, at utter variance with God's wisdom, and mercy, and love,[2] while others are just as rife with celestial beauty and truth. In short, his is a Protestant instance, as there have been many Roman Catholic ones, of that state of abstraction, coupled with

---

[1] Alle sprechen aus ihm und wie er, wie er aus seinem Innern hinaus Sie sprechen machte. Also durchaus eintönig, daher das Lesen dieser Schriften so sehr ermüdet. Herder, *Werke*, B. IX. S. 95. *Psychologische Erklärung der Swedenborg'schen Geschichte.*

[2] Wer in lebendigem religiösem Glauben lebt, verklärt durch denselben alle Erscheinungen um Sich her, und jede Begebenheit erhält ihm göttliche Bedeutung. Er glaubt an das Walten Gottes in der Natur, aber er darf weder Hässliches noch Unmoralisches zulassen, sonst wird sein Glaube Aberglaube. Das Beispiel des unglücklichen Swedenborg, der die einseitige Verfolgung der hochsten und reinsten Gedanken, deren der Mensch fähig ist, in unheilbaren Wahnsinn fuhrte. *Swedenborg und der Aberglaube.* Schleiden, *Studien, Leipsig*, 1857.

corporeal hallucination, which ends by mistaking its own conceptions for outward realities. But spiritual truth, since it is clothed with everlasting sanctions, needs no preternatural utterances, and certainly not those of the Swedish seer, whatever.

309. LOVE AND FEAR.

Religion has been regarded through the medium of love and of fear. The advocates of sombre faiths adopt the latter. They tell their dear ones, their children, else so accessible to all spiritual affections, to fear God. Ah no, were it with my latest breath, I should employ it to say, respecting themselves and the spiritual nature that is within them, love God only, sublime yet simple element of all religion, all morality. For we have only to fear ourselves, our passions, prejudices, shortcomings, ignorance, weakness, and nothing else in this world.

310. HUMAN DWELLINGS.

Municipalities and capitalists should reconstruct, but with every appliance of order, purity, and decorum, the dwellings of the working-classes, the poor. Great then would be the saving in the matter of preventible disease, great the avoidance of physical suffering, moral stagnation and decay. For all rule, with all government, whether on the large scale or the small, avails only, as furthering individual development and wellbeing. The more general diffusion indeed of aesthetic culture, in which architecture holds so prominent a place, would subserve the better interests of our kind.

311. LOST IS LOST.

Lost is lost and gone is gone.[1] I attended once a shipwright, one who built stout ships to navigate the seas, who died of hot fever in the place where I reside. And he was a comely youth as he lay upon his bier. But he is lost, he is lost, exclaimed his sorrowing mother, he is gone, he is gone. Then she praised him for what he had been and done. And now, she cried afresh, he is lost, he is lost, he is gone, he is gone. There were just the mother and her dead son by the cold hearth-stone. Together, they abode in life, and now, too, are they together in a land where stout ships are no longer needed, and where stalworth sons do not leave fond mothers to struggle with penury and care.

312. MUNICIPALITIES.

Federal, elective institutions and municipalities, the latter in Niebuhr's most true estimate the very basis of political life and liberty,[2] should subsist throughout Britain and the world. They have worked well wherever they have been introduced, and along with trial by jury, lie at the very foundation of civic life and liberty.

313. THE HOLIEST AIR.

The holiest water is water to drink, water to maintain the body's purity and furnish refreshment for man. The holiest earth is that which bears corn, and wine, and oil, for his sustenance, hides the wasted frame when God's good work is done. And the holiest air is

---

[1] Und hin ist hin, verloren ist verloren.   [2] Freie Verwaltung.

pure air, air untainted by the odour of decay, air fresh, in short, as that which plays on the lea-field or drives the salt-sea wave. For cleanliness, and sustenance, and order, are needful to all, and holy, indeed, are the earth, the water, and the air which subserve these precious exigencies.

314. A WISE IGNORANCE.

There are things of which the brevity of life and the limits of man's intelligence require that we should remain ignorant.[1] But there are also things which concern us all to know, things, as Elizabeth Carter remarks, essential to our present condition and prospects, and to the investigation of which our faculties will invariably be found adequate.

We cannot afford to remain blind to religion, and science, and poesy, and literature, and art. For this were a sottish ignorance. Yet some, alas, are all but unaware of truth's divinest elements, the glorious wealth of art, the spirituality of our affections, some to whom aspirations too deep for words, conceptions holy, just, pure as the heaven from which they spring, seem little better than dross and forgetfulness.

315. A GOLDEN THOUGHT.

The golden thought flashed this morning with peculiar vividness on my soul, that we were, indeed, members of the divine commonwealth, part and parcel of the glorious congregation of God's creatures, worlds

[1] Humanae enim sapientiae pars est, quaedam aequo animo nescire velle. Scaliger.

stretching beyond worlds into space illimitable,[1] and that infinite intelligence, and love as infinite, took concern of us for ever. For the present and the future are as one great Now, and the soul's pulses of the moment, are the same throughout eternity.

316. THE EXHIBITION.

Pictures there were, and statuary, at the recent Manchester exhibition, that one could wish never to forget, pictures, statuary, that imparted new faith in spiritual purity, and goodness, and truth. There, was witnessed a surpassing loveliness, immortal truths were inculcated, affections instilled, such as tide men over the sea of life, and into the wide-spread ocean of eternity.

317. DOGMATIC THEOLOGY.

Dogmatic theology, at least as it is held by multitudes, is in much the same transitional state, abounding in mysticism, error, and other shortcomings, that dogmatic astronomy, dogmatic chemistry and physics, dogmatic physiology and psychology, were in some two or three hundred years ago. You might not safely reason on physical science then, you must not, according to some, reason on religion now. The Scripture text is admittedly not conclusive as against physical demonstration.

[1] Die Grösse Gottes wird nicht durch Sternenweiten gemessen. Die Unendlichkeiten der Sonnenwelten, die Aeonen der Weltgeschichte sind ein Nichts gegen die geringste Erscheinung geistiges Wesens und Lebens. Das Gefühl für Schönheit in der Natur, welche uns, wenn auch unsagbar, die ewige Liebe hinter den körperlichen Erscheinungen ahnen lässt, wird nicht gemehrt durch die Siriusweiten des Sternenhimmels, nicht gemindert durch die Kleinheit des funkelnden Thautropfens. Schleiden, *Studien*.

But adds a writer in the Edinburgh Review,[1] is it conclusive against moral induction and metaphysical inquiry. We cannot indeed reason too much, provided only we observe the laws of reason, the well-prescribed limits of our intelligence. For religion should be the measure, not only of our affections and our love, but also of our best knowledge, our awakened capacities, our ripest intelligence,

> The nobler husbandry of mind,
> And culture of the heart.[2]

318. DISEASE AND DECAY.

Ah, poor sufferer, if thou wast only not so impatient. For consider, disease, and sickness, and the wreck of temporal things, are also avenues to the better, the hidden life,[3] smooth many times the approach of death. Be not then so much solicitous about the body, as of the soul's heal, and wast thou sick, then shouldst thou be well. For happiness depends not on fortune only, but on things yet more divine.[4] Then should celestial messengers conduct thee to the heavenly mansions, and the fountains of eternal joy.

319. THE INSANE.

The least fallible, indeed the only sure method of treating the insane, is by ceaseless, intelligent, attractive occupation of body and soul. We have not, perhaps, as Descartes remarked, entire power of self-

[1] Oct. 1850, p. 351. [2] Drennan's Poems, 2d ed. Dublin, 1859.
[3] Krankheiten sind Lehrjahre der Lebenskunst und Gemüthsbildung. Novalis (von Hardenberg).
[4] Juliani Imp. *Ad Themistium*, Opera. Parisiis, 1640.

conservatism, for this is reserved by Another who unites in himself the perfections which are wanting in us, yet to us not the less has been imparted the keeping of our own souls.

It needs culture, ceaseless appeals to all the extant faculties, the better affections, continual repetition, to lay the foundation of healthy moral and mental habits. No one who has not had intercourse with the mentally perverted and debilitated, can imagine how imperfect is their self-control for good, how inferior their addictions, how frequent their lapses, ere they regain, if it ever existed, their lost self-control. Their souls, like those of the imbecile and idiotic, have to be treated as we treat some forms of paralysis, supplying effort, at first passively, by and through the intelligence of another. It is a most noble task to reintegrate the ruined soul, set right the perverted intelligence, in short, restore the spiritual harmony and completeness, which, assuredly, it is the divine intention should subsist in all.

320. THE MARSEILLAISE.

Once again, perchance, shall the Marseillaise, sublime hymn, echo over the freed soil of France. Her beauteous plains shall cease to be deluged with blood. Culture, amenity, and joy shall subsist in her borders, hand in hand with all the virtues, all the arts. Never must we believe that providence designs for Italy, Poland, Hungary, France, any of the great European populations, in fine, perennial convulsions at the dictation of political despotism, or religious fanaticism.

There shall one day ensue a real, indeed, a holy alliance between the nations,[1] overawing, and, if needs be, crushing, with mightiest, truest purposes, tyranny and despotism whenever they may be found.

321. FEAR, A BLIGHT.

There have been periods in the history of our kind when blighting fear exerted dread supremacy. The cruelest kings, some Russian Ivan or Spanish Pedro, found reverence from a barbarous race. African Landor saw trees hung thick with human skulls, grim fruitage of the superstition that wars with glorious aims, sees in the life beyond the grave but dens of endless suffering. The red hand, blood impressed, records in central America the sacrifices of a revolting past. But too long has religion been infected with the same drear leaven. Diabolical agency, which even Luther held by, was believed in for ages, and weird wild legends still linger by many a hearth. Yet, one day all shall learn that God, and, subject to him, their own souls, are the fountain and supreme tribunal of that truth of which formulas and confessions are the more or less imperfect utterance. For the laws of nature and of our own being, are as thoughts of God, and science and religion are entirely at one, all existence is a revealing, and light, at once material and spiritual, a proclamation to nations, realms, and times. Everything that appeals to the higher faculties, appeals also to the divine life, the eternal, the golden aspirings within.

That sin introduces moral death is indeed most true,

[1] Durch Einheit zur Freiheit.

but that it introduced physical death, is contravened by the evidence of actual science, quite as clear and demonstrative in geology, as was in Galileo's time and is now, the evidence for the world's revolvings round the sun. For religion needs no untruth whatever, to aid its blessed, its eternal sanctions. Man advances in intelligence and holiness with an impetus that increases with his spiritual growth. All existence is a kingdom of reason, a region in short of the kingdom of God. And the pursuit of science in a sense is religion, as the pursuit of duty is holiness.

There is indeed a soul in nature and that soul is God.[1] There is a perfect consent, harmony the most absolute, between natural science and religious truth. Whatever be the obstacles occasioned by the stupifying yoke of habit, the difficulty of altering past modes of thought, we must not the less cultivate spiritual sympathy with the entire universe, abandon the folly of thinking to save life or soul by superstitious observances, in short, address ourselves to the nobility of thought, the moral elevation, and entire truthfulness, that lead from the comparative narrowness of earth to the enduring greatness of heaven.

322. THE NAVIGATORS OF OLD.

It is touching to peruse the relations of the early navigators, how, in some remote island of the ocean,

---

[1] Εἷς, ταῖς ἀληθείαισιν, εἷς ἐστιν θεός,
ὅς οὐρανόν τ' ἔτευξε καὶ γαῖαν μακράν
πόντου τε χαροπὸν οἶδμα κ'ἀνέμων βίας. κ.τ.λ.
Sophocles, *Fragmenta ex Incertis Tragediis*, LI. Brunck ed.

the birds, devoid of fear or dread, lighted on their persons or walked amid their feet. The Indians welcomed the Spaniards, the people of Otaheite the English, as gods. Alas, we do not requite the dear children of nature as we ought. A traveller, in America, speaks with rue of a butterfly, the imprisoned seraph as he sweetly terms it, months after its impalement, raising its beautiful wings.[1]

If some rare and lovely winged creature, bearing the divine signature from regions afar, light upon our shores, it is forthwith despatched by some fool, and thrust, a mere waste of feathers and skin, into a glass box. Birds, too, are massacred in preserves, nay, animals are followed into their native wilds, and destroyed with no view of lofty science or human conservancy. Surely a time may come, when we shall again walk among the creatures of God, and without the infliction of needless suffering, share with them our common heaven.

323. MONEY.

The excessive inconvenience and even misery, so often induced by monetary derangements and monetary frauds, should lead to efficient efforts to rectify certain malpractices and misconceptions in respect of money itself. For money, capital, in a word, stripped of economic verbiage, is simply an expedient for doing away with the immediate exchange of objects of prime necessity. Silver, platinum, gold, really anything but stationary in their values, are not alone adequate as a

[1] *The Shoe and the Canoe.*

basis of exchange. With due care, a paper money, sufficient to facilitate exchanges, limiting all transactions between individuals to a cash standard, might be made to represent not merely the precious metals, but other values. Banks issuing notes,[1] but acting as comptrollers of credit, proportioning loans to capital, should be placed under municipal or government control, and the entire system of fictitious values and false credits brought to a close.

324. GUARDIANSHIP OF SOULS.

The better principles are guardians and conservators of men's souls. Self-respect alone, did it pervade all bosoms, would infallibly elevate the whole family of man. And he who justly valued himself for the divine, the noble gifts of God, sum of all his worth, his every capacity, would necessarily appreciate them in his kind. That these gifts constitute man's entire excellence, is a truth which no convention, no prejudice, can set aside. For the kingdom of truth and of reason, which is also the divine kingdom, can never be at variance with, or wanting to itself.

325. FILIATION OF CRIME.

There is not a folly, a superstition or a crime, unatoned for, which, by the natural filiation of cause and effect, does not produce its dreary crop of bale and suffering. The horrors related in the daily press, are at once a rebuke to our sottish self-esteem, and an urgent plea for the more effective culture of our kind.

[1] Smith, Say, Gray, Freedly, Senior.

326. THE VISIBLE WORLD.

It needs a sort of sensuous, as well as intellectual new-birth, rightly to appreciate the wonders of the material and moral worlds, the conception of an all-wise and infinite God. The uncultured man, the savage, and the child, live amid creation almost without once imagining that any thing spiritual underlies or earth, or sea, or sky. They feel, indeed, but do not know, they think, but hardly appreciate thought. The unconsciousness, however, so lovely and appropriate in the child, is out of place in the man. Although religion, and philosophy, and poesy, and science, teach better things, he is all too prone to view the material world, the old atheism, as the one and only existence. Yet, the visible heavens and the visible earth, with all their sublimities, are but as an appearance, declaring order and reason, celestial harmonies, laws divine, in which matter has no share.

327. LIFE'S MISSION.

Life is or ought to be a ceaseless development, no gospel of negations, but the marriage of philosophy with faith, the religion of the heart, a building-up of truths to be written on the countenance,[1] and pondered in the soul. For this is the free spiritual activity which makes us indeed children of the divine, compelling the revelation of nature's secrets, penetrating to the idea through the senses, aiming in hours of inspiration

[1] Hominem liberum et magnificum si queat, in primore fronte animum gestare. Apuleius.

at everlasting truths, continual action in goodness and intelligence, in short realising the faith, the charity, and the hope, which are of the very light and glory of heaven.

328. PIOUS FRAUDS.

Let us hold with Coleridge that religious frauds are the worst of frauds, bearing dreary crops of misery, deceit, and crime, at utter variance with the faith, the trust, and the truth that lie at the root of the spiritual life of man. For we may not hold back a truth, utter an untruth. The freest disclosure alone combines safety and peace. Faith must not be at issue with itself, religion cannot be irrational or untrue. We may not conceive God otherwise than as absolute truth, perfect goodness, infinite wisdom. And to God and our own conscience are we alone accountable for discerning those attributes in him.

Earnest is life. Each soul must digest the heavenly manna for itself. For every sorrow the heart has turned from, we lose a consolation,[1] for every fear we dare not confront, we forfeit some of our hardihood, and for every truth, I will add, that we fail to cherish, we forego a portion of our very souls. Reason, faith, philosophy, must contract divinest nuptials. Then should we have the universal church, the progressive, the pure,[2] a church true to man's best interests, because true to truth, to hope, to thought, to feeling, and to affection, without sacrifice of reason or of love, but combining these in one sacred, one celestial whole.

[1] Ruskin.   [2] Ὁ καθαρός.

329. PSYCHOLOGY.

Psychology, as a science, is natural and demonstrable as any other, takes account of man's inner nature, the good, the beautiful, the true. So far from self-observation being impracticable, everything, even that material science by some thought alone accessible, comes to us through the medium of the inner, the unseen life.[1] Psychology, rightly understood, resumes all other sciences, for it is the science of the living soul. It is intimately connected with religion, of which it is the sure and certain ally, and vain are the efforts which have been made, or ever shall be made to decry it.

330. PURIFICATION THROUGH LOVE.

The doctrine of purification by fire, was adopted, perchance to escape the not less absurd than drear alternative of ceaseless pain. But, unhappily, it was applied to this life, as well as to the life to come. Arrested by the Inquisition of Venice, Giordino Bruno was sent to Rome, where two years' imprisonment, with death impending, did not suffice to abate his constancy. On the 9th of February, 1600, after being excommunicated, he was handed over to the secular power, in order, as the mocking formula ran, that he should be punished with the utmost clemency, and without effusion of blood. He heard his sentence with intrepidity, merely saying to his judges that perhaps it caused them yet greater terror than it did him. Eight days after, he suffered the accursed infliction to the end.

[1] Das höhern selbst, der innere Sinn. Fortlage, B. ii. S. 251.

Would that the reformed churches, rightly rejecting the revolting doctrine of a fiery, had adopted that of a universal spiritual purification. The world, however, knows not God through science only.[1] For love, it is,[2] which exalts us to the great conception of the ultimate regeneration, not of a selected few, but of man's whole kind. This view claims to be revealed by the conscience, and not merely by the fancy, a distinction first insisted on by the distinguished philosopher above named.[3] As for the doctrine itself, it is entirely consonant with the goodness, clemency, and power of God, and as such commends itself to our entire adoption.

331. GROWING OLD.

It is an illusion about growing old, for how can the soul grow old. Gradations, which we term the approaches of age, sickness also, mask transition, and with many a change bring the frame to its term. But it is our duty to be unmoved by any such. For the countenance, if young, should be the prophecy of a joyful future, and if old, the record of a glorious past.

332. SINCERITY A TEST.

Sincerity is the correlative of every virtue. The eyes were given to man to look, the tongue to speak the truth. All falsehood, every disguise, is a horror, a misery, and a sin. Directness is the very essence of genius, and loyalty, and grace, and with all goodness

---

[1] Οὐκ ἔγνω ὁ κόσμος διὰ τῆς σοφίας τὸν Θεόν.
[2] Offenbarung durch Liebe.
[3] Bruno, *Dialoghi dell Causa, Principio, e Uno.* Venice, Lond. 1584.

proceeds straight to its aim. Let us be direct, then, even as God is direct.[1] Divinest truth is set forth in the revelations of nature as in those of man's soul. For the world, the entire universe, is as a volume making truth more visible, goodness more divine. The untainted soul abhors cunning and duplicity, and strong indeed must be the perturbing influences that can set aside its natural proclivity to truth.

333. A MIGHTY AIM.

Mighty was the aim that would rouse the dead,[2] the dead in spirit, from their trance-like repose. For whether in the seen or the unseen life, there is no other death than spiritual. He whose soul is well awakened can never die, and he whose soul is not awakened, is in effect dead, in spirit dead, whether in this life or in the life to come. Spiritual insight, as we learn through the psychology of faith, increases with our spiritual knowledge itself. The soul awakened, presses upward and onward to the eternal goal, is impelled to acts of mercy and of truth, and realises the ecstasies of heaven in the end.[3]

334. CONSCIENCE.

While I agree with Herbart,[4] not the less would I affirm, that each moral aptitude is inborn in the soul.

---

[1] Faciem semper monstramus.   [2] Ἐγείρειν τοὺς νεκρούς.
[3] Ex his clare intelligimus, qua in re salus nostra seu beatitudo seu libertas consistit, nempe in constanti et aeterno erga Deum amore, sive in amore Dei erga homines. *Benedicti de Spinoza Opera quae supersunt Omnia.* Ethices, Pars. v. Prop. 36, Schol.
[4] Vid. § 188.

The capabilities, beauties, grandeurs of the visible and invisible life, are so many sweet and beneficent incentives to the formation of conscience and the growth of its binding roots within the heart. For conscience, union of faith, and love, and truth, is needful to man, yields the great abiding basis of his convictions, and prepares us for realities to come.

335. THE PRICE OF PROGRESS.

The revelations of the divine, whether in nature or man's soul, are indeed ceaseless, but our appreciation of them is commensurate with our spiritual efforts and aspirings, till by degrees they come to grow and glow within. There is an ever-present, a most true inspiration, causing heaven to dwell potentially, as it might actually, in every breast. The celestial life, overcoming sloth, error, fear, is entered upon by many and successive stages. For as Plutarch in his treatise on superstition observes, though reason sleep, fear watches always.[1] Yet, no true affection is ever lost, no elevated taste is cultivated in vain. The revelations of the higher life are symbols of the holy, the glorious hereafter, of love, and purity, and truth to come.

336. SAVING ANGELS.

The disinterested affections are as saving angels. In truth, they are divine. They must be taken into consideration in respect of any just estimate, not only of aesthetics, morals, philosophy, but of every true belief. They instil indeed, the nearness and the reality

[1] 'Ονειρώττει μὲν ὁ λογισμὸς, 'εγρήγορε δὲ ὁ φόβος ἀεί.

of invisible things, bring us within hearing of the hymning angels of paradise, the merciful city, all the glories of space and time, and, as allied to conscience, are the very marrow and glory of life. For although reason may falter, the affections never falter. And if alone they show man's limited, dependent condition, associated with reason, they free him alike from dejection and fear, exalting him to love, and hope, and every heavenly thing.

337. REAL GROWTH.

The only real growth is spiritual growth. Behind the physical, the savage sees a demon, the civilised man a soul. Philosophy, indeed, will bake no bread, but it will procure us God, freedom, immortality.[1] It is the marriage of nature with the human soul.[2] The principles of psychology, of all philosophy, like those of all religion, all truth, have subsisted from the beginning, not so, however, man's appreciation of them, which is progressive.[3]

The soul, observes a recent writer, in its attempts to bring the divine into closer union with the consciousness, has gradually built up its appreciation of the character of Christ.[4] And thus it is more or less in our delineations of all greatness and goodness, our conceptions of the ideal and its realisation in man.

It has been asserted that psychology, in place of cor-

[1] Die Philosophie kann kein Brod backen, aber sie kann uns Gott, Freiheit, und Unsterblichkeit verschaffen. Novalis.
[2] Die Ehe von Natur und Geist. *Id.*
[3] Wachst die Stärke der psychischen Anlagen. Beneke.
[4] *Westminster Review*, April, 1855.

recting, ratifies the delusions of ordinary thought.[1] This, however, must mean an erroneous psychology. Otherwise, we may gladly subscribe to Ferrier's eloquent remark, that all God's truths and man's blessings lie in trodden ways, and that intellect and genius are but the power of discerning wonders in common things.

338. GROTIUS.

I have frittered life away, exclaimed Grotius dying, in busy idleness.[2] Not so, good Grotius, for even to think busily, were to do well. This very desire to amend, to act better, is itself derived from the past, and without it could not be. Yet, should we also busy ourselves with things that subserve the soul's immortal purposes, mighty issues that renew life, and hope, and youth, for ever. The world, indeed, should prove a ceaseless development, with life not death, divine realities and goodness unspeakable, at its close.

339. A PROGRESSIVE LIGHT.

Let us share with the sectaries their exalted spiritual convictions, their heart-communings, but with their errors and shortcomings have nothing to do. Religion, truly, is of the life, and love, and thought, of earnest souls, whose views are carried to the great account of humanity. For life is no poor dream, but a great, and good, and glorious thing, progressive faith, a growing light, with every just conception that can satisfy the intelligence, every loving one that can solace the heart.

---

[1] Ferrier, *Institutes of Metaphysic*.
[2] Vitam perdidi operosè nihil agendo.

340. DEATH, LIFE.

Each occurrence, and very especially death, fosters the perception of moral certainties. But death, ill understood, looming so largely on the horizon of our hopes, frightens men from their propriety, prevents them from taking the same clear simple views of it, as of any other natural and necessary thing.[1] Too long, indeed, has this great mystery been made small change for superstition. Of this we may be well assured, that the spiritual law, charity to others, personal dignity, and divine sincerity, in fine, every lofty, generous sanction, will follow us in the life to come, and however augmented and expanded, prove not less certain and obligatory than here. For all law is in truth divine,[3] deriving its origin and sanctions from the common Author of nature and nature's laws,[4] and revealed to all mankind.[5] Would then that those, who linger in prospect of the mighty change, could but perceive that it is life which it ushers in, indeed a new life, with all good, and holy, and exquisite things.

The vital faith and vital truth which appertain to our moral nature, should not be permitted to stiffen into dogmas, but with every sweet and spiritual grace enter warm and living into our souls. Men spiritually

---

[1] Dass das Aufhören unsers Lebens mit Angst verbunden wird, ist ein Phantasiebild. Fortlage, B. ii. S. 221.
[2] Hobbes, De Cive, § 34.
[3] Bishop Cumberland, *Law of Nature*, Part ii. Chap. v. § 1.
[4] Id. § 19.   [5] Id. § 51.

dead and apathetic, are unfitted to pluck, much more bestow, the golden apples that ripen in eternity. For their exquisite savour they have no relish, by their heavenly beauty they are not touched. Divinest truth, simple because divine, has ever found acceptance with upright souls, among the real children, sons indeed, and daughters of God, those fitted to inhabit the beautiful city, our true and final home. For it is not only spiritual knowledge, but the habit of seeking it that is required, not only the highest speculation, but the discipline that wields it.[1] The spectacle of the good and beautiful in nature, reflecting the divine, refreshes the percipient spirit, reassures our intelligent faith.[2] Inward lights break continually on the soul, and man realises community with heaven.

341. CONSTANCY.

Constancy amid snares, defections, and distractions, is among the angelic virtues. Having once grasped a principle, let us cling to it for ever. Only abandon evil, and God will absolve you. There neither is nor can be any absolution save this. For principles, true principles, are indeed the keys of paradise, of life, of eternity, and of time. You desire proof of the divine, behold it within you and around. The higher convictions cannot come at second-hand. We seek materials, from long agone and from afar, for the faith which is to live and burn within our breasts for ever, yet see, they are even here, they are also now. Supreme

---
[1] Pattison, *Oxford Essays*, April, 1855.
[2] Guyot, *Earth and Man*, Preface.

intelligence and love are at work ceaselessly. For the divine is always present, and God is ever nigh.[1]

Every generous sentiment is nourished by the discharge of duty, by commerce with the elevated and the unseen. Whatever draws the heart out of itself, wraps the soul in conceptions at once truthful and beautiful, also raises it for the time to heaven. Short of vital influences, religion and morality declaim in vain. Yet have we enchanting objects of contemplation, if we only hold by them, celestial love, ravishing tenderness, lofty magnanimity, the unspeakable beauties and declarations of this world, and effluences from the unseen. Thus, we feel and know that our affections extend to all things, and that faith and hope declare alike for the life which is to come.

342. ART'S REALITIES.

If artists would but go more out into nature, and leave the murky studio where they hope, too often vainly hope, to arrest grace and beauty, all the loves, upon the wing. Else why is so much of art the pale and faded thing it is. If men, having conquered mechanical difficulties, will not look with the eyes of the spirit, how are they to gain the perception of that unspeakable loveliness which may not, cannot die. For art must be true to living nature, beautiful nature, else it strives in vain.

[1] Unser Gott geht uns nicht verloren, wenn wir die Natur naturwissenschaftlich erklären und verstehen lernen. Gerade dass wir ihn unmittelbar in der Natur niemals finden, macht uns ihn unverlierbar und gross. Schleiden, *Studien.* Dritte Vorlesung. Die natur der Tone und die Tone der Natur.

Would that I could but reproduce on canvas or in stone, as some Sant, or Millais, or Foley, or Thrupp, or Lough, or Bailey might do, but a few of the groups which subsist, sculptured, minted, for ever in my heart. I could wish to sketch the little girl with kerchief knitted around her brow, as I saw her by the hospital pallet, where her father, a poor ouvrier, bayonetted by a brutal soldier, waits, wistfully gazing, to die. Life, and time, and eternity, all were in that gaze, but ah, she knew it not. And fain would I limn that brawny mariner, stripped to his belted waist, as with lighted portfire he pauses to hurl red destruction on yonder bounding bark, whose flashing deck swarms with swarthy forms not less eager than his own. The old helmsman, bronzed by many a sun, who grasps with iron hand the circling wheel, while the rolling wave mounts high above the stern. Those dark-hued men who pace by twos and threes Erie's forest-bordered strand. The negro brothers fast clasped in each other's arms. That ebon Hercules who holds aloft his gigantic opponent, ready to hurl him on the snow-white sand. Those lithe African maidens, too, who poise the water-jar, or, with many a strange wild chaunt, impel their swift canoe along yonder enchanted stream. Lastly, I would pourtray the lady as she stands upon the green hill-side, caressing her beautiful steed, or feeding him from her hand, while the tepid winds blow aside her habit-folds, or play amid her clustering hair. But subjects for art are boundless as is the nature which supplies them, varied as the spiritual loveliness which burns and glows in all things.

343. A PROGRESSIVE FAITH.

I would not utter a word unfaithful to truth, unworthy of the spiritual power which I adore. For I would incite to the love of the good, the true, in fine, the unutterable grace and excellence which teach us to aspire to heaven, and fit us to abide there. And I would not have a petrified, but a progressive faith, faith in God's infinitude, and the fulness of his love. For this, indeed, is the very rock of ages, which never can be stricken down or overwhelmed.

344. HARMONY OF EXISTENCE.

There should be a perfect harmony between the speculative and practical life. Moral science, indeed, is now mainly given up to the control of reason, that reason which is bound to decide on truth and falsehood as with the voice of God. But reason is not enough, we need love also, all the affections. For the ideal must come through the real, the angelic through the actual. The dogma which affirms that labour is a curse, is only worthy of some Indian fakeer, since labour, at once of body and soul, is our life, our hope, our stay,

> And heaven itself but work
> to surer issues.[1]

The love of God is indeed the beginning of wisdom, but it is also the end. How beautiful is the Christian doctrine of repentance and change of soul.[2] And how admirable in respect of the spiritual economy, is the

[1] E. B. B.   [2] Μετάνοια.

law which exacts various effort in order to nourish spiritual power. For thus do the sweet affections grow, and the heart is turned to a very Eden, enchanting counterpart of the budding universe which the first man, like the last, saw upon his awaking. For indeed, the real Eden is within. There, and there only, and not in some outside paradise merely, as those who hold by the exoteric letter, heedless of the esoteric truth, are wont to imagine, does the divine Eden flourish and grow. The development in unity and harmony, in purity and truth, of man's whole nature, nothing less and nothing more, is the gospel which Providence has preached from the beginning, and shall surely preach on to the close.

345. THE RELIGION OF THE SOUL.

Each one views religion according to the level of his intelligence and his heart, paints heaven with colours drawn from the complexion of his own soul. The stern reformer of Geneva, when he consigned dissentients to destruction beyond the grave, but imputed to divine providence what he himself perchance would do. His harshness towards the Libertines, so named of Geneva,[1] to Pierre and Mme Ameaux, Castalio and Gentili, the Perrins husband and wife, was indeed great. The noble Francesca Perrin he names Penthesilea,[2] and

---

[1] Adversus Anabaptistas et Libertinos. *Calvini Tractatus Theologici Omnes.* Genevae, 1597.

[2] Penthesilea certe brevi nobis reprimenda erit, et furiose defendit, denique fronte meretricia agit et loquitur. *Calvini Epistolae et Responsa.* Hanoviae, 1597, p. 159.

having thrown her and her husband into prison, derides their sufferings.¹ The beheading of Jacques Gruet, July 26, 1547, after a month's preliminary torture, however conformable to the sad excesses of the times, was only second to the immolation of Servetus, of whom Calvin spoke,² and towards whom he acted, with immitigable severity. Countenanced, indeed, by certain of the Reformers, Calvin went to the saddest extremes. From a frightful dungeon, with violent death imminent, Servetus sought reconciliation of Calvin, unhappily his persecutor and betrayer, and was repulsed.³ It was even reported that the latter was seen to smile when he saw his victim led past to the stake,⁴ a thing which, for the honour of our common nature, we must utterly refuse to believe.

Alas, the errors which cling to our conduct and our creed, often prove of serious detriment to the holiest interests of our kind. Religious error is often the travesty of a philosophical truth. The doctrine of predestination is a misconception of the law of moral causation, or what some have named philosophical necessity. The

¹ Perrinus cum uxore fremit in carcere. *Calvini Epistolae, &c.* p. 162.
² Quanquam inter alia errorum portenta, quibus Satan renascentis evangelii lucem hac aetate obruere conatus est, apprime detestabilis est impietatum congeries quam Michael Servetus libris editis evomuit. *Fidelis Expositio Errorum Michaelis Serveti.* Op. Citat. p. 686.
³ Servetus capitis damnatus, a Calvino damnatore suo veniam petit. Calvinus veniam Serveto neque viventi dedit, neque mortuo. Castalio, *Contra Libellum Calvini.*
⁴ Sunt qui affirmant Calvinum cum vidisset ad supplicium duci Servetum subrisisse, vultu sub sinu vestis leviter dejecto. Castalio, *Contra Libellum Calvini, in quo ostendere conatur Haereticos Gladii Coercendos esse.* M.D.I.C.X.I.I.

arms of a true faith, however, are not fire and sword, but, as St. Paul has greatly said, doing the will of God from the heart.[1] It is, indeed, one thing, as the defender of the memory of Servetus remarks,[2] to speak of burning, away from the pile, another to be sprinkled with sulphur, and to have it thrust by the executioner into the face and eyes.[3] In the very church at Geneva, where Calvin taught, another doctrine now prevails.[4] New England, too, has changed, while in Scotland itself, as a recent writer declares, there is great spiritual restlessness under the old dogmatic bonds.[5]

When old light merges into new, when Calvinist, Arminian, and Arian, faith, and love, and charity, bridging over the gulf of ages, become as one, then, and not till then, shall the blood of the tortured and heroic Servetus, cease to have been shed in vain. For, see, no creed can invade moral distinctions with impunity. That misconception of the divine which places the greatest saint who does not receive a given doctrine, beneath the greatest sinner who does, must of necessity die away. The passage to the spiritual life, indeed, is attended with many difficulties. Jouffroy gives a touching picture of his regrets on the loss of his early beliefs.[6] Yet, like Descartes, and every one who has

---

[1] Ποιοῦντες τὸ θέλημα τοῦ Θεοῦ ἐκ ψυχῆς.

[2] Credite mihi lector, aliud est de igne sub umbra loqui, aliud videre se a carnifice sulphure aspergi, et faciei in orbem admovere. Castalio.

[3] Combustus est Servetus, anno 1553, die 27 Oct. *Id.*

[4] Letter in the *New York Christian Inquirer.*

[5] *Leaders of the Reformation*, by J. Tulloch, D.D. Ed. Lond. 1859.

[6] *Cours de Droit Naturel, Professé à la Sorbonne.* G. Planche, *Revue de Deux Mondes.* Paris, Mai, 1855.

thought and felt, avowing his ignorance, he resolutely accepted the distress of his intelligence, in the hope through labour and reflection of acquiring a more enduring belief, the true conception of faith, and hope, and love, and immortality.

346. MENTAL SCIENCE.

Ferrier parades the evils of psychology, or rather, as I conceive, of what he so misnames. Yet what does it signify how mental science is called, provided we associate right ideas with the terms. Matter and mind, with their correlatives, as we know them, are but forms of our conscious experience, which no sane individual can ever fail more or less correctly to discriminate. Ferrier, with Hamilton and others in England, Beneke and Fortlage in Germany, have, however, thrown much light on a difficult branch of inquiry, and any one who imagines that he appreciates mental science, without being fully aware of what they have written, will be very apt to fall short.

347. THE OPPRESSOR AND THE OPPRESSED.

The oppressor is even more to be pitied than the oppressed, the persecutor than the persecuted, the slave-driver than the slave. We should rather stand up at the stake with Servetus, than sit with Calvin on the judgment-seat. We should prefer to eat a crust with Chatterton rather than partake of certain repasts, in short to fare with Lazarus instead of feasting with Dives. This brief life once closed, all tyranny is at an end, but how shall it fare with the tyrant before the chancery of heaven. Alas, he knew it not, or knowing, felt not what he did. Be ye comforted then brother, for the developed soul will rue the evil it has done. The victim shall have compassion on his oppressor, and divinest compensations be rendered before high heaven. For God having made man for an excellent end, will not abandon the development of his destiny.[1]

348. LIFE A RELIGION.

How different is the aspect in action, at least, of those grand conceptions which we term Christianity, its vast establishments, countless teachers, and multitudinous professors, as contrasted with the period when twelve poor men, with their great Leader, essayed to plant new standards of spiritual truth before the world. Then, Christianity sought, now it claims a hearing. Religion, however, should be acted as well as spoken. Incredible, almost, considering the immensity of the means, seems, too often, the paucity of results. But the church which is to consummate religion's precious work, ruling by love not law merely, must be unfettered by formula or creed. Yes, a mighty purpose, a united faith, shall one day address themselves to the elevation of the downtrodden, the reclamation of the vicious and incompetent, the inculcation of rectitude and truth, and the beauty of charity, on all.

349. SPIRITUAL RENEWAL.

Man is a spirit, and not a clod of earth. It is a spiritual, not a material renewal that is needed, unend-

[1] Cousin, *On The True, The Beautiful, and The Good.* Preface.

ing purity and truth, not endless torment and spiritual death. God's violated laws do most assuredly vindicate themselves. There is a spiritual as well as a material responsibility, that nothing, for a moment, can evade, a real, not a fictitious responsibility, most certain, eternal, unrelaxing, and true. The neglect of this vital distinction indeed, lies at the root of the inefficacy of religious culture, the vice and dreary wretchedness that so beset the world.

A spurious morality, artificial, unreal sanctions, too much replace the divine mandatories, usurp wholly or in part, the stead of the sacred issues which God and nature demand at our hands. I would not offend by a hairsbreadth, the convictions of the humblest worshipper before God's throne, but I feel, I know, that reason and religion, the heart and the understanding, must unite as one, and thus abate effectively, the disease of body and of soul which so sadly tortures and afflicts our race.

350. A TRUE IDEAL.

Women prove, or ought to prove, not only their own guardians and conservators, but also guardians and conservators of our kind. In the presence of consummate purity and grace all base thoughts fall aside, and these angel potencies assert their celestial sway. Oh why should any woman suffer want or physical wretchedness. Yet, the only way in which this can be for ever stayed, is by disciplining the will, the intelligence, and the heart, in all. As the loveliest statue lies hidden in the stone, so the sweetest ideal, seeds of all holiness, and excellence, and truth, lie imbedded in every breast. Very especially must the heart be cultivated, since from it, great thoughts most do spring. Amor and Psyche, as of old, must contract celestial nuptials in the human soul. Force, too, and strenuous purpose, must be imparted to the will, since short of these, we cannot have freedom to love, to be, and to do, cannot truly feel that God and heaven are nigh. For with discipline, intelligence, and love, duty would be as some polar star, sure Pharos on the sea of endless life. We should indeed be as husbandmen of God, and the soul would reap the harvests of eternity.

Then, ah how great might be our part in the progress of the world, owing, as we do, our fellows, those who live beneath the same empyrean of our hopes, the benefit not only of our acts, but of our aspirations, nourishing, ere we sleep the last sleep, dream the last dream, patience, endurance, and self-control. Peal it then, through furthest heavens, no one is good in vain. He who raises a brother, a sister, from the slough, has done as God himself would wish him to do. For each woman, indeed,

> Her dress just like the lilies,
> Her heart as pure as they,
> One of God's holy messengers
> To walk with us each day,[1]

has her claim on the sustentation of every man. And every good and elevated woman is as an angel of mercy and consolation to her kind.

[1] Longfellow.

351. THE ANGEL OF DEATH.

Death is not the hideous spectre which superstition has set up, but as philosophy, and faith, and true religion teach, twin-brother of love,[1] beauteous, smiling, and crowned with stars. The absurd, pitiful, in truth, insane dread of death, nurtured by fanaticism and fear, stands in the way of the assertion of every elevated principle. We continually see death described as the end, whereas it is only the beginning, a second birth, indeed, the entrance to a new career. Life once ended, men will recognise the blessed agency of death's angel, who shall charm away their pains, as the angel of sleep does their cares.[2]

352. HIDDEN INFLUENCES.

It is interesting to witness puritanical influences cropping out even in Emerson, and Hawthorne, and Carlyle. Their God is a somewhat bright, and cold, and glittering Being, remote enough from human loves and sympathies. Hawthorne, perhaps, is the most spiritual of the three, morbid, dreary, weird, yet often beautiful. Emerson's terse concision and massive thought, are all his own. Carlyle, as to his second style, has moulded himself on Jean Paul, whose remote analogies, extraordinary fancies and elliptical inversions he successfully enough imitates, less successfully

---

[1] Fratelli, a un tempo stesso, Amore e Morte
Ingenero la sorte.
   Giacomo Leopardi, *Opere*. Firenze, 1856, Tom. I. p. 132.
[2] Krummacher, *Parabeln*, Tod und Schlaf.

perhaps, though a man of great and various parts, the genial humour, breadth, and mighty heart of that good and true soul, whose tender, loving strains, as he enlarges on the bounty of God and the affections of man, shall render his name, and even the ponderous tongue in which his frequently glorious thoughts are clothed, loved and cultivated while the world endures.

353. A DISCOURSE WITH GOD.

In one sense the world is a conversation, a ceaseless communing with the Divine, enlarging ever on the spiritual ideal, on freedom and truth, and providence, and immortality. Heaven, indeed, invites us to intercourse, not in order that we should pretermit our efforts or our vigilance, but that we should cherish the holy frame of mind which renders duty easy and labour light, makes each day a loftier hope, a greater joy, ourselves wiser, better, more loving, and more true. For although we may sleep, God never sleeps. Though we may forget, he never forgets. Although we may pause, he never pauses. And in this infinitude of action, of perfection, and of care, in the least as in the greatest things, his most glorious attributes are seen.[1]

---

[1] Elle revient, l'ideal divin, en quelque sorte á vous par tous les chemins, à tous les moments de votre vie. Vous trouvez le grand Ouvrier tout entier dans la plus humble de ses oeuvres. Simon, *Religion Naturelle*, 2d. Ed. Paris, 1856, p. 184.

ASPIRATIONS

FROM

THE INNER, THE SPIRITUAL LIFE.

BOOK VIII.

INDEM wir die Einheit des Menschengeschlechtes behaupten, widerstreben wir auch jeder unerfreulichen Annahme von höhern und niedern Menschenracen. Es giebt bildsamere, höher gebildete, durch geistige Cultur veredelte, aber keine edleren Volkstämme. Wenn wir eine Idee bezeichnen wollen, die durch die ganze Geschichte hindurch in immer mehr erweiterter Geltung sichtbar ist, so ist es die Idee der Menschlichkeit, die Vervollkommnung des ganzen Geschlechtes, und die gesammte Menschheit, ohne Rücksicht auf Religion, Nation, und Farbe, als Einen grossen, nahe verbrüderten Stamm, als ein zur Erreichung Eines Zweckes, der freien Entwicklung innerlicher Kraft, bestehendes Ganzes zu behandeln. So fest gewurzelt in der innersten Natur des Menschen, und zugleich geboten durch seine höchsten Bestrebungen, wird jene wohlwollend menschliche Verbindung des ganzen Geschlechts zu einer der grossen leitenden Ideen in der Geschichte der Menschheit. Kosmos.

ASPIRATIONS.

354. SAN JANUARIUS.

DURING the late earthquake at Naples, the so-styled blood of San Januarius, according to Salverte,[1] some alcanet-stained admixture of spermaceti in ether, liquifying with the heat of the hand, was brought out with a view to stay the ravages which occasionally attend this great natural phenomenon. Here, clearly, it is an appeal on the part of the unreflecting affections, which continually essay to set aside the physical order, the material and moral government of the world, results which may not, cannot be. How much better were it, therefore, that love and reason should go hand in hand. For a true Catholicism asks no sacrifice of the understanding, since its best dictates are ever in holiest unison with those of the heart. We are, indeed, to appeal to no idols, whether of the feelings or the intelligence, but to Him only, the one Lord of the intellect and the affections, to Him who framed the soul, and bestowed upon it those precious capacities which we are not at liberty to throw away.

355. HUMAN VICTIMS.

Vanini, Bruno, Huss, Lollard, Servetus, and Aikenhead, were martyrs in behalf of the great principle

[1] Onosma. *Philosophy of Magic*, Chapter xiv. Thomson's tr.

of the free assertion of opinion. Vanini, hapless sufferer, taking up a straw, on his trial at Toulouse, is reported to have said, from this also could I prove the divine.[1] Vain averment, his tongue having been cut out, he was thrust by cruel men, in the year 1629, era of another tortured sufferer, into the flames, where, after unspeakable suffering, he expired.[2] His ode to God,[3] translated into German by Kosegarten, transcribed by both Herder and Fichte, is full of touching elevation and devotion to the mighty Author of men and things.

Bruno, originally a Dominican monk, was eminent

[1] Amphitheatrum Aeterae Providentiae, Lyons, 1615. *De Admirandis Naturae Reginae Deaeque Mortalium, Arcanis*, Paris, 1816.
[2] Bayle, *Dictionnaire*, Art. Vanini.
[3] DEO.

Dei supremo percita flamine
Mentem voluntas exstimulat meam,
Hinc per negatum tentat alta
   Daedaliis iter ire ceris.

* * * * * *

Origo rerum et terminus omnium
Origo, fons et principium sui
Suique finis terminusque
   Principio sine terminoque.

* * * * * *

Tu meta, pondus, Tu numerus, decor
Tuque ordo, Tu pax atque honor atque amor
Cunctis, salusque et vita et aucta
   Nectare et ambrosia voluptas.

Tu verus altae fons sapientiae,
Tu vera lux, Tu lex venerabilis,
Tu certa spes, Tuque aeviterne
   Et ratio et via veritasque.

for speculation of a pantheistic turn. After visiting England, France, Switzerland, he was arrested in Venice, then transferred to Rome, where, as I have said, he was burnt quick in the Field of Flowers. Huss, too, in infamous violation of the safe-conduct of the Emperor Sigismund, died of the torture by fire, at Constance, in 1414, where a Council profaning religion's sacred name, then met. Lollard met his end at Cologne. The tower called after him, in London, is still blazoned with the signatures of those who bore and suffered for the name.

Among illustrious Spaniards, was Michael Servetus, of Villa Nueva in Aragon. Distinguished for physiological and theological inquiries, he was the first to assert, momentous averment, the lesser circulation, or that between the heart and lungs, of the blood, and the elimination of its impurities, through the medium of the respiratory process, from the lungs.[1] The narrative, by a contemporary,[2] supposed to be Sebastian

[1] Ex expiratione in fuligine expurgantur. Servetus, *Christianismi Restitutio*.

[2] Ita ductus est ad struem lignorum, erant autem fasciculi querni virides, adhuc frondosi, admixtis lignis taleis. Impositus est Servetus trunco ad terram posito, pedibus ad terram pertingentibus. Capiti imposita est vel straminea vel frondea, et ea sulphure conspersa. Corpus palo alligatum ferrea catena, collum autem fune crasso quatriplici ant quintriplici laxo, liber femori alligatus. Ipse carnificem oravit ne se diu torqueret. Interea carnifex ignem in ejus conspectum, and deinde in orbem admovit, homo viso igne ita horrendum exclamavit, ut universum populum perterrefecerit. Cum diu langueret, fuerunt ex populo qui fasciculos confertim conjecerunt, ipsa horrenda voce clamans. Jesu fili Dei aeterni miserere mei. Post dimidiae circiter horae cruciatum expiravit. Castalio, *Contra Libellum Calvini*.

Castalio, of his sufferings and death at Champel, near Geneva, October 27, 1553, while slowly roasted in a fire in part of green wood, his head covered with straw, his body chained, his neck bound with a thick rope to the stake, while the executioner thrust the burning fuel about his face and eyes, cannot even now be perused without a thrill of mingled horror and incredulity.

The case of Thomas Aikenhead, as coming still nigher our own times, and in the country, too, where the dying sobs of Margaret Wilson and Margaret M'Loughlin had echoed from Wigton Bay, is, if such, indeed, be possible, yet more distressing.[1] Some eighteen years of age, doubtless with parents, sisters, brothers, friends, of whose agonies however we hear little, he was a student in Edinburgh, where his license of speech, in the estimation of some, having outran his boyish discretion, the lad, after a vain pleading for mercy to those who ought to have been to him as angels of light and of love, was offered up a sacrifice by the common hangman, December 23, 1696, on the slope between Leith and Edinburgh, in the presence of those who made him die.

These sorrowful excesses have ceased. Would that denunciation, and slander, and imputations, hardly less reprehensible, had ceased along with them. Religion's gentle empire does not reside in such, but only in confidingness and good will. Force or fraud never constrained opinion since the world began, never will constrain it while the world endures. For love and truth, with firm resolve, alone win souls to heaven.

[1] *Macaulay's England. J. Aikenhead,* by *J. Gordon.* Lond. Whitfield.

356. NO SIN, NO SOIL.

Some, it has been said, are so intoxicated with their own misery, as to have neither heart nor soul to rise above it. Yet, God wills that we should realise, not wisdom and goodness only, but also happiness. We owe it, indeed, to him to be our best, our most cheerful selves. For every noble aspiring prophesies its fulfilment, and man's great destinies. There is, indeed, infinity for the having, and infinite purity and goodness along with it. It is only to ask and to obtain, to seek and to find.[1] Like those wells in Artois, whose waters, once reached, flow up and on for ever, there are in men's souls depths of spiritual affluence, fountains of holiness which never can run dry. For God is the fountain, and man's soul the eternal recipient. If we only listen to the spirit's voice, we shall be free. There is never, indeed, a spiritual beauty or a grace, which, if we have but faith, may not one day be ours.

The certainty, the great reality, of a nigh spiritual world, are announced to us in the sighing winds, the water's rush, the wind-bent trees, the beauty of the perfumed flowers. Nothing short of implicit trust can still the cravings which assail us, the liabilities and the limitations which heaven indeed permits, but not for ever.[2] Each deep and earnest soul feels the necessity of a higher life, as well as of the discipline by which alone we are to attain to it. Either we must cultivate

[1] Αἰτεῖτε καὶ δοθήσεται ὑμῖν, ζητεῖτε καὶ εὑρήσετε, κρούετε καὶ ἀνοιγήσεται ὑμῖν.
[2] Dios consiente, pero no para siempre.

our spiritual powers or bury them. They are not merely lent, but given for increase. Our obligations, let us be assured, will not be discharged for us. We must order the body so as to strengthen the soul, the soul so as to fortify the body, and both to compass heaven.

357. RELIGIOUS PERSECUTION.

I cannot explain the terrific severity exhibited by the Roman Catholic Church, else essentially humane and gentle in its ministries, towards the Albigenses and Waldenses, the Moorsmen and the Jews, the excesses in the Low-Countries and the Indies, the Dragonnades at Toulouse and other where, the revocation of the Edict of Nantes, the persecution of the Huguenots, the holocausts of the Inquisition, except upon the presumption that within its pale, as in other churches, there were men without or heart or soul, men who, however sincere in their convictions, mistook the very essence and requirements of religion. But in the courses of the centuries, such evils must pass, nay, already have passed away. Love and charity, the soul's life, shall prove religion's staple, when distinctive creeds, themselves, shall be no more. A noble moderation will become universal, and religion, true religion, sympathising with each new spiritual fact, shall one day resume the faiths of all mankind.

358. PROTESTANTISM.

That Protestantism, when animated by a spirit of charity and love, has produced most noble fruits, there cannot be a doubt. But Protestantism, too, has shed innocent blood, and in these latter days leaves children incult, permits the poor to die in the streets, or too much disburthening itself of house to house visitation, huddles the destitute and the criminal together into the workhouse. Protestantism was cruel to its slaves, is still so in Protestant America, yet has freed West-Indian serfs in the mass, rushed with regal munificence to the relief of Irish distress.

The daily records of violence in Protestant England, of wife beating and child murder, are simply frightful. Protestant Britain suffers women to be driven to unhealthy, unremunerative employments, or consigned through want to the streets. Protestant England, in times happily never to return, first impoverished Ireland by prohibitory enactments, endless confiscations and neglect, the sufferance of perennial absenteeism, then, in terms of stereotyped contumely,[1] has closed or tried to close the avenues of employment, unless when that employment was to die.

Protestant Scotland, by the abrogation of free discussion, the idolatry of days and forms, clinging to the means instead of to the end, has drawn the people in part from nature's ways, which are God's ways, yielding occasion to pernicious, unnatural excess.[2] When nature is too heavily burthened, it either breaks down or is carried to the opposite extreme. For no one, not even the greatest puritan of us all, believes a Jewish Sabbath either binding on Christians or possible

[1] No Irish need apply. *Times* Advertisement, Jan. 1, 1858, p. 2.
[2] James Stirling, *Failure of the Forbes Mackenzie Act*.

in modern life.[1] There are those, observes Donaldson, who accept as exclusive salvation their admixture of Judaism and Calvinism, and who would construe the prohibition of labour on the Jewish Sabbath into the prohibition of innocent recreation on the Christian Sunday.[2] Religion, indeed, does not consist in mere outward observances, but in sobriety, charity, kindness, all the days of the seven.[3] It consists in subjection to the law of truth and love, rendering, not only every day, but life itself, a perennial sabbath. Then, Protestantism, itself, streaked with gentleness and love, would become generous, just, and true, and faith and reason prove correlatives for evermore.

359. CHILDREN.

Children, it cannot be too often repeated, are the grace and solace of life, gems of earth, the very creatures and populace of heaven. The cry of a child in agony or distress, lacerates the heart, in very truth is too intolerable to be borne. Yet does Protestant Britain incarcerate children in her gaols, and, mercy of God, scourge those who are of the celestial cohort, those of whom Christ has said, they are of heaven.[4] But these, we shall be told, are criminal children, yet why criminal, for this is a yet more evil incident than the scourge. For Protestant England, if she had but heart enough, would snatch these dear ones from

---

[1] *Edinburgh Review*, Oct. 1850.
[2] *Christian Orthodoxy*. Lond. 1847, p. 341.
[3] Letter in the *Daily Scotsman*, Oct. 13, 1859.
[4] Των γὰρ τοιότων ἐστὶν ἡ βασιλεία του Θεου.

filthy lane and den, and every vile environment, teach, and train, and tenderly rear them, conformable to their divine origin, born indeed of woman, and candidates for heaven.

Yes, paradise, the gentle empire of heaven, is revealed to us in our childhood. Infancy, with its most sweet and precious instincts, has immediate commerce with the seraphic, the angelic world. Savage brutes, the wolf even and the bear, have been known to come in contact with childhood and to respect it. Very touching is the narrative of the English child, who, in India, somehow made acquaintance with a serpent, and brought it milk daily. The little creature was watched, and the friendly serpent, one is almost constrained to regret, was slain. For, indeed, the great aim of humanity is to extend the light, and love, and glory of childhood into man's estate. I never see a soiled, neglected infant, without desiring to deliver it from material and moral stain, to foster it with woman's love, and to place it in some good and fitting environment, in short, the very atmosphere of the heaven in which it was born.

True genius, love and intelligence holding celestial commerce together, is in part the reflection of childhood. To genius is the spiritual vision which the child has already had in its commerce of love. For genius, also, is of heaven, a ceaseless craving and aspiring, mightiest longings after truth and purity, each sweet celestial thing. Yes, the loftiest genius, the deepest love, shall unite one day, to rescue and preserve the heaven of our childhood, prolong it into ardent youth, manhood's best and wisest prime.

R

360. TRUTHFULNESS.

It is a mighty virtue ever and always, in act and in thought, in word and in look, to declare for truth. An inflexible conviction in its efficacy would go far to redeem the world.[1] But truth, whether of the heart or the intelligence, is sometimes coy, and will not come at our call.[2] Let us only go straight to our aim. We are never alone in our inquiry, since God and all the angels are there. For truth is the staple of the moral law, conscience its test. Truth incites to noblest deeds, declares for eternal life, the mighty realities of the world unseen. And philosophy is truth, and religion is truth, and science is truth, and art is truth, in fine, it is the soul's centre, the very basis and keystone of heaven.

361. DEATH.

The soul remains, but phenomena are transitory. Death, indeed, seems essential to the spiritual elevation of our kind. As regards the developed heart and intellect, death, in truth, is bereft of power. For it is but an appearance, dissolves the barrier between the visible and the invisible, things that belong to earth from those that relate to heaven. Its sublime serenity should elevate, its stillness and impassibility not too much oppress, the soul. How the sentient principle

---

[1] Aucun esprit ne peut refuser son assentiment aux démonstrations qu'il a comprises.

[2] En tout, restez un peu sur vôtre faim, si vous ne voulez point connaitre le deboire de la satieté.

may be circumstanced in respect of the phenomena which we here term matter, what, in short, the spiritual aspects of the latter may prove, we do not indeed know, enough that every object has its spiritual side. But if there be any truth or certainty in the spiritual world, death has no power over our affections or our intellectual perceptions.[1] If it be a negation, it is at least one pregnant with eternal life, mightiest evangel of wisdom, and goodness, and love. For we have need of ceaseless activity, and we feel assured that that activity can never die. The beauty which Plato terms the reflection of the good, that beauty which is of the intellect and affections, shall in truth endure for ever.

362. RENUNCIATION.

Renunciation is the power of sacrificing the temporary and present, for the permanent and eternal. It is man's desert to endure and to wait, to suffer, and yet be strong. If one would not forfeit one's peace of soul, one must learn to bear for a space the base and brutal things which are permitted here below. For these, as the Stoics said, are indeed external, and there should they be suffered to remain.

Without self-development, the beautiful thoughts, free gifts of a spiritual God, will not descend upon our souls. Alas, then, for those who have not had ex-

[1] Das arme Herz hienieden
Von manchem Sturm bewegt,
Erlangt den wahren Frieden
Nur wo es nicht mehr schlägt. u. s. w.
    Salis.

perience of the higher affections and the paradise which they are calculated to bestow. Renunciation, in truth, is needful to the life of man. Here, all the great teachers of philosophy and religion, the wise and good of every age and time, are at one. What shall it avail, they continually cry, though a man should gain the world and lose his soul.[1] The material world, that green hill flooded with softest summer morning light, the white cloud resting on its brow, shedding a glory like unto paradise, is indeed beautiful. But it must give place to the spiritual, which is at once of earth and of heaven. For the soul is the true Eden, very garden in which God walked in the beginning, even as he walks to-day. And our powers, virtues, and affections, are the plants thereof, indeed life's very tree, watered with the waters of the river of life, blooming with celestial flowers, yielding fragrance and fruitage for ever.

363. ROADS TO EXCELLENCE.

Let us only habituate the young to excellence, to self-culture and self-mastery, holy thoughts, self-denying strivings, which lead to heaven. Our conceptions of moral greatness will perhaps for ever surpass our realisation of them, yet these conceptions enhance that realisation. For as spiritual knowledge enlarges, so ignorance and superstition degrade the soul. We are surrounded by abysses of being, the meaning of which we cannot penetrate, but not the less do we know that energetic moral action is conducive to the soul's weal.

[1] Τί γὰρ ὠφελήσει ἄνθρωπον, ἐὰν κερδήσῃ τὸν κόσμον ὅλον, καὶ ζημιωθῇ τὴν ψυχὴν αὐτοῦ.

What can be more simple, natural, pure, than Christ's teachings, what more conflicting, intricate, and unsatisfactory, than the doctrinal structures which have been reared upon them. For Christ's one, his single mission, was to exhort to goodness, and the imitation of God.

Unless there be spiritual culture and development, doctrine is meaningless. The gentle truths of God can in no otherwise expand. The ideal, the flower of our higher nature, can only be converted into the real, by vigorous action in the outer as in the inner, and in the inner as in the outer life. Effort alone, with ceaseless aspiring, confers spiritual strength, renders us akin to heaven. And all the years that are given us, be they many or be they few, can have no higher object than self-renewal, unlocking the golden gates, realising paradise in our midst, bringing us into relations with the divine life, and the loftier developments of eternity.

364. ART.

Ancient art, with its sculptured grace and loveliness, some temple of Theseus or Minerva cutting the clear blue sky, is exquisite beyond the power of language to pourtray. But there is a filiation in all art, as in all excellence. How charming is the representation of the sensuous beauty which also comes from God, consummating the union of the visible with the invisible, of the earthly with the divine, that records on canvas or in stone, truths most rare, most spiritual, truths that cannot die.

Lofty art takes cognizance of the vast topics of time and eternity. Yet all art is also world-art, and, like all excellence, appreciable by the great family of our kind. Art-poesy is given to smooth the rough places of this beautiful world. It acknowledges no bondage save to the mighty laws of spiritual life.[1] Embodied art includes as it were the Roman Catholic doctrine of good works, while in its spiritual features it recals the doctrine of grace of the reformed church, true consummation of faith, grace, and works, which, if only extended to man's life, would transfigure and renew the world. Beautiful art, indeed, excels some nature, yet not all nature. Art, exalted by truth, partakes of the divine. But the doubting, and merely sensuous in art, is for ever by, and art's celestial accords are in strictest harmony with religion, and philosophy, and truth, bearing ceaseless increase on God and man's behalf.

The arts will yet work out a spiritual brotherhood in the better education of our race. Perfected art looks down on human griefs, as angels might do, and as wise. For lofty art, true art, is also a gospel of mercy, bestows freedom and love and token of immortality on our kind, holds us in accordance with the spiritual life, and with the power which will not suffer its most sweet and precious work in any respect to fall through or fail.

365. DIVINE ENERGY.

Would we have a conception of inexhaustible goodness and energy, behold it in the production of souls.

[1] Tout assujetissement du monde moral et social à des lois invariables, est maintenant représenté par certains raisonneurs comme incompatible avec la liberté de l'homme.

A soul is the divinest thing, greater, grander than any material creation whatever. For nature is unconscious, knows not God. The material, in truth, is as nothing without the percipient principle, short of which, it could not even so much as exist or be. The soul, indeed, is our all in all, recipient of our faculties and affections, divinest bond of union at once with God and with heaven.

366. THE BEST OF MEN.

How exquisite are these lines by Decker,

> The best of men
> That ere wore earth about him was a sufferer,
> A soft, meek, humble, patient, tranquil spirit,
> The first true gentleman that ever breathed.

Or these by Shelley.

> Spirit, patience, gentleness,
> All that can adorn and bless,
> Art thou. Let deeds not words express
> Thine exceeding loveliness.

An atmosphere of moral purity and truth is not readily borne, unless by those who seek and are fitted for it. Corporeal hindrances and death, vain constraints, too often have beset the leaders of our race. Faith, hope, and charity, by angels termed love, greatest of the three, very echoes from a higher world, are not indeed to be put down. Would we win the better life, we must aim at God and heavenly things.[1] But genius and goodness are endowed with celestial energy, the adamantine will which nothing can subdue or quell. What, indeed, would become of the world, what of humanity, of the

[1] Viser Dieu.

very treasures of heaven, all the precious interests of eternity and time, of liberty, happiness, truth, justice, were either to submit or yield.

For genius, allied to goodness, the angel in humanity, must strive with ceaseless tenacity of purpose, if it would win. If it only persist, the multitude will bend the knee, as once it did by some Columbus, but if it persist not, precious though it be, it will be rent and trampled in the mire. For genius and goodness cannot be, and suffer soil, that soil which it is their ceaseless effort and divine mission to thrust from themselves and from the world. In truth, they shrink from contamination as from fire. Nor is there any better way than, with whatever toil and care, to build up the spiritual house, in which we are to abide for ever. Then should the soul, holding divinest interviews with excellence, and full of costliest flowers, be cultivated like the paradise of God. Each incident, every elevating influence, would be turned to account, spiritual sympathy would breed fresh insight, till by degrees a holy tenderness, the very reflection of heaven, should pervade the soul.

For the whispers of the heart, the many-tongued voices of nature, the magical accents of childhood, the enchanted aroma and infinite delicacy of love, all the felicities of the spiritual life, each noble and generous impulse, every golden sinless thought, and pure passionate emotion, the living voice, affection's tones, eyes that beam with hope, and truth, and every celestial thing, these, and far more than I can declare, reveal realities infinite as the universe, enduring as the stars of heaven.

That great thoughts and pure affections have exerted a mighty share in the destinies of our race, I hold as immutable truth. Such might well be termed the religion of humanity, were there not a yet loftier, more excellent faith, that of one high and ever-present God, light and pharos of the world, one law of duty, one truth, one aspiration. For love alone realises the conception, the certainty, indeed, of immortality, the inner worship which is the essential all in all, the faith, in short, in which a man may sweetly live, and without a fear may die.

367. HOUSE OF TRUTH.

Lead me only, says Goethe, into the house of truth, and there shall I abide for ever.[1] So indeed say we all. But Comte would lead us into a house, which, in respect of spiritual considerations, is not the house of truth at all. The human mind, he most erroneously declares, is competent to observe all phenomena except its own. His intelligence drew him to the reformed church, which he disliked, his heart to the Roman Catholic, which he disbelieved. In after years, indeed, when the great realities and requirements of the living affections appeared for the first time to strike him, he recognised the necessity of a cultus of some kind, and accordingly inaugurated humanity as his God.[2] The doctrinal pride of the reformed churches, unhappily, has led them to make too little account of the affec-

---
[1] Führte man mich in der Wahrheit Haus,
    Bei Gott ich ging nicht wieder heraus.
[2] Etre immense, éternal, l'humanité.

tions, else turned to purpose by the more ancient faith. For not the intellect, only, but the affections, must unite to realise the religion of the heart, our loftiest aspirations, our purest hopes.

368. BROAD PRINCIPLES.

Bodily purity is essential even to the soul's weal, for health, vigour, strength, all that purity sums up, are needful to conquer the moral, not less than the material world. Body and soul must be developed alike, else many a satisfaction is lost, many a germ of excellence thrown away. Breadth of culture, indeed, abates the petty and contingent, approximates us to the infinite and the supreme, which is in synthesis with all things.

369. NEEDFUL EFFORT.

Too often we would win the guerdon we have not toiled for, reap the crop we have not sown. Yet is effort pleasurable for its own sake, as well as for the sake of that for which we are to contend. There cannot be victory without a struggle.[1] Each one must bear his own burthen, yet a word of aid, direction, or advice, when we meet the generous being, some Prince of Orange or Francis of Lorraine, able and willing to afford it, may prove of mightiest efficacy. All, in truth, that I have heard or read or seen of the magical potency, the fascination of personal influence, some Mme Recamier or others, stimulating the powers, quickening germs of excellence, I believe. If men only felt, knew, what a

[1] Kein Sieg ohne Kampf.

divine power it lends, I say divine, for of such is the influence of heaven, many, indeed, would claim to exercise it.

370. THE SOUL'S BRAVERY.

It needs bravery to assail the spirit of convention when it bars the road to progress, would combat excellence. Failure and disaster too often are ascribable to want of courage and indolence, alone. Would we only persevere, we should arrive at a living conviction of the efficacy of the power which lies latent in every heart.[1] Nor man nor nation, indeed, should despair. Lost temporalities may be replaced, other losses restored, but for him who gives himself up, there is nor hope nor safety more.[2]

371. LIVING FOR GOD.

Fenelon, and Oberlin, and Neff, lived but for God and their kind. They perfectly understood the doctrine that to work is to pray.[3] To recite what they taught and what they did, were to recite much of what is excellent and good in humanity. They had, indeed, that insatiate craving which Boehm styles the life of the spirit, the hunger after better things, the highest good, the crown of pearls, seeking the divine kingdom,

---

[1] Unglaublich ist es was ein gebildeter Mensch für sich und Andere thun kann wenn er das Gemüth hat.

[2] Un hombre, una nacion, no deber jamas creer que su fin hayo llegado. La perdido de los bienes temporales puedè ser reparada, otras pérdidas pueden alivierse por el tiempo, y solo haya un mal qui no puede tener remedio, qui es el hombre que se desespera de se mismo.

Memoirs of Oberlin, Lond. 1838, chap. iv.

and the ever merciful and nigh God, whose image is generated within.[1] And thus, indeed, do God's cohorts and his children prepare for the life to come.

372. THE REAL AND THE IDEAL.

The scanty appreciation too often awarded, as well as the yet more serious wrongs inflicted upon the great and good, forms a blood and tear-stained chapter in the annals of our kind.[2] Alas for sublimity at issue with baseness, the ideal with the real. What do we not then owe to those blessed succourable influences which yield to genius the inch of footing needful even to the poorest material sustenance on the solid earth. We too, had we been by, would have comforted Cervantes, aided Camoens, rescued Chatterton, yet not the less, too often, do we suffer worth and genius to perish at our very doors.

After all, it is of little moment to genius, which brooding over truths that cannot die,[3] the conditions of celestial things, heeds not the asperities of the rugged path, but aspires, and ever must aspire to heaven. For what, after all, are such, but as wayside accidents on the path to the stars. And, I am not sure that genius, sublime, and to itself all-sufficing, has been happier, more uniformly fortunate, feted and feasted, than hooted and disowned by the world. Let no one

---

[1] Barmherziges Gott. *High and Deep Search concerning the Threefold Life of Man.*

[2] Es liebt die Welt das Glanzende zu schmutzen.
Und das Erhabene in dem Staub zu ziehn.

[3] Du nur Genius mehrest in der Natur die Natur.

then, however he may sympathize, presume to pity genius, which knows full well to suffer, and, if needs be, to die.

373. UP AND DOING.

Religion's great task is, while we neglect not the present, to grasp also at the future and the unseen. For it needs, indeed, divinest influences, courage, prudence, and self-mastery to animate the soul. Thus, speaking of Wieland, Goethe truly said, there was nothing about him petty or unworthy, nothing out of keeping with that moral greatness, dignity, and honour which he all his life maintained. We cannot all be Wielands perhaps, yet we, too, may reach the goal. One's own guidance avails much, and now and then a happy providence when least expected, aids.[1] The needful thing is to be up and doing, and to allow boundless scope to the soul.[2]

374. PEARLS AND DIAMONDS.

Pearls and diamonds, jewels of exceeding price, lie in our daily path, to be gathered and worn if we will.

[1] Der Zweck der Erziehung ist die Kinder dem Spiele des Zufals zu entreissen. Wäre es nicht die Ungewissheit, der man nicht Raum geben darf, so sollte Man lieber an gar keine absichtliche Bildung junger Leute denken, denn oft erzieht der Zufall viel besser als die grösste Sorgfalt der Eltern und Lehrer. Herbart, *Kleine Philosophische Schriften.*

[2] Il-y-a tant de nuances de caractere chez les individus, tant de dégres differents dans la conception du vrai, tant d'aspects variés de la riche nature qui crea la genie humaine, qu'il est absolument necessaire de laisser à chacun les conditions de sa vie morale et les élémens de sa force d'action.

Smiles celestial betimes irradiate features which else were cold and apathetic as the stone. The rustle as of seraphs' wings is heard, and rays are shed from loving eyes, like gleams from some star-gemmed heaven.

375. A NIGHT AT SEA.

It were well worth a fragment of one's existence to spend a night between the tropics at sea. Oh, to behold the great undulating deep, welling up like diamonds and pearls, to see the stars blaze and sparkle in their exceeding loveliness, like carbuncles plunged in sapphire blue, to breathe the tepid life-sustaining element, converse long hours with the tempest-tost mariners, mariners over whom the ooze and slime of ocean have washed for many a year, to watch the tall masts writing incessant hieroglyphs on the sky, the star-stream weltering in its own exceeding glory, while, presently, spire on spire of crimson light, joyous messengers of heaven, reveal the exultant dawn.

376. PHILOSOPHY AND RELIGION.

We are so tied down by conditions as often to find it difficult to obtain release.[1] For it needs effort to rise above our position, and dispassionately to consider the true relations of things.[2] There are few, observes Morell, who, uninfluenced by the spirit of the age, can

---

[1] Welche wohl bleibt von allen Philosophien, ich weiss nicht. Aber die Philosophie, hoff ich, soll ewig bestehn. *Schiller.*

[2] Denn das ist das Schicksal auch des fruchtbarsten menschlichen Geistes, dass er mit Ort und Zeit umfangen, in Gewissen, Ideen, Gleichsam aufwachst, und sich nacher nicht ohne Mühe von ihnen zu trennen vermag. Herder, *Seele und Gott.*

look through the forms and utterances of Christianity, itself, and gaze face to face on the eternal ideas which they embody.[1]

377. LIVING FOR EVER.

Oh thou good teacher, exclaimed a youth to Christ, what thing of excellence must I do, so that I too may live for ever.[2] And this is a question, which, some time or other, each soul must address to itself. For, dost thou not perceive, oh youth, that noble aspirings, a lofty aim, persistence in purity and well doing, is already on earth to win the reversion of heaven.[3] Since to be and to do, in faith and in love, is the end and object of all religion.[4] Shame, then, be upon those who, understanding these things, have failed to make them known to the world.[5]

378. MOTHER AND CHILD.

I saw this day, seated by the way side, a mother and her child. The mother was squalid, the child was soiled, alas, miserable embodiments of motherhood and childhood, else the very counterpart and correlative of relations most divine. We gaze upon the ideals of a Raphael or

[1] *Historical and Critical Review of the Speculative Philosophy of Europe.*
[2] Διδάσκαλε ἀγαθὶ, τί ἀγαθὸν ποιήσω, ἵνα ἔχω ζωὴν αἰώνιον.
[3] Glücklicher Säugling dir ist ein unendlicher Raum noch die Wiege.
   Werde Mann, und dir wird eng die unendliche Welt.   Schiller.
[4] Was auch als Wahrheit oder Fabel
       In tausend Büchern dir erscheint,
       Das alles ist ein Thurm zu Babel,
       Wenn es die Liebe nicht vereint.   Göthe.

[5] Honte à ceux qui ont compris ce devoir et qui se soucient encore d'avoir en partage le bonheur et le répos sur la terre.

Murillo, and are entranced. Yet every mother should realise as sweet an ideal. For see, each mother, with her infant, is, or ought to be, in effect, a Madonna, living counterpart and grace of heaven.

379. WARRING WITH DESPAIR.

It is the office of the intellect, as monarch of the soul, to bear up against emotion whenever it would impair and lessen its powers. Of all those who have succeeded in doing so, Boetius, as we see in his treatise on consolation,[1] perhaps comes in most for our applause. After cruel torture and captivity at Pavia, he liberated himself from the thrall of desolation and despair, looking with dauntless courage to the time, when, as he said, he should be freed, not only from Pavia, but the prison-house of the world.

380. PROGRESSIVE INFLUENCES.

Were one to live a thousand years, never could one exaggerate the potency of progressive influences. The mightiest river, the most impetuous torrent, may be turned by the foot at its source, or crossed at a bound. That heavy-browed man, who checks no appetite, hesitates at no crime, was erst a gentle, innocent child. That moody lunatic was once both decorous and self-possessed. In truth, the evil principles that tend to insanity and crime, like the roaring lions of the Christian allegory, seek continually whom they may devour. Yet, every influence, whether for good or for ill, is feeble at its outset, might be crushed or fostered in the very

[1] *De Consolatione Philosophiae*, Lib. V. Venetiis, 1492.

bud. The sane might continue sane, the innocent innocent, and moral worth and lofty intelligence be minted on each soul for ever. For it is true as heaven, whether as regards the heart or the understanding, that man's faculties need ceaseless, watchful culture and effort, in order to realise the divine.[1]

381. KNOWLEDGE AND FAITH.

Each one must ascertain through labour and resolve, whether he be worthy to take a flight above life's individualities, and grasp existence as a whole.[2] Our moral, not less than our material likeness is stamped on the souls of our fellows. Some, indeed, there be, observes Von Muller, who, even when called to a loftier destination, impress their image with all the fulness of life on the hearts and affections of the latest generations, glorious evidence of the moral grandeur which a firm pure will achieves.

So soon as we set out from the principle, says Goethe, that knowledge and faith are not given for mutual destruction, but to supply each other's deficiencies, we shall arrive at a just estimate of the right. This position accords well with Kant's categorical imperative, as he is pleased to style the moral law, and the obligatoriness of duty.[3] For if we err in one

[1] Chez les hommes dont la volunté paresseuse néglige la direction de certains facultés, ces facultés semblent s'accoutumer à cette indépendence et ne se laissent reprendre et gouverner qu'avec une incroyable resistance.

[2] Marx, *Akesios*.

[3] Il veut nous apprendre par un seul mot, que la morale n'est pas l'interêt bien entendu. Barni.

direction, in respect of the moral law, we are liable to err in all.

382. REMORSE AND SUPERSTITION.

There is not a horror or a degradation which superstition and fanaticism, fellow fiends, have not caused man to inflict or to endure. It was in the thirteenth Louis' reign, August 18, 1634, that Urbain Grandier, fourteen magistrates sitting, was burnt alive. The Maréchale d'Ancre, adjudged of sorcery, forsooth, was condemned to die, 8th of July, 1617, and burnt on the same day. Through faith in truth, only, with action conformable, can man gain purity of soul, alone realise on earth the comity of heaven.

383. FAITH AND LOVE.

The doctrine of the soul's immortality is a real victory of reason over the imagination and the senses. Instinctive faith, however unable to discriminate between the double forces, the twofold order of phenomena in our nature, has ever looked upon death as the beginning of a new life.[1] The soul was life indeed, immortality a resurrection. Plato, in the Phaedo, insisted on the unity and simplicity of the soul, the immortality of reason, Aristotle and his followers on the eternity of the thinking principle, for which Kant would substitute our individual humanity.

---

[1] Aus dem Leben sind der Wege zwei dir geöffnet,
    Zum Ideale führt einer, der andre zum Tod.
  Siehe wie du bei Zeit noch frei auf dem ersten entspringest,
    Ehe die Parze mit Zwang dich auf dem andern entführst.

Every true inquiry into the soul's powers, conscience, reason, imagination, confirms the great conquest, shows how the heart and intellect are beset by the longings after infinitude. For each several faculty that aspires to immortality and cannot else be satiated, has its origin and principle in God. Nor does this exclude scope for faith and love,[1] which, in regard of questions which the intellect alone is unable rightly to grasp, supplement the understanding, and, in a degree, precede its dictates.[2]

384. THE SOUL'S LIBERATION.

What purpose can be loftier than to free the soul from ignorance, and passions still more degrading. Delivered from grovelling error, and yet more sordid fear, man, calm, resolved, might enter the future, as he would enter a father's mansion, and a father's home. Nor weakness nor irresolution should stay the needful effort,[3] only condition on which excellence can be won. For heaven, the heaven of the heart and of the will, lies ever nigh, is evinced in the mother's quenchless love, the infant's dawning smile, every successful

[1] Ah, sans doute c'est par l'amour que l'eternité peut être comprise. Il confonde toutes les notions du temps, les idées de commencement et de fin. De Stael.

[2] Du hast Unsterblichkeit im Sinn,
Kannst du uns deine Grunde nennen.
. Gar wohl. Der Hauptgrund liegt darin,
Das wir sie nicht entbehren können. Goethe.

[3] La faiblesse et l'irresolution sont inapperçues de celui qui les a, et prennent à ses yeux dans chaque circonstance une nouvelle forme. Tantôt c'est la prudence, la sensibilité, ou la délicatesse qui eloignent de prendre un parti, et prolongent une situation indécise. De Stael.

struggle to improve our position, enhance the wide dominion of the soul.

385. THE HAND.

We cannot sufficiently admire the hand's exceeding excellence. It is evinced in every attitude, before the lathe and in the forge, in the factory by the loom, at sea among the ropes, afield among the potherbs and the corn, in securing the child's mantle, in smoothing the invalid's pillow, nay, in the last offices to the dead, in fine, in countless acts of devotion and love. Thus, some mother attiring her babe, or lady with wet and jewelled fingers amid her plants and flowers, shall all unconscious realise Correggio's divine ideal of modesty and grace.

386. NECESSITY AND FREE-WILL.

I am not sure that Morell quite succeeds in reconciling the antinomies of necessity and free-will.[1] In nothing, in truth, is the variousness of human culture more conspicuous than in the treatment of such subjects. There is no greater necessity in morals and religion, than in chemistry or astronomy, and no less. For necessity, rightly understood, is but another name for order and law. And if we admit, as we needs must admit these, we may term them liberty, the liberty of submission and assent, indeed, if we will.

The true theory of causation must be founded on man's whole nature, as governed by his position and his powers. For heaven itself conforms to law, the rule

[1] *History of Speculative Philosophy.*

of right. Bad habits, observes Hegel,[1] in golden words that should be preached to all mankind, rob us of our liberty, but the habit of what is right, everything that morality approves, that is liberty. Man cannot realise greatness or goodness, wisdom or learning, without having recourse to means, in fine the influences productive of such results. For a ceaseless unity pervades all phenomena, every power and affection of our souls.

387. TRUTH NEVER TRITE.

No truth can ever become trite, though truth may be tritely rendered. Can there, indeed, be a spectacle more pitiful than the pursuit of honours, wealth, distinctions, without a redeeming feature, or sense of better things. For life is not meant to be a sorry game of material profit and loss merely, but a scene of iron persistence in welldoing and co-operation in laws divine.[2]

388. THE INTENT OF DEATH.

One of the intentions of God's providence in the institution which men term death, is doubtless to foster faith unlimited in his divinest wisdom and love.[3] Thinkest thou, said Goethe, to frighten me with a coffin. What signifies death, exclaimed Albert Dürer, in the cause of truth.[4] A fool with cap and bells, after

[1] *Encyclopaedia*, § 410. *Werke*, Berlin 1844, 5.

[2] Alle Philosophie müsse geliebt und gelebt werden.

[3] *M'Cormac's Philosophy of Human Nature*.

[4] Qu'importe la mort. L'immortalité et l'eternité nous attendront au seuil du paradis. Un peuple, un homme, qui ne sait pas affronter la mort ne vivra jamais.

all, is not the fit emblem of life, any more than a grotesque and hideous spectre is of the evils and shortcomings of the world. Teachers, apostles of the mighty truth, that knowledge, which is of the light divine, was made to comfort, to elevate, and to bless, shall one day assert in loftiest accents the dignity and brotherhood of man. And truth and love having once consummated celestial nuptials, shall be separated no more.

389. TRUE NOBILITY.

Let us not too much compassionate the sufferings of the noble and the good. There are sufferings, let us be assured, transcending in their spiritual compensations most enjoyments. There is solace, indeed, in the inner sanctuary before which the waves of human suffering roll by and are stilled. Bright great thoughts, the sunshine of the heart, all that makes existence beautiful, man's soul like unto an aroma of paradise, are there, and there shall subsist for ever. For greatness and goodness vindicate themselves, and a true nobility of character holds on, and so will hold on to the close.

390. A RAVELLED SKEIN.

It were easier, such is the clinging nature of every sin, to loose a ravelled skein than to rectify a corrupt heart. Elevation of character, indeed, cannot stoop to meet wile with wile. But as the swift arrow distances the winding snake, so shall directness of purpose, coupled with goodness and intelligence, in most cases baffle the insincerity which confides in nothing, not even in itself.

391. COURAGE AT HEART.

Some degree of boldness is essential to intellectual and moral worth. The famous French factionary but uttered the truth when he asked for courage, and more courage, and always courage. For he too needed it, since on the morrow he had to die. If you do not strangle the lion in your path, you he will assuredly devour. Eternal forces are at work. You must defeat them, when adverse, or be yourself defeated. Be earnest, exclaims Boehme, for hell cannot be destroyed without earnestness or the heavenly kingdom won. Yet, I do not term it defeat, when a man dies at his post, for here non-success is not defeat. He is the sentinel in the breach, the standard-bearer who winds his colours round his body, or hands them to his successor. Though bound to hold firm to the death, still, it is victory enough to have done all that man can do. And were it not for firmness, the ceaseless combat, the unconquerable will never to submit or yield, where should we be now, freedom of thought in chains, humanity in the dust.

392. POVERTY OF SOUL.

Poverty of soul is often a more irredeemable evil than some downright sin. For this, penitence may atone, but for that, what shall atone. How, then, to infuse the sacred fertilising fire which is to animate the else dead and worthless machine. Any spiritual convulsion or sorrow, almost, were preferable to a hard unyielding heart, intolerable alike to man and heaven.

393. THE LIFE WITHIN.

Spiritual food for hunger spiritual. The thirstier the soul of man or angel, the more freely does God pour his free grace upon it, till the soul becomes as it were another soul, seeks but to accomplish the purposes of heaven. Hence came Howard's intense determination, throughout his mighty task, till brought by death to bay at last, on Kherson's wind-swept plains. It was Fichte's unflinching perseverance, amid pinching want and hardship, which enabled him to accomplish so much in the higher walks of thought. What is it, indeed, exclaims Jacobi,[1] which so excites our admiration in a Bayard, a Ruyter, a Douglas, or a Montrose, what, but that, each and all, they did not cling to the life of the body merely, but rather to that of the soul. We must, indeed, stand firmly by the living law, ascend from platform to platform, and from arena to arena, till we reach the empyrean of our hopes at last.

394. MODERN SPECULATION.

The amount of modern speculation is something enormous. Descartes, Spinoza, Hume, Malebranche, Berkeley, are, indeed, of moderate dimensions, not so Fichte, Schelling, Kant, Hegel. Like Milton's demons,

> discoursing high
> Of providence, foreknowledge, will, fate,
> Fixed fate, free-will, foreknowledge absolute,
> And found no end in wandering mazes lost,

---

[1] Fliegende Blatter. Erste Abtheilung. *Werke*, Leipsig, 1812.

their writings would consume no mean portion of a life to appreciate. Hegel would have us to believe that man thinks over, re-creates, so to speak, the conditions of the universe. But even Hegelians are at issue as to his views. Heine, himself a Hegelian, spent a couple of years in writing out a summary, then burnt the manuscript. If the truth must be told, he says, I seldom quite understood him, and then only as an afterthought, and do not think he even meant to be understood.[1] It seems to justify Heine's irony when we find Hegel affirming that the stars are but as a luminous eruption in the sky.[2] Whatever Rosenkranz[3] or Vera[4] may say, there is dross to be eliminated from Hegel's gold.

According to Spinoza, and so far as I can discern, Fichte and Schelling, God is the immanent, intransient source of all things.[5] In Hegel, pantheism takes a yet loftier flight, man, in short, is the Absolute.[6] This conclusion seems to resume his entire philosophy, thus

[1] Ehrlich gesagt selten verstand ich ihn, und erst durch späteres Nachdenken gelangte ich zum Verstandniss seiner Worte. Ich glaube er wollte gar nicht verstanden sein. Heine, *Vermischte Schriften*.

[2] Ein leuchtender Aussatz am Himmel, *Id*.

[3] Wer so wie dieses König im Reich des Gedankens, einen neuen Bandes Wissens gegrundet hat. Freiheit, Freude, Frieden hat er uns gegeben. *Hegel's Leben*, Grabrede.

[4] Nous ne hesitons pas a proclamer Hegel comme un des plus puissants penseurs qui ait jamais existé. *Introduction à la Philosophie de Hegel*.

[5] Est omnium rerum causa immanens.

[6] Das Selbst ist das absolute Wesen. Hegel, *Phänomenologie des Geistes*.

rivalling the Sankhya of Patandjali, the Buddhist doctrine of the Nirvana. With Spinoza, indeed, man is God, with Hegel and Schelling God is man, nay, man is everything, the individual nothing. The world is a flower, the ceaseless becoming, proceeding eternally from a single germ, the absolute concrete idea, genesis of the divine in the human soul, itself the Absolute and substance of the universe. According to Hegel, the object of religion and philosophy is the determination of eternal truth, in a word, consciousness in God, philosophic consciousness, the idea conscious of itself, producing and reproducing itself for ever.

Whatever may be thought of these mystical speculations, they are, at least, capital as dialectic exercises. And it might be well for any one who prides himself on his acuteness, to take in hand one or more of the volumes which contain them, say Schelling's Bruno,[1] in which Anselmo thus sets out. Wilt thou, O Lucian, repeat to us what thou didst yesterday maintain on the subject of truth and beauty while discoursing of the mysteries. From this to the end of the dialogue, when the advancing night and the light-shedding solitary stars admonish the friends to retire, matters of infinite moment, the connexion of man and nature, the human and the divine, the development of consciousness, the interpretation of life, the religious idea, are treated of after the fashion of the Kant, Fichte, Hegel, and Schelling school. Yet were Kant's merits great, most momentous his firm insistence on the subjection of all creeds to the interpretation of the moral law, never subordi-

[1] *Bruno, oder über das natürliche und göttliche Princip der Dinge.*

nating the great ends of existence to any temporary expediency whatever.[1] The great ability of these ever-remarkable writers, the purity of their lives and moral doctrines, with the exalted nature of their speculations, command our attention and interest, though it did not suffice to shelter them, any more than it did Jean Paul, and others, from the imputation of atheism, an imputation to which Fichte has adverted with touching earnestness and ability.[2]

395. CREATIVE POWER OF LOVE AND ART.

God is praised in every successful effort of creative skill. As in art the glories of form, the exquisite purity of the beautiful, raise in us yet higher conceptions of spiritual purity and truth, so love, likewise, is a creative power, elevates us from the sensuous, merely, to the supersensuous, from the perishable to the imperishable. It is, indeed, the living link between God and man, the golden bond by angels held, clew between earth and heaven.

396. SPIRITUAL LIFE.

No tongue may recount the soul's combats, combats which even the best, at times, might hesitate to avow.

[1] Summam crede nefas animam praeferre pudori,
Et propter vitam vivendi perdere causas.
[2] Aber selbst wenn ich bestimmt sey die unzäligen Opfer, welche schon für die Wahrheit fielen um eines zu vermehren, so musste ich doch noch meine letzte Kraft aufbieten, um Grundsätze in das Publicum bringen zu helfen welche wenigstens diejenigen sichern und retten könnten, die nach mir dieselbe vertheidigen werde. *Werke.* Appellation gegen die Anklage des Atheismus.

But in the spiritual life all shall be cleared up. The seeds planted here, shall there bear fruit and flowers for ever. For see, there is but one heaven and one joy, seated, not beyond stars or distant space, but in the soul's depths, the very, the inmost heart of man.[1]

397. LOVE OF ORDER AND OF TRUTH.

The love of truth, purifying the desires and ennobling the will, is as a golden lamp to illumine and direct the world. But habits of accurate thought and strict precision are needful, and such had Lessing in perfection. Montesquieu's prudential economy was ever subordinate to benevolent and generous ends. His conceptions of human nature were remarkable as was the dignity with which he lived up to them. Like the Chancellor D'Aguesseau, who, in retirement drew on the almost infinite resources of a well-stocked mind, never, it is said, did he experience an ennui which an hour's study, or, in his advanced years, being read to by his secretary or one of his daughters, failed to dissipate.

398. MEN OF PROGRESS.

There are those whose every feature is indicative of spiritual ennoblement, the impress of struggle and of victory. Turning over the leaves, one day, of a rare French folio that treated of men and things gone by, I found, among others, likenesses of Von Sickengen

[1] Es gibt nur einen Himmel,
Den ew'gen Sitz der Lust.
Sucht ihn nicht in den Fernen,
Sucht ihn nicht über Sternen,
Sucht ihn .   . in Eurer Brust.

and Ulrich Von Hutten, the latter clad in armour, the portraiture he loved best, and displaying a countenance of uncommon firmness and resolve. For me, he said, repose is death.¹ And speaking of the German people, he exclaimed, their misfortunes are yet greater than their souls.² His epistles, or reputed epistles, of obscure men,³ written on the occasion of the persecution of Reuchlin at Cologne,⁴ came like a thunder-clap on the opponents of progress, rescuing humanity from torpor and from chains. Never, says Hamilton, were unconscious barbarism and sanctimonious immorality so ludicrously exposed as in the letters ascribed to Hutten's pen. He was to Luther a vigorous, and sometimes troublesome, coadjutor. This most noble man, and dauntless combatant in the cause of humanity, died at the early age of thirty-five, greater, it has been said, than all the reformers together.

Defoe, with less elevation and pretension, was nevertheless a man of similar stamp. His short way with the Dissenters, produced much the same effect in England that the epistles of obscure men did in Germany. To Defoe's force of character, contempt of bigotry and danger, and tireless constancy, the dissenters mainly owe it that their own great protest against Protestantism, the efforts of the establishment, notwithstanding, proved successful. The burning of Joanna Bocher and

¹ Strauss, *Ulrich Von Hutten*, Leipzig, 1858.
² *Klagschrift an alle Stand. Auferwecker der Teutcher Nation.*
³ *Epistolae Obscurorum Virorum*, Venet. 1516, Lond. 1859.
⁴ Reuchlin, wer will sich ihm vergleichen,
    Zu seiner Zeit ein Wunderzeichen. Göthe.

others, in the reign of Edward VI, with the execution of Henry Barrow and his associates, at Tyburn, April 6, 1593, for writing and publishing certain books, alleged to cry down the Church of England, and the then Queen's prerogative in matters spiritual, yields bitter evidence of the intolerance of the times.[1]

399. CONCEPTION OF THE DIVINE.

War and death, and the ceaseless clash of forces, tend, or often tend, to raise us from the material to the immaterial, from the sensuous to the supersensuous, from man to God. Men or nations that sink into contented sensuality, perish as to the spiritual. For we cannot satisfy ourselves with things of sense, and save the soul alive. If not by and through our own efforts, God will tear us from our security, and thrust action upon us perforce.

Fichte dwells much on the means to which Providence resorts for evoking the conception of the divine, and to which everything immoral is opposed.[2] For God's revealings announce him as a moral, not an immoral lawgiver. Promises and threats are alike opposed to pure morality.[3] Not for its own sake, observes Fichte, can I esteem this world. The mind can

---

[1] *Egerton Papers.* Camden Society. Lond. 1840, p. 166.

[2] Alles was unmoralisch ist widerspricht dem Begriffe von Gott. Jede Offenbarung die sich durch unmoralische Mittel angekündigt behauptet, fortgepflanzt hat, ist sicher nicht von Gott. *Versuch einer Kritik aller Offenbarung,* § 10.

[3] Angedrohte Strafen oder versprochene Belohnungen zum Gehorsam, können nicht von Gott seyn, denn der gleichen Motive widersprechen der reinen Moralität. *Versuch.*

take no hold of it, but rushes upward and onward to a future and better state of being. His efforts, indeed, were unwearying to exalt the inner, spiritual consciousness which alone is life and happiness unchangingly.[1] For this is the true life with its thoughtful intelligence, its obedience, its enjoyments, and its love. If I may not, observes Fichte, alter what is without, let me at least try to alter what is within, and thus approximate to the eternal, the divine.[2]

400. THE BETTER LIFE.

Endless almost is the testimony of the wise and good, of all nations and times, to the better, the celestial life, the boundless region which we term the soul of man. Blind, suffering, almost hopeless, exclaims Thierry,[3] I can yield the assurance which from me at least will not be questioned, that if in this world there be a thing which avails more than another, which is better than fortune, health even, it is devotion to science. Very affecting are the astronomer, Arago's last

---

[1] *Anweisung zum Seligen Leben, oder an die Religionslehre.* Erste Vorlesung. *Sämmtliche Werke.* Berlin, 1845—6.

[2] Ein heiliger Wille lebt,
Wie auch der menschliche wanke,
Hoch über der Zeit und der Raume webet
Lebendig der hochste Gedanke.
Und ob alles in ewigen Wechsel kreist,
Es beharret im Wechsel ein ruhiger Geist.

[3] Aveugle et souffrant, sans espoir, et presque sans relâche, je puis rendre ce temoignage, qui de moi ne sera pas suspect, il-y-a au monde quelque chose qui vaut mieux que les jouissances materielles, mieux que la fortune, c'est le devouement à la science. *Etudes Historiques,* Préface.

words, when blind and dying, yet still resolved, he hands over his hardly completed task to the care of those who are to follow him.[1] And if we except Fichte's prayer, neither Schelling nor Schleiermacher, nor Hegel, ever delivered himself of anything more beautiful than Kant has done, when he speaks of the starry heaven above, the moral law within, the invisible self, our everlasting infinite worth.

401. EXCELLENCE, OF NO SEX.

We discriminate between masculine and feminine perfections, nevertheless, the more nearly these approach each other, the more exalted do they become. The highest virtues and affections, in truth, are of no sex. The more men and women rise in the scale of psychical being, the loftier their intelligence, the more exalted their tenderness and grace, the more closely will they be found to resemble each other. For the virtues, let us ever repeat, are faculties as well as qualities, and it requires no insistence to prove that the heart's best endowments are supplemented by those of the understanding, while these again receive their proper complement from the heart. It is indeed owing to our partial culture, that while the virtues of the mother, as has been too often observed, realise virtue in her offspring, those of the father, confer only fame.

---

[1] Pour moi dans l'état de santé où je me trouve au moment où je dicte ces dernières lignes, ne voyant plus, n'ayant que quelques jours à vivre encore . . . F. Arago, *Astronomie Populaire*, Avertissement. Paris, 1855.

402. THE DIVINE TREASURY.

My failures in the pursuit of virtue, observed Blanco White, were their own punishment, are the punishment, indeed, of us all. He entertained the loftiest views of truth, deepest convictions as to the divine presence and perfections. He had escaped from the restricted arena, restricted as to the intelligence, of Roman Catholicism, into the comparatively freer atmosphere of Protestant life and speculation. I have contributed my mite, he said, to the liberties of mankind. It is cast into the divine treasury. He stood on the rock of providence, the inner light, the infinite rationality of the infinitely perfect God. His friends he sweetly termed representatives of the merciful compassions of God. Five days before his decease, this most upright and enlightened Spaniard, and suffering tried man, exclaimed, that whatever may prove the difficulties in the course of this life, there are more than compensations.

403. THE PAST, AT OUR DOOR.

Who would now address a reproach on the score of the horrors of Smithfield or those of St. Bartholomew, the hangings and scourgings of New-England, the destruction of Servetus or Aikenhead, unless it were sought to justify the excesses of the past, for then, indeed, we become as participators in them. We are to be ashamed of our unworthy predecessors, not because they were of this sect or that, but because they were men, and because, on any pretext, they could so outrage the reverence due to heaven and our kind.

404. THE CROWN.

And he that overcometh, shall inherit all things. I will be his God, and he shall be my son.[1] Than this, indeed, there is no more joyous utterance in the wide category of celestial things. All nature proclaims it, the universe proclaims it, and the human heart, which God has so graced and endowed, proclaims it. For if we only overcome, we shall inherit, with all its infinite belongings, the better life, become at a bound free of it and of heaven, the joyous brotherhood to whom the glad fruitions of the spiritual life are for ever known.

Ah, the very conception teems with ecstasy. The denizens of eternity shall take us by the hand, and welcome us to their starry homes. Nor is it a selfish or exclusive joy, for heaven eventually must include all the children, sons, indeed, and daughters of God. All must become participators in the blessed life, the manna of God's unwearying love. For each several virtue flows from him, from him derives its celestial quality and origin. What, then, do we not owe to our infinite benefactor and friend. This, indeed, we do owe, that man is to strive to become still more deserving to claim him as a Father, still more worthy to be named a son.

[1] Ὁ νικῶν κληρονομήσει πάντα, καὶ ἔσομαι αὐτῷ Θεός, καὶ αὐτὸς ἔσται μοι ὁ υἱός.

ASPIRATIONS

FROM

THE INNER, THE SPIRITUAL LIFE.

BOOK IX.

GREAT truths have been gradually buried under a hard incrustation of human dogmatism, till the deep life beating within is scarcely any longer perceptible. Christianity will then resume its apostolic fervour and simplicity, when, going back to the original fountains of faith in the human soul, and renouncing the fruitless controversy about forms of opinion which derive all their value from the intellectual wants of different minds, it shall throw itself once more, without distrust or reservation, on that eternal religion of the heart and conscience, which is the utterance of God's spirit within us, which Christ acted out in the narrow circle of Palestinian life, and which his followers, believing in the perpetuity of his heavenly life, have been striving, with varying success, for nigh two thousand years, to spread over the world.

National Review.

ASPIRATIONS.

405. SPECULATION.

THE vast accession of intellectual ability, as displayed in the Bacons, Miltons, and Shakspeares of England, the Herders, Wielands, Fichtes, and Richters of Germany, is mainly owing to the prodigious impulse derived from the Reformation, itself a result of the renewal of letters, liberating thought and opening the floodgates of speculation.

The English have made of Shakspeare a sort of household divinity. He excelled, indeed, in a fine perception of the essences and relations of things, in virtue of which he is cosmopolitan, belongs not merely to England, but to humanity and the world. He is no sectarian either, but a proper member of the universal, the invisible church. And, then, he is so gentle, so good, so humane, the tenderest, manliest affections find in him fitting voice and utterance.

The poets of Roman Catholic lands, however able their delineation of the passions and the conduct of the drama, some Dante or Boccaccio, who themselves protested, excepted, rarely give expression to the combined sublimity of sentiment and thought. There is little for example, in Lope de Vega's fertile pages that we should desire to preserve.[1] And even Calderon, though combining many excellencies,[2] wanted the spiritual discernment which his narrow convictions could not well supply. But Protestantism, itself, is anchored to a formula, already far in the misty rear. The good ship of human progress, however, freighted with the mighty destinies of man, will be held by no such anchor of human forging, but will on and on, till the cares and uncertainties of this rich yet exacting existence shall vanish, and the abounding wonders of a higher life rise in sunny splendour on the soul.

406. OUTWARD OBJECTS.

The reciprocal action of soul and body, the forces which link matter with mind, mind with matter, we do not know. The motion of my hand over this paper, the gaze of these unresting eyes, are marvels, indeed, as great as the courses of the heavenly orbs with their wondrous impress on the soul.

407. THE PROMISED SHORE.

God has not laid too bare the avenues to the better land, yet it is already here, it is also now. Gaze through the nighest casement, and infinity is before you. Look into the soul's depths, and it meets you there. And God, also, is here, that God whom we only see or can see, with the soul's eyes, and spirits of the invisible,

---

[1] *Holland's Lope de Vega*, Lond. 1806. Bouterwek, Lond. 1847.

[2] Fue el oraculo de la corte, el ansia de las estrangeros, el padre de las musas, el lince de la erudicion, la luz de las teatros, la admiracion de los hombres. *Vida.*

with whom the body or what we so term, alone prevents us from communing. Therefore, dear heart grieve not so much, thy child is not really dead. Its bright intelligence, with every dear affection, remains intact as before. And divinely prepared, you too one day shall rejoin it, and so abide without pause or severment, for ever.[1] For life is only the pronaos and forecourt of eternity. Material barriers, indeed, shall be abated, but the affections shall flourish like the souls whom their possession has made divine.

408. IDEAS NEVER DIE.

Ideas slumber, but never die. Emit some divine truth, and straightway it becomes immortal, survives the wreck of ages and of time.[2] No, adamant is not more permanent than are the regenerating influences, the deathless principles, indissolubly associated with the advancement of our kind.[3]

409. TO BE GREATLY GOOD.

To be greatly good, a man must sympathise with others, make their pains and pleasures his own. To

---

[1] Deine Lieb' hat sie umfangen
    Ehe sie die Welt umfing,
    An Dein Herz ist sie gehangen
    Ehe sie auf die Erde ging. Herder.

[2] *Buckle on Civilisation.*

[3] Les Idées, grâces à Dieu, ne périssent pas. Une fois semées dans le monde, tôt ou tard elles portent leur fruit pour la postérité. Les vérités éternelles ne s'oublient plus, ne se perdent jamais. Et l'humanité avance toujours vers son ideal, vers la vérité qui est son étoile. Jules Simon, *Histoire de l'Ecole d'Alexandrie*, Tome ii. p. 583. Paris, 1845.

be greatly wise, he must dare to confide in the soul's resolves, and without or fear or dread carry them through. A resolute will, in truth, is the tough cable whereby we hold on by the fast anchors of trust and hope. The strenuous determination never to submit or yield, comes from striving alone. Acts of sublimity multifold, creations springing from the misty realms of uncertainty and nothingness, assert the dignity of man. No difficulty could daunt Mozart, or induce him to lay aside the firm resolve, which only exhaled itself with life, and the mighty requiem with which its close was sung.

410. A GREAT SOUL.

Greatness and goodness, for all the virtues are supplementary to each other, twin angels both, should hold joint tenancy together. There is, in truth, consecration in a mighty purpose, wrestling with difficulty, converting it into excellence for body and soul. For the least trace of magnanimity lights up the possessor, fascinates our kind.

411. TO KNOW GOD.

God wills that we should know him and inquire into his power.[1] He demands no pitiable degradation, no wallowing in the mire. Some earth-born despot may desire it, but not our Father and our God. He requires us but to love him, to think nobly and well. He demands not prostration, but elevation of soul, not blind adoration, but appreciation, our best, not our lowest

---

[1] Dieu veut qu'on le comprenne et qu'on discute sa puissance.

intelligence, all our science, and all our powers. And these are the soul's true healing, best extinguishers of superstition, all the unholy, unworthy things falsely written in God's great name, these, the sure preventatives of religious madness, that utter ruin and prostration of the faculties connected with erroneous, perverted conceptions of almighty goodness and power. That God, of whom the immense heavens reveal the glory, the lucid firmament and the wide-spread universe the mighty handiwork,[1] seeks, indeed, our obedience and our affections, but no, ah no, not our degradation or our despair.

412. LIFE'S TREASURES.

New truths, purer, more exalted, emotions directed to the beautiful and the good, are the soul's conquests, life's best treasures. Strength indeed, and gentleness should go hand in hand. It is surely of the province of our sisters, the womanhood of earth, to instruct oftener than they do. But superstition, on the one hand, an arrogant civilisation on the other, reject their precious aid in leading souls to heaven.[2] For woman, in truth, is a moral providence over man, and guided

[1] I cieli immensi narrano
Del grande Iddio la gloria.
Il firmamento lucido
All' universa annunzia
Quanto sieno mirabile
Della sua destra le opere.

[2] L'instinct moderne reprouve une morale qui proclame les inclinations bienveillantes comme etrangères à notre nature, qui méconnait la dignité du travail jusqu' à le faire dériver d'une malédiction divine, et qui érige la femme en source de tout mal.

by a developed intelligence, her influence should extend to every individual of our race.[1]

413. TORN AWAY.

I feel wrung at heart when I call to mind the numbers, treasures, I may well say, of goodness, sweetness, and intelligence, torn by consumption from this earth's life away. Yet, consumption there could not be, were the twice-breathed atmosphere avoided, which arrests the discharge of bodily waste, and alone causes it to be deposited as tubercle throughout the frame.[2] For, indeed, the air we breathe, at night in especial, should be pure as that which flits across the lea-field, or floats on the salt-sea wave. And were it only suffered to do so, this our life's elixir would rush into our chambers, kiss each sleeper's brow, and, with divinest pharmacy, refresh his blood, and banish fell disease away.

414. HUMANITY, ONE.

All men, the white man and the black, the red man and the brown, are of one species.[3] It matters in this respect not the least, whether we spring from one origi-

[1] Une profonde tendresse constitua toujours le meilleur préservatif du libertinage.

[2] M'Cormac *On Consumption*, Lond. 1855. M'Cormac, Letter to the Imperial Academy of Medicine, Lond. 1858.

[3] Das Gefühl von der Einheit des Menschengeschlechts, das Princip der individuellen und der politischen Freiheit ist in der unvertilgbaren Ueberzeugung gewurzelt von der gleichen Berechtigung des einigen Menschengeschlechts. So tritt dieses als Ein grosser verbrüderter Stamm, als ein zur Erreichung Eines zweckes, der freien Entwickelung innerlicher Kraft, bestehendes Ganzes auf. Alexander von Humboldt, *Kosmos*. Stuttgart und Tubingen, 1847, Zweiter Band, S. 235.

nal stock, or from many, like the plants and the flowers. Wandering princes are we, as Channing with truest illumination declared, sons of the Great King. For the real attributes of humanity, capability of culture, and self-consciousness, in short, union with the divine, attach to all our race. Nor is there a savage, in sunny southern isle, or deep continental recess, who is not susceptible of spiritual influences, in fine, all the development of our kind.

415. YOUTH, INNOCENCE.

Passing recently through the streets, I heard a child addressed by other children. His first reply was an execration, his second was an impurity, hideous in itself, yet more hideous in one so young. But a new phasis of culture, a better carrying out of the divine evangel is needed. Philosophy and religion must come down from the desk, and vice and ignorance be fought with in their own dark lairs. Each child, compulsorily if needs be, should frequent the model school. Every aptitude, moral, industrial, artistic, intellectual, coupled with all possible appliances of order, cleanliness, neatness, and decorum, ought to be developed. All sweet and precious culture should be enforced, lived up to as well as professed, with teachings calculated to instil the love of God and of our kind, and action conformable thereto. The laws of the material and moral worlds, the certainty and permanence of the spirit-life, of God, and providence, and immortality, should be proclaimed at every turn. And these will be found in eternal unison with an unadulterated Christianity, views of life, and types of piety which afford their own intrinsic vindication apart from all extraneous or merely verbal authority.[1] For indeed, training in action and not in words merely, is needed to evangelise the world, to instil practically and for ever, the simple yet heavenly truths in which all morality, all philosophy, and all religion are at one.

416. MUSIC, DIVINE.

Music, as an element of spiritual culture, is not yet turned to best account. If children were only fitly trained by masters of their art, and without too much theory, how quickly would their voices mellow, and the love of God and all excellence find sweetest acceptance in their souls. For music steals into the deep recesses of our being, evokes conceptions of the unseen, the divine life, purity ineffable, emotions too deep for tears, too exquisite for words. It leads to faith and hope indeed, sympathy with goodness, ousts all animosity, fills us with sentiments of ineffable tenderness, and purity, and love. It tends to an unquenchable belief in the regeneration of humanity. It discourses in celestial accents of the higher life, assures us that refinement and goodness never die. It reveals infinitude, in short, evokes emotions which partake of heaven.

For like religion, the music is worthless which does not spring from the heart and find its way there. Difficulties, indeed, occur in the pursuit, but they must be vanquished. They are but as means to ends, for if thrust into prominence, the beautiful takes to flight,

[1] *National Review*, April 1859.

and wings itself for ever away. A girl singing at her work, a reaper among the corn, some boy with snatches of wild melody, shall perchance touch the heart more than any Pasta or Grisi. Sometimes it is the song of the wild bird holding mysterious accord with the rippling deep, as it mounts the wave-washed strand. It is the sailor chaunting his lay to the sea, while the bellying sail and the heaving ship keep time. It is an emigrant singing with tears of the soil he shall never tread again. Some mother with tireless constancy lulling her babe to rest, or angelic Mara rescuing souls from else cureless grief and care. In fine, music is among the zests of existence, very aroma and food of heaven.

417. A THOUGHT OF GOD.

It was the noble conception of Oersted and Schelling, as it was of Plotinus[1] long before them, that the divine will was one of reason, and that the world was a thought of God. What we term nature, is, thus, an eternal discourse on love, and truth, and every heavenly thing, between man and the divine. Tepid breezes fan the infant's cheeks, pleasant perfumes salute his nostrils, the gay parterre his eyes. He is conscious, as the lower animals are conscious, but in a little he begins to discern the intent of creation and of his own soul, and straightway that sacred, that holy converse begins, which, unless interrupted by sin, endures for ever.

And thus do we commune, as in a paradise, with the

[1] Ἀρχὴ οὖν λόγος καὶ πάντα λόγος. *Ennead.*

divine, in the heavenly garden, which is in man's soul, as in the ambient world. Viewed in this light, thought is of yet greater moment than the mutations of a world, since each thought is a reality, in short, a soul. And wherever the soul feels, and is conscious of what it feels, it is conscious of everlasting life. I feel, and think, and love now, and, therefore, I shall feel, and think, and love for ever. God, who might have made us from the first, as he shall one day make us, very angels of purity and perfection, requires us to co-operate in the mighty work, the spiritual elevation and security of our own souls. It is nothing, indeed, or next to nothing, to have, or even to know, but it is everything to be.[1] As our capacity increases, so shall we hold yet diviner intercourse with celestial things, true bond between earth and heaven. Then, the world becomes too narrow for the soul, which asks infinity and obtains it.

Inquiries thus exalted, as Huyghens remarked, have this character of sublimity, that it is a glory to arrive even at a probability in respect of them. For truth divine, although discerned as a glimmering spark at first, expands into a sun of light, transfiguring the conscious soul at last.

418. SPECULATIVE ABILITY.

It is of the last importance to the individual and the species, that constructive speculative ability should be maintained in activity and vigour. We should welcome the whole family of thinkers and inquirers, those

[1] Es ist kein Gluck viel zu haben, sondern viel zu seyn. Zschokke.

of Germany among the rest, although they, or rather some of them, have undertaken tasks, than which it were easier to raise water in sieves, or twine ropes of sand. Yet, have they helped to rouse man to a higher sense of the divinity of his nature. For without God and the spirit-life, I hold with Schleiermacher, there cannot be a world. But any attempt to chain human thought to a formula, tends to deprive man of the privilege of seeking truth for himself, and thus realising community with heaven.

419. THE ANGELS BY OUR SIDE.

As the poet sings,

> 'Tis only when they spring to heaven,
> That angels reveal themselves unto you. They sit all day
> Beside you, and at night lie by you, who
> Care not for their presence, muse or sleep.
> And all at once they leave you, and you know them.

Many such angels have I known, some in their prime, others in their sere, discharging in their sweet measure the charities of God. They were of both sexes, and some hardly of any, since they vanished so young, almost unwitting of the change, unless it were, as they lisped, to go to heaven.

420. THE HIGHEST BEAUTY.

The highest beauty, says Winkelman, resides in God alone. And for this one saying, for in it resides the discernment of celestial truth, since God is the great Artist as he is the great Chemist and great Geometer, his name should never perish. Peace, my heart, he exclaimed, thy powers yet surpass thy cares.¹ Beauty, with all its countless utterances, is of the dialogues which God maintains with man's soul, inciting, urging, calling upon, intreating it, to realise the purity which is of heaven. For there is never a smiling babe or ruddy rose, which does not tell, or long to tell, of heaven. Beauty, indeed, archetype and divine ideal, is of the very atmosphere of paradise, of that life wherein no impurity can dwell, and where the soul which is susceptible of it, holding communion with its Author, is exalted more and more, and for ever.

421. DIVINE PROGRESS.

A writer in the Edinburgh Review remarks cogently, that it is the special comfort and consolation of those who would abate abuses, that these have within them a principle of decay which renders them amenable to the assaults of advancing civilisation. And this is true of all evil, all falsity, whether in the visible or the invisible life, that it is of necessity impermanent, incompatible with nature, and order divine.

The very conception of eternal evil and suffering, is only less immoral than it is irrational. For spiritual progress must needs triumph over sin and suffering, and this so surely as that God is light, and truth, and love, and will not suffer his precious creatures, or his good work to remain under any blight or taint of imperfection, whatever. For He is the true liberator and reformer, preserver, indeed, and Saviour of mankind.²

---

¹ Paix mon coeur, tes forces surpassent encore tes soucis.
² Καὶ ἠγαλλίασε τὸ πνεῦμά μου ἐπὶ τῷ Θεῷ τῷ σωτῆρί μου.

422. SPIRITUAL PARENTAGE.

We owe love and reverence to our bodily parents indeed, but we also owe something to those, who, heralds and interpreters of the divine, awaken and rouse within us the lofty consciousness of spiritual things. Reflect well then, ye who would elevate your fellow man, that for each true and noble thought which you inspire, you raise souls to veriest paradise.

Appreciation surely, is the meed of those who would exalt the spiritual condition of their kind. The true poet-artist, consummate philosopher, the man, in brief, in whatever way inspired by God, becomes as an angel of light to his species, lifts them from the slough, and by a sort of divine coercion, draws them into the charmed circle, beyond the power of the fiends of vice and sensuality, and into the very precincts and atmosphere of heaven.[1]

423. FIXITY OF OPINION.

The fixity of human opinions is less real than apparent, for they fleet and fleet, and speed as speeds the rack away. Even sects that boast the greatest enduringness, undergo continual development and change. We submit, because we must, to the sweet influences of the ages. The Roman Catholicism of to-day is no longer that of the past, and even Calvinism, except

---

[1] Das Leben ist höhern Ursprungs, und es steht in unserer Gewalt, es seiner edlen Geburt würdig zu erziehn und zu erhalten, dass Staub und Vernichtung in keinem Augenblicke darüber triumphiren dürfen. Tieck, *Phantasus*, Erster Theil, Berlin 1828.

perhaps in the printed tenets, is not the Calvinism of the days of yore.

Mere faith, observes Chalybaeus,[1] as a blind traditional belief, has lost its hold on the minds of men of education, who can never again regain their whilome conviction, peace, and satisfaction, except through science alone. Nothing, indeed, will now satisfy us except a free personal conviction. Faith, and reason, and science must unite at last.[2] Science and religion, as Steffens said, will realise the loftiest faith when they penetrate the earthly life, and the sensational and earthly shall cease to be regarded as the higher element.[3] Our yearnings, meanwhile, are ever towards the good and the true, and to the period when faith and reason must coalesce to part no more.[4]

424. TRUE CAUSATION.

The current of experience though never so constant, might still, urged Hume and others, vary. To this it was replied, that so long as man was man, the laws of thought must remain unaltered. The laws of outward nature, however, whatever Hume may allege about the variableness of impressions and the force of habit, are not less stable. Both, in truth, are secure enough, yet

[1] Der Philosophische, selbstdenkende Mensch ist auf immer dem Gebiete des blossen Autoritätsglaubens, dem unreflectirten Dafürhalten entführt, und nie wird er den Rückweg zu seiner alten Ueberzeugung, Ruhe, und Befriedigung anders finden als ganz durch die Wissenschaft. *Entwickelung der Speculativen Philosophie.* Dresd. und Leip. 1848.
[2] *Morell's Modern German Philosophy*, Manchester Papers.
[3] Oersted, Leonora and Johanna Horner's translation.
[4] Und mich ergreift ein längst entwöhntes Sehnen
Nach jenen stillen ernsten Geisterreich.

love and faith alone can turn aside the barbed shafts sped from the well-bent bow of the Scottish dialectician. With these and these only, the world, man's soul, and immortality, are safe from such assaults for ever.

425. THE ROAD TO GREATNESS.

Men arrive by different routes at greatness. Kant never left his native Königsberg, whereas Descartes and Liebnitz sought out the world which came of its own accord to him. Descartes, indeed, by his clearness of style, and perpetual appeal to consciousness, as the organon of mental science,[1] has left eternal impress on the intellect of his kind. Liebnitz, likewise, philosopher and mathematician, aided by a good mother and the library which he inherited, found his own road to distinction. Men, he observes, in his noble essay on God's greatness, man's liberty, and the origin of ill,[2] employ words as they would algebraic symbols, with little sense and less sentiment. Speaking of formulas, he says that too often they stifle devotion and obscure the divine light. Faith and reason, virtue and intelligence, he would couple together. This is eminently

---

[1] Il a reconnu et fait définitivement triumpher le vrai principe de la certitude, l'autorité de la raison et de la conscience, invincible barrière à tous les efforts du scepticisme et d'une théologie aveugle enemie de toute philosophie. Il a mis hors de doute cette vérité profonde, l'ame se conçoit mieux que le corps. Descartes, *Dictionnaire des Sciences Philosophiques*, Tome ii. Paris, 1854—52.

[2] Par sa sure méthode, par l'indestructible vérité de l'optimisme, la Théodicée reste la plus solide monument que des mains humaines aient jamais élevé à la gloire de Dieu. Jacques, *Oeuvres de Leibnitz*, Introduction. Paris, 1846, 47.

a Protestant conception, the Roman Catholic satisfying himself with good works and the development of the affections.

Leibnitz carefully distinguished between what is above and what is opposed to reason, which fanaticism and superstition never do.[1] Else, not to know what the great Master designs we should not know, is, as Joseph Scaliger twice variously declares, a warrantable ignorance.[2] Satisfied with heaven and the universe,[3] Leibnitz, like Cardan, who, old and blind, would not have exchanged with ignorance and youth, also yields his testimony to the divine superiority of the inner life.

426. NATURE, MAN, GOD.

It was Schelling's notion that there was an unconscious intellectual activity in nature, of which man indeed, became conscious. Nature, he would have us to believe, acts blindly and unwittingly, without forecast or design, in virtue of an immanent principle, which, although unreasoning, acts like reason. This, he would further illustrate by the latent intelligence of the slumbering babe, the operations of genius working almost unwitting of results. For to describe nature as

---

[1] Il nous suffit d'un certain ce que c'est, τί ἐστι, mais le comment, πῶς, nous passe et ne nous est point nécessaire. Il nous suffit que la chose est ainsi, τὸ ὅτι, sans savoir le pourquoi τὸ διότι, que Dieu s'est reservé. *Théodicée*, Discours.

[2] Nescire velle quae magister optimus docere non vult, erudita inscitia est.

[3] Il n'est pas peu de chose d'être content de Dieu et l'univers, de ne point craindre ce que nous est destiné, ni de se plaindre de ce que nous est arrivé. *Théodicée*.

fulfilling certain ends, is, he most erroneously conceives, to impair our sympathy with it.

We may acknowledge the charm which Schelling found in nature, the ripple in the current, the song of the birds, the music in the breeze, without however depriving it of an associated intelligence. The divine, indeed, is at one end of the chain, man's soul at the other. For nature, although unconscious, the earth and lofty heavens alike, bears traces of God's own hand, and every heavenly signature. Its divine, though unwritten[1] laws, are laws of reason, its empire is reason's empire. In all its parts, there are connexion and filiation. And the sciences are but as one science, the science of God, of nature, and of truth.

427. TAKING THE VEIL.

Taking the veil is, in a measure, the counterpart of the Indian Suttee. In the latter, the woman sacrifices life indeed, but in the former she sacrifices her affections, mortifies her natural feelings, in short, surrenders that which makes existence desirable. The world, in truth, is the handiwork and paradise of God, the very arena of duty, whereas the conventual retreat, as such, is opposed to reason, a flying from obligations really divine. For men and women reverence and serve God best, by discharging life's sacred trusts, regulating not crucifying the affections. There have doubtless been angels in nunneries, but is not a woman who discharges the world's duties, relieves the suffering, succours the distressed, in very truth angelic. And so long as there

[1] Νόμον ἄγραφον καὶ θεῖον μάλιστα. Plotinus.

are sisters, mothers, wives, daughters, friends, so long, at least in this life, will the world prove the highest arena of a woman's duties.

A Sarah Martin, Florence Nightingale, Elizabeth Fry, some good sister, daughter, or wife, is surely as much a child of God, as ever was nun, were it in Protestant Holstein or Kaiserwerth, who washes out a refectory, makes her own couch, or leaves the impress of her knees beside her desk of prayer. Irrespective of the languor of disease, the convent, alas, must be weary, weary, the scene of many a childish contention and illspent hour. Mme Reybaud's tale of Felise, Courier's comments on celibacy,[1] and Drummond's plea,[2] yield many a painful detail. For I, too, have seen poor nuns, like caged birds, flit across their iron-belted, yet, unless to coerce, why iron-belted, casements.

There is in the possession of the Prince of Prussia a picture, the nun, by Von Hoyol. Below are the words. All sprouts, and buds, and blooms, but my world is dead.[3] Drear despair, as she gazes on scenes to which she must not return again, is stamped on every lineament. But heaven meant woman to beautify and adorn, not to forsake the world,[4] gifted her with life and liberty, and freedom, to assert, reject, inquire. Spiritual direction, every form of despotism or dictation, in fine, which, under colour of confession or otherwise,

---

[1] *Oeuvres Complètes*, par A. Carell. Paris, 1834, Tome i. p. 299.
[2] *Plea for the Liberties of Women*, Lond. 1851.
[3] Alles sprosst, und knospt, und blühet, aber mein Welt ist tedt.
[4] Elle est soeur, elle est femme, peut-être mère, et doit être la joie, la sainteté, le conseil, et la dignité du foyer domestique. *Figaro*.

assumes to disqualify the mind for directing itself, enfeebling the moral sense, annihilating freewill, and all nobility of action[1] along with it, can neither be the intent of Providence, nor the interest of thoughtful, progressive humanity.

428. UNSEEN ENEMIES.

It is not so much the seen as the unseen enemies, and they are legion, which we have to dread. Let us shun them when we can, else by subduing, gain a position, which, if possible, shall elevate us above them for ever. Yielding fullest scope to the divine within us, as Hierocles urges,[2] is to insure renovation, and goodness, and truth, return to God, and converse with the divine. And thus, as the poet says,

> Rock-bound and fortified against assaults
> Of transitory passion,

We shall bear down sensationalism and materialism, the great idolatry as Carlyle terms it, give ourselves up to the worship of the invisible, to spiritual liberty, and the faith which conquers death, realises the divine, and a life beyond the grave. For spiritualism it is, which, from Plato down, has formed a portion of every just and generous conviction, has taken the part of right against might, in opposition to all fanaticism, atheism, and materialism, and which, essence and grace of true religion, has ever pleaded for a spiritual and merciful God, for truth, for freedom, and for immortality.

---

[1] Bungener, *The Priest and the Huguenot*, Chap. 53.
[2] Ἀλλὰ σὺ θάρσει, ἐπί θεῖον γένος ἐστὶ βροτοῖσιν.

No view of our nature that excludes the celestial element of the feelings and affections, can be complete. It is the absence, more or less, of this element, that mars so much of the philosophy of the ideal, Kant's among the rest. Jacobi it was,[1] who added moral and spiritual truth to German rationalism, what in art is termed genius, in philosophy feeling, in religion faith, in life enthusiasm, sure preservatives against philosophic hardness, as against mere ritualism and formularism.

429. PICTURES.

Pictures there are, such as the Sybil in the Borghese Palace, Poesie by Carlo Dolci, Guido's Beatrice Cenci, Scheffer's Mignon, from which spiritual truth and excellence stream as from some star-lit heaven. Their enchanting grace and loveliness make us, too, aspire to that heaven which art, in its sweet measure, helps to realise for us all.

430. MUSIC'S EFFICACY.

The harsh, unsympathising character of some forms of sectarian asceticism, was never more fully displayed than in the attempts made to discourage, nay, to crush music. It seems, indeed, almost useless to argue with those who mistake a total ignorance of the sacred things of art, for a higher sense of the proprieties of religion.[2] And why should any innocent enjoyment, and very especially the solace of music, be tampered with. Does any one suppose there shall not be music in heaven. For music, in its degree, some ecstatic Scottish or Irish

---

[1] Morell.   [2] Music, Lond. Murray, p. 44.

melody, Latin mass, or German oratorio, is of the very staple and food of paradise, passport and key to heaven. No day, indeed, is too good for good music, and good music is good enough for any day. It is the nature of the enjoyment, the highest that sense can yield, to win men from base addictions.

Some richer pasture in truth, is needed for the feelings and affections than what a harsh sectarian asceticism, adverse to all the arts, can yield. It will not tolerate the gentle culture in which men both good and wise, can see no sin. That divine Being who has implanted the love of music, with that of every pure and innocent enjoyment in the human breast, will not be dictated to. The feelings may not be hardened with impunity. Sweetest influences, would we only listen to them, are ever at hand, a visible and an invisible world of endless grace and beauty, all the lovely things of earth and heaven, bringing comfort to the often torn and shattered heart of man, a world in which the rich cup of pure, and sweet, and innocent enjoyment, filled by God himself to the brim, shall not always be rudely dashed aside, much more exchanged for rioting and sin.

431. ENGLISH CHARACTERISTICS.

There is an occasional harshness in English characteristics, which, notwithstanding the great good sense and surpassing excellence of the people at large, compassing earth and sea with their beneficence, sometimes brings the nation to grief. To what else, if not to this, are we to ascribe the arrogance which induces Englishmen to look upon all other communities, even those living under the same dominion with them, as inferior, which has made them dreaded and disliked on the Continent and even nigher home, which induces them to term Sepoys niggers, brutes, and alas to treat them brutally,[1] which has led to the infliction of torture for the collection of Indian revenue, the sale of Hindoo children for improper purposes,[2] which has tolerated solitary confinement, scourgings and puttings to death in gaols, which has crowded male criminals in penal settlements, and given rise to penal settlements themselves. Were all Englishmen only as some, nay, happily as multitudes are, such anomalies would cease, and England might indeed become the paradise, Englishmen the exemplars of the world.

432. RECEPTIVITY OF MAN'S SOUL.

There is, perhaps, nothing which more bespeaks man's mighty eventual destinies,[3] than the facility with which he takes in the various features of his position. We envy the owners of some lordly palace, whereas the owners themselves long since are wearied of it, will not, perhaps, reside in it. Palaces, indeed, become common-place to him to whom one day shall be laid

---

[1] Special Correspondent on the Conduct of Europeans towards the Natives in India, *Times*, Oct. 20, 1858. Debate in the House of Commons on the Massacre of 500 unarmed Sepoys by the Deputy Commissioner of Umritzur, March, 1859.

[2] *The Friend of India*, June 3, 1858, p. 507.

[3] Der heilige göttliche Geist ist es, der uns als Ziel unseres Daseins die allseitige Vollendung einer schönen, reinen Menschlichkeit an uns selbst zeigt und zu erreichen antriebt. *Das Evangelium der Natur*, Manheim, 1853, Band I, S. 91.

open the palaces of infinity, and kingdoms are quickly traversed by souls shortly to traverse the kingdoms of eternity.[1] For such is the spiritual in man, which nothing limited or temporary can satisfy, and which must proceed from conquest to conquest, and from possession to possession, for ever.

433. CULTURE.

Our taste becomes developed by an acquaintance with lovely scenery and specimens of finished art, our moral susceptibilities by meditating on goodness and excellence.[2] No time can be considered misspent that enables us to fathom truth. Huyghens, Wallace, Galileo, Bernouilli, Kepler, Hooke, struggled, year after year, to grasp some principle, accelerating force it might be, impact, or collision, which, thanks to them, is now found in every treatise.[3] But we are to cultivate the whole soul, all the faculties, little enough for the joint requirements at once of earth and heaven.

434. AMALGAMATION OF CREEDS.

When one takes up a German or English catalogue, some Bent's list or Leipzic book circular, one marvels at the wealth of active intelligence which it displays. But what will it be when the united culture of literature, religion, science, art, shall pervade every intelligence, soften every heart, leading as it must one day

[1] Wie milde redet uns die Ewigkeit an mit ihrem majestätischen Antlitz, wenn wir auch das nur als Schatten und Traum besitzen, oder uns ihm nähern können was, das Gottlichste dieser Erde ist. Tieck.
[2] *Wayland's Moral Science.*   [3] *Mechanics' Magazine*, May, 1847.

lead, to the amalgamation of creeds, realising, in very deed, the mighty conception of the solidarity and brotherhood of man.

435. RELIGIOUS ESSENTIALS.

The Sunday stillness in some Scottish village or homestead, keeping off the wretched boothy to which the farm-labourer is now so frequently consigned, is most impressive. Yet the worship of days and hours alone is of no avail. For, although a day of rest prove a day of infinite price, humanity is not, therefore, to be sacrificed to a form.[1] Gentleness and sweetness, indeed truth and loyalty to God, with action suitable,[2] adding charity, and faith, and love, are the religious essence without which creeds, and confessions, and times set apart, are but as husks in the yellow corn.

436. THE DIVINE IN ART.

When one contemplates the thrice-admirable Francesca da Rimini and Marguerite at the fountain, of Scheffer, the Gabrielle and St. Cecile of Delaroche, Schopin's Paul and Virginia, one is filled with admiration at the spiritual excellence which these miracles of art display. All the wealth of human grace and loveliness, and woman's sweetness is there. They show us, indeed, of what humanity is capable, reveal, in part, the eternal capabilities of our kind, lead us, in short, into

---

[1] Τὸ σάββατον διὰ τὸν ἄνθρωπον ἐγένετο, οὐχ ἄνθρωπος διὰ τὸ σάββατον.

[2] Die Religion ist Wahrheit und frohe That. Aber ein freudiges Bewustsein und ein geistiges Leben sind die Hauptsache, der Stempel der Göttlichkeit.

the inner recesses and very sanctuary of heaven. Ary Scheffer and Paul Delaroche are now no more, but they shall hardly witness in the unseen life diviner fruitions than what their genius and their tenderness have evoked while here.

437. GENIUS.

Men of genius, Shakspeare, Cervantes, Swedenborg, Retsch, often discharge an exoteric and an esoteric part. Thousands admire the dramas of the great Englishman, yet with little suspicion of the jewels that house within. The Spaniard enchants the multitude for reasons very different from those which complete the satisfaction of the man who reflects. The Swedish mystic delights at once the philosopher and the sectary, but on grounds essentially distinct. While the German, in his chess-players, grandly, yet not grandly enough, delineates humanity doing battle with sin and spiritual death.

Had Cervantes but dared to utter, without disguise, the divine truths with which his spiritual romance is full, the swart tinder is not blacker than they would have scorched his frame. To true chivalry, indeed, he was not opposed. He only sought a vehicle for the truths which must make his book endure, while language itself endures. The Don is the exemplar of the ideal life, sacrificing material advantages, showing, by every possible device, how absurd it were to look for a spiritual heaven, and lead a false and sinful life preparatory to it. He is the very soul of chivalry, which Cervantes, so far from overthrowing, upheld with all his might, but also unworldly, fantastic, impracticable.

Sancho, on the other hand, sagacious, sturdy, prudent, but withal pusillanimous, grovelling, sensual, represents the naughty, calculating, material world. The antithesis, indeed, is pursued throughout, till the Don land in that better life for which he was, in some respects, so much better fitted than the actual one. The author, with sly evasion, makes knight-errantry the source of what men would term the knight's madness, but angels his inspiration. Cervantes himself, indeed, in the world's esteem, came off but indifferently in the great duello between the real and the ideal.[1] But the world happens to be mistaken in this matter as in many others, both in respect of his life and of his death, for he realised the crown, and victory, and dominion, so far at least as it is given to man to do so, for ever and for ever.

438. HEART'S CO-OPERATION.

If teachers did but know it, they would resort to pleasurable, rather than painful influences, to discourse of heaven rather than of hell, of joy rather than suffering, of blessings instead of curses, God's approval sooner than his frown, appealing, in short, to the better affections, in place of realising at one time apathy and indifference, at another, perchance, horror and despair.

Mendelssohn, the great and true composer's grandparent, was accustomed to gather young persons about him in the morning hours, and to discourse with them about God, and truth, and freedom, and immortality. He encouraged them to comment upon what was said, to

[1] Der Zwiespalt des Lebens.

interrupt him even, and each other, being of opinion that philosophy, like religion, should be learned first by use and then by rule. Thus originated his book, his famous Morning Hours,[1] like his Phaedo and other philosophical works, composed at intervals when nervous weakness and exhaustion permitted the effort. They afforded his youthful hearers the most attractive culture, renewed afresh his intercourse with philosophy,[2] the associate of his better years, his single comfort in all the contrarieties of existence. In him, indeed, as was well borne out in his life and conduct, human well-being was the aim of all philosophy.[3]

439. GLORIOUS TRILOGIES.

Side by side with the glorious trilogy of God, freedom, and immortality, there is yet another trilogy of truth, and beauty, and purity, which, through the infinite bounty of heaven, we also appreciate. The capacity, indeed, is born with us. So soon as religion, so soon as art, assert their great ideal, infinite desires take possession of the soul.[4] If, indeed, the world be the work of divine reason, man's soul, his affections, and capacities, are not less surely the work of divine love.

[1] *Morgenstunden, oder Vorlesungen über das Daseyn Gottes.* Berlin, 1777.
[2] Sie war in bessern Jahren meine treueste Gefährtinn, mein einziger Trost in allen Wiederwartigkeiten dieses Lebens. Vorbericht.
[3] Die Glückseligkeit des Menschen der Philosophie, als Ziel versteckten. Ulrici, *Grundprinzip der Philosophie*, Dritte Abschnitt.
[4] Dès que l'on presente à l'homme, comme le font la religion et l'art, un certain ideal de bonheur et de perfection absolus, on éveille par là même dans son esprit des désirs infinis. Vera, *Introduction à la Philosophie de Hegel.* Lond. 1848.

Reason and love, then, not one but both, celestial duality, preside and rule over the mighty universe. And if it be our task to think after the mighty Being that thinketh all things, not less is it our duty to love after Him for he loveth all things.[1]

We are not all powerful in the world of objects, but we are approximatively so in the world of the soul, the sweet world of faith, and thought, and hope, and love. Yet, the outer world with all its wealth of light, and beauty, and excellence, nature, the universe, is also made for the soul, and in the soul finds its beginning and its end.[2] With the exercise of each affection the soul expands, and, wonder of wonders, discerns in spiritual and material nature fresh truth, further goodness, beauty yet more exquisite. For man is as the slumbering infant till he find in alternate action and repose, the play of his intellect and bodily powers, the struggle with the passions, his real happiness. If the soul, then, be under a necessity, springing from the inner life, of conforming to the eternal laws of order and beauty, after all the only liberty and best deliverance, so likewise must it conform to the law of love, of all the affections, that which in life and in death approximates us

---

[1] Da waltet Gott in Glanz und Herrlichkeit.
Wo Liebe lächelnd Mensch an Menschen bindet.
Und wo die Liebe herrscht, hat alle Zeit
Das wahre Glück sich seinen Thron gegründet.
Du kannst nicht glücklich ohne Liebe sein,
Und aus der Liebe redet Gott allein.

[2] La lumière, l'oeil, le corps, la nature entière en un mot, est faite pour l'esprit, et trouve dans l'esprit son principe et sa fin. Vera, *Op. citat.*

more and most to the celestial, the divine. For truth, and spiritual beauty, and love, all triumph over and indeed destroy death,[1] liberate us from bondage, the shadows which envelop the life of sense, conduct us to eternal realities, and the consciousness, ever true, ever new, which has no end.

440. THE HIGHER LIFE.

Every thing about us, would we but take heed to it, urges the surpassing importance of the higher life,[2] the spiritual world on whose threshold we subsist, not, indeed some mere passive state, but one in which we shall live, and love, and learn, for ever. Let us, then, only destroy the serpents, the false desires, which gnaw continually at the root of the tree of life, and would consummate its decay. Grief even, and care, combating, sacrificing, enduring, bestow divinest compensation in the clearer insight which they afford, the spiritual direction which they yield, the putting to flight of every littleness of thought and feeling, results so hard for ordinary natures during uninterrupted prosperity to compass. Spiritual teachers, too, abound as in days of yore, saintly persons, who, in spoken word and loving act, urge us on our onward way, so that, as has been said,

> Our hearts in glad surprise,
> To higher levels rise.

Then, since God has imparted to us capacities unutterable, opened to us every gate of paradise, let us,

---

[1] Εσχατος εχθρὸς κατεργεῖται ὁ θάνατος.
[2] Βίος ἀγγελικὸς, βίος ἀσωμάτων ἐν σωματι.

seeking development after development, and insight on insight, strive upwards and onwards for ever.

441. OUR OUTER EXISTENCE.

As we have to dwell not only in the inner but the outer life, so should purity, and sweetness, and brightness, rendering the living frame, the humblest abode, acceptable before God, subsist in all things. In some African Tunis, or Asiatic Damascus, interior amenity is often wonderfully realised. Painted tiles and silken hangings adorn the walls. There are marbled floors and terraces, ceilings glowing with colour, and fretted with silver and gold, while in the open courts, parterres of flowers, the orange and the fig-tree, the lemon, the jasmin, and the vine, meet the gratified senses at every turn. Here, wealth alone may compass such luxuries, yet the morning-bath and an untainted night atmosphere might be realised by all. Alas, too often we deface, instead of embellishing and perfecting, the sweet handiwork of God. Hideous maladies, frightful shortcomings, self-entailed, harass the frame. Life's purposes are insufficiently realised, and beauty and health, of body and of soul, wayside sacraments indeed, are cast to every wind.

442. LIFE, SPIRITUAL.

Man, though he lapse, shall rise again. Though his sins, as the ancient Seer,[1] with heavenly insight has worded it, were red as crimson, yet shall they become white as wool. Yes, this I believe with my heart of

[1] Isaiah.

hearts and my soul of souls. Inward purity and a harmonious life, not creeds, not professions, not formulas merely, afford the one clue to spiritual safety,[1] and favour divine. But the relinquishment of evil is indispensable. It is the alpha to which there is no omega, that first to which there is no last.

Man's soul is as a ship, life is the surging wave, the favouring gale is the better principles which have root in our spiritual nature, opposing currents are the obstacles that beset our course. No great thing can be accomplished without toil, and suffering, and liability to error. But life's uncertainties here, and the mighty certainties to come, should nerve us to utmost effort. For the spirit-life, let us only reflect, can never die. Heaven cannot, will not, forsake us, and the favouring gale of God's providential love must overcome all obstacles, and land us in the lofty heavens, at last.

443. THE WILL OF GOD.

The one end and object of all religion is obedience to the law of love, the moral law. For man alone becomes divinely free through obedience to the will of God. In this, and nothing else, does the soul's safety, and liberty, and man's chiefest welfare reside. Let instructors, then, take it to their very hearts, utter it with their lips, and act it in their lives, till nations peal their glad assent, and sects and sectaries be no more.

How else shall it be possible to reclaim the vicious, bring over the ethnic swarm, while each and every sectary denounces his sectarian brother, and tenets too

[1] Τὴν σωτηρίαν.

often are urged which are an affront to the divine. Is it not enough to obey the sweet will of God. If, indeed, we set so much stress on man's esteem,[1] why do we not labour to secure His, to whom our disputes are as nothing, less than nothing, the shadow of a dream. How is it that we cannot bear the aspect of our own souls, but rush into every distraction to avoid it. Yet, all evil, with every shortcoming, must be looked at, combated, and overcome. For, in veriest truth, the measure of our moral greatness resides, not merely in our unwonted efforts, but in our daily life and bearing.[2] There can be nothing save humility in the sight of God, not indeed the humility of debasement, but that of souls aspiring to heaven.

Infinite perfection, and truth as infinite, are before us for ever. Each man, moulding his soul to purity, must for himself interpret his wants to God. We are the possible incarnation of every thing excelling and divine.[3] Yet, let us ponder it well, we cannot realise a higher heaven than we bring. If, indeed, we would have heaven, we must be of heaven and not otherwise. Knowledge, and truth, and love, are the soul's clothing, very fruitage of the celestial tree. Let us then be constant, and whatever be our sacred purpose, carry it faithfully and resolutely through.[4]

[1] Et toute la felicité des hommes consiste dans cette estime, l'estime d'une ame. Pascal, *Pensées*.

[2] La vertu d'un homme ne doit pas se mesurer par ses efforts, mais par ce qu'il fait d'ordinaire. Pascal, *Id*.

[3] *Parker's Sermons*.

[4] Sei beständig und was einmal göttlicher Beschluss in dir bedungen, daran setze alle Kräfte, dass du es zur Reife bringest. Göthe.

444. SPIRITUAL CONSTANCY.

There is, so to speak, a reasoning as well as an unreasoning ignorance, a reasoning as well as an unreasoning faith. The developed man knows his ignorance, whereas the undeveloped man knows it not. Things seem to the latter much as they did to the blind youth whom Cheselden couched, a present reality in need of no explanation. He discerns nothing, in truth nothing of the most wonderful of all wonders, that the universe is resolvable into simple forces, of which we only know that they are.[1] It is a sort of intellectual as well as moral new-birth, when the soul wakens up to perception and self-reflection, and finds its actual position in the world. Would, then, that we were but true to ourselves, neither sacrificing the heart to the intelligence, nor the intelligence to the heart,[2] but elevating and consecrating both.[3]

445. TRUST AND TRUTH.

Paul was a prince and leader, in truth a mighty expounder of celestial things. Like Christ, like Augustin, observes Pascal,[4] like the good John also, Paul aimed less to instruct than to animate, to instil God's gentle kingdom into the souls of men. Some, indeed, there are who would tie down the spiritual life to cer-

---
[1] Durch das ganze Weltenall die gleichen Naturgesetze ewig gleich wirken.

[2] Die Herrenhuter annihiliren ihre Vernunft, die Empfindsamen ihren Verstand, die Leute von Verstand ihr Herz. Novalis.

[3] Comme on se gâte l'esprit, on se gâte aussi le sentiment. Pascal.

[4] Leur but principal n'était pas d'instruire, mais d'échauffer.

tain beliefs.[1] Yet, the spiritual life is often realised in spite of error, and sometimes even despite of sin.

While to the intellect there are many truths, to the heart there is indeed but one. Love, with all goodness, contrary to the prepossessions of most theologians, may be associated with almost every form of error and illusion. It is of yet greater moment that the heart should be right than even the intellect. For the necessity of love is instant, whereas truth most times must wait. Full many a heart is animated with the consciousness of obligation to God, overflows with love, and faith, and every gentle thing, which yet has but dim perceptions of many a spiritual truth. Nevertheless, love coupled with intelligence, cherub and seraph, divinely loving, knowing divinely, shall yet join hand in hand, and faith, and knowledge, and love, united for ever, shall stand before God's throne.

446. SOLIDARITY OF MAN.

Scenes take place in Paris, London, Vienna, Dublin, Stockholm, Edinburgh, New York, in fine all large towns, which are simply outrages on our common humanity, insults to human dignity and the God who endows us for better things.

For in evil as in good, we are akin. Each deed of self-abnegation, of magnanimity, devotion, with every pure and holy thought, benefits, let us be assured, the entire family of our kind. So each wicked, unmanly thought and feeling, every act of meanness, hardness, cruelty, and selfishness, each and every insult offered

[1] *Jowett's Discourse on Righteousness by Faith.*

to the shrine of eternal purity and truth, that houses or should house in the human breast, is, so far as it extends, ruinous to the best interests of our race. For God and God's servants, visible and invisible, and heaven and the kingdoms of eternity, are with us and about us at all times. If the better influences, ministers indeed divine, the philosophers, conservators of heavenly truths, were to enlarge for ever and for ever, they could not set forth any greater or more momentous thing, than that no one, whether for good or for evil, lives for himself alone, but for his fellows also, and the mighty universe of God.

447. ECSTASIES.

There are conditions, associations of idea, and sensation, and emotion, of body and of soul, not often adverted to by metaphysicians, or even by medical inquirers, which as yet are only in part appreciated.[1] Most of us can remember, while speculating on things of the visible and invisible life, to have experienced emotions which savour of very heaven. Quietism and mysticism have had to do with these elements of our common nature. You cannot, observes Plotinus, apprehend the infinite except by a faculty superior to reason, states in which you are your finite self no more. And what are these but ecstasy, by him first so named.[2] I have realised them, he adds, but twice, and Porphyry not once. Yet are they conditions which may occur to any one. They furnish no necessary criterion of truth, whether human or divine, and cer-

[1] J. Frank, *Praxeos Medicae*. [2] Ἔκτασις, Plotinus.

tainly do not for a moment encourage the idea of commerce direct with heaven.

448. ONE REASON.

All reason is God's gift, and, therefore, divine, the common treasure and inheritance of humanity. For it is as respects our intelligence and our affections, and not otherwise, that we are made in God's image, and by God.[1] The same in kind though different in degree, there is perfect consonance between man's reason and God's reason. For so long as reason continues right, it cannot possibly dissent from divine reason.[2] It is of a moral necessity, a law natural to God, and, even from the first moment of its existence in man, united with trust, and obedience, and love, confirms, as the good Bishop of Peterborough tells us, the divine authority, as it has confirmed it from all eternity. Were it otherwise, reason, instead of proving a guide, would indeed be a delusion and a snare. For why, as Aristotle said, there is a parity in reason.[3] It is truth in unison with itself.

There is an apprehension that human reason, as it has been termed, is at issue with divine reason, but this cannot be, since it is of divine origin and God's gift. Therefore, in so far as it is a right reason, man's reason and God's reason, like God's love and man's love, are in absolute accordance. Reason and religion,

---
[1] Ingeneratum a Deo. Cicero.
[2] Bishop Cumberland. *Inquiry into the Laws of Nature*, Cap. v. § 20. Cap. ix. § 2.
[3] Ἰσότης τοῦ λόγου.

true reason and true religion, never were at issue, never will be at issue, while the world endures. For truth is truth, at once with man and with heaven. And general reason and individual reason, general reason and divine reason, are absolutely one and the same.[1] Philosophy, indeed, appeals to the thinking faculty, but religion speaks to the affections also, or, as Cousin puts it, the whole man.

Philosophy addresses the elect, the vanguard of humanity, whereas a spiritual religion addresses all, but takes its more immediate colouring from the spiritual character of God, surrenders the conflicting passions and egotisms of our nature to the guidance of the divine spirit.[2] True religion and true philosophy, then, are alike inseparable and divine. It is only a mistaken religion and a mistaken philosophy that quarrel.[3] Religion and reason are indispensable to themselves and to each other. The more we cultivate both, the more certain are we to earn the approbation of heaven. For it is at once the mission and the glory of humanity to cherish them, until they shall expand into the divine presence and the more perfect day.

[1] En dernière analyse c'est donc à la raison qu'il en faut revenir. C'est son temoignage qui mesure toutes les autres témoignages. C'est sur son autorité qui reposent toutes les autres autorités. Si cette autorité est purement individuelle, il n-y-a plus de certitude au monde, plus de vérité universelle. On ne peut s'empêcher de sourire en voyant une secte protestante, apres s'étre séparée de l'église au nom du droit du libre examen, finir par renier l'autorité de la faculté qui examine. Cousin, *Fragmens Philosophiques*, Preface.

[2] Unspiritual Religion, *National Review*, Oct. 1857.

[3] C'est toujours la mauvaise philosophie et la mauvaise théologie qui se querellent. Cousin.

449. SCULPTURED EXCELLENCE.

There is about successful sculpture an exquisiteness, to which successful painting, even, does not always, if indeed it ever attain. For sculpture seems to suggest, nay to realise, a higher ideal, stands out more, comes more within the boundaries of space and time, than do those other miracles of art that spring from the easel and the pencil. Its beauties are various almost as the beauties of nature herself, and from the absence of colour and other distracting accessories, perhaps yield a larger scope for the imagination and the feelings. We are, indeed, astonished at the successful efforts made by the ancients to overcome the difficulties of the material, and to impress marble with the characters of life.[1]

Art is alike beautiful, in the Grecian delineations of passionless loveliness, the simple outlines of lofty intellect, the granite chisellings of the Egyptians of old, as in modern sculpture, whether in forum or market-place, crumbling vault or dim cathedral, over some well-loved child or woman's tomb. In Lichfield's aisle Chantrey's twin children, with arms entwined, sleep sweetly on their couch of stone. In Romsey church, Taylor has raised an infant's memorial. The child reclines upon its little pallet, a moss-rose snapt in its hand. The hair, says Ruskin, speaking of a memorial to Ilaria di Caretto in Lucca cathedral, is braided over the fair brow, the eyes are closed, the tender lips are set, neither death nor sleep, but the pure image of both.

[1] Winkelmann, *Histoire de l'Art chez les Anciens.*

Things in truth there are, some dead virgin robed in white with wreath upon her brow, pomegranate in her hand, written on the impassive stone, which touch the heart to the core, bear us into the celestial presence, and into an atmosphere of goodness, and holiness, and truth, where nothing mean or low can dwell, and where the anxieties of this rich, yet often troublous and necessitous existence,[1] like some rent and shattered garment, are put for ever away. For what is art if it serve not to evoke emotions which are as the very salt and glory of life, to hold out almost living copies of goodness, and beauty, and grace, and truth, to deter the base, solace the miserable, raise us above the calculus of mere material gain, the sale of the soul with all its precious powers for gold, in fine to elevate us from all that is inferior, to hope, and life, and the blessed fruitions which are to come.

450. THE SOUL'S IMPRESS.

Some appear worse, others better, more spiritual than they are. Without subscribing to Lavater, the countenance is a mighty page and index of the pregnant soul. Hieroglyphs in truth are there, which no hierophant shall decipher ever. Nevertheless, by omission or commission, from what is there, and what is not there, each feature tells its tale, the legend of a fiery or an imbecile past. Some countenances, indeed, evoke no love, elicit no response, whereas culture will impart a cast of intellect to the features, and eyes beaming with celestial light shall render them divine. So, a

[1] Das beengte Leben, die Schwere des Daseyns. B. Auerbach.

single pursuit will often raise us from the slough, a mother's love bring parity with angels, and sympathies that distil fragrance from celestial flowers, furnish the key to heaven.

The features, above all the eyes and mouth, are the outer citadel, mintage and impress of the soul. Many a face wears token of celestial commerce, bears us to paradise away. And often, when least expected, perchance in some lone cabin, on hospital pallet, or in sickbed watch, some dead hero or maiden, mother it may be or infant in its coffin, a countenance shall startle us with seraph's features and revelations from the infinite.

451. CHARLOTTE BRONTE.

Women are more conservative, because more timid than men. But when they overcome this, and learn to launch out into the free fields of speculation, there is little, unless it be a loftier tone of sentiment, to distinguish what they say from men's best efforts. Mme de Stael and Mme Roland, with others, displayed the courage of men, and of very good and wise men too, enhance our conceptions not only of the sex but of mankind.

The growth in heart and intellect of the Bronte sisters is of striking interest. They evinced, indeed, the vivid power and fervour betokening their Irish stem, and I had Charlotte Bronte's own assurance that she loved the Irish suffrage so largely accorded to her. What a soul the wise and good little creature had, and how wondrously did her genius expand, ere she took her daring flight above the dust, the moulder, and the sere of common things.

Plainly does she tell us of the hell of our own meanness, the glorious task of bettering our nature and our race, carrying knowledge into the realms of ignorance, substituting peace for war, freedom for bondage, religion for superstition, the hope of heaven instead of the fear of hell. Life to her was all too short to spend in registering wrongs, nursing animosities, since eternity was to be our rest and mighty home. Injustice never crushed, revenge never worried, degradation never too much depressed her. She lived on calmly looking to the end, forgiving the criminal though abjuring his crime.

Charlotte Bronte had not, perhaps, the exquisite appreciation of outward nature with which a Bettina Arnim was graced. Her home and chief walk lay in the deep heart of humanity itself. Like each great, and good, and true-souled woman, who opens to us glimpses of the sunny heavens, she exhaled, indeed, an odour of divinity,[1] made thousands, nay, millions, think and feel as they might else have never thought or felt, and well deserves the lasting homage of our kind. And now, her work well ended, and her toils of sweetness closed, her loved remains repose beside her sisters, by their tranquil moorland home.

452. THE PARADISE WITHIN.

Something of sweetest interest, even in Milton's history, attaches to the lines, tribute to his sleeping grace, which the lady left within his passive clasp. What would ye do, they say, if open, ye starry mortal eyes,

[1] Getta quasi un odor di regina. Firenzuola.

when closed ye thus destroy me.[1] But then she beheld those features, the moulded form which Villa praised. How sweetly does Milton, himself, hymn of paradise, and of the

> Flowers which never can in other climate blow.

For his was of the mighty minds of which the Reformation, with the literary revival which originated it, that in part has helped to liberate mankind, was parent. Milton's demon, indeed, is much at variance with the theological one. The tameless democrat, resolute nor to submit nor yield, was but an exaggerated type of powers which Milton directed to the service of his kind. Turn to his immortal lines,

> to obey is best,
> And love the only God, to walk
> As in his presence, ever to observe
> His providence, and on him sole depend,
> Merciful over all his works, with good
> Still overcoming evil, and by small
> Accomplishing great things.
> This having learned, thou hast attained the sum
> Of wisdom. . . . . Only add
> Deeds to thy knowledge answerable, add faith,
> Add virtue, patience, temperance, and love,
> By name to come called charity, the soul
> Of all the rest. Then wilt thou not be loath
> To quit this paradise, but shalt possess
> A paradise within thee happier far.

[1] Occhi, stelle mortali,
Ministre de miei mali.
Si chiuse m'uccidete,
Aperti che farete.
                Guarini, *Madrigal* xii.

ASPIRATIONS

FROM

THE INNER, THE SPIRITUAL LIFE.

BOOK X.

It cannot be that earth is man's abiding place. It cannot be that we are cast up by the ocean of eternity to float a moment on its waters and sink into nothingness. Else why is it that the glorious aspirations which leap like angels from the temple of our heart, are for ever wandering about unsatisfied. Why is it that the rainbow and the cloud come before us with a beauty that is not of earth, and pass away to leave us to muse on their faded loveliness. Why is it that the stars hold festival around the midnight throne, above the grasp of our limited faculties. Finally, why are brighter forms of human beauty presented to our view, then taken from us, leaving the thousand streams of our affections to flow back in Alpine torrents upon our hearts. We are born for a higher destiny, a realm where the rainbow never fades, where the stars will be spread before us, and where the beautiful beings that pass before us here, shall abide in our presence for ever. Anon.

ASPIRATIONS.

453. NATURE'S REST.

WHEN we commune with nature very closely, it almost seems as if we became part of her. In all our troubles, wearinesses, perplexities, she preaches patience, ever patience. Wait, only wait,[1] she says, and thou, too, shalt rest. Her gentle inspiration meets us everywhere. One can sit by the shore of the great sea, when the stars are slowly waning, and sweet, and calm, and clear the night,[2] while the moon holds sway aloft, revealing the quiet hills, and the phosphor-lighted wave laps, laps upon the strand, and still she whispers patience, only patience. The glowing sunsets and the angelic messengers of heaven reveal it, and the carol-

[1] Ueber allen Gipfeln
   Ist Ruh.
   In allen Wipfeln
   Spürest du
   Kaum einen Hauch.
   Die Vögelein schweigen im Walde.
   Warte nur, balde
   Ruhest du auch.
                         Göthe.

[2] Dolce chiara è la notte e senza vento,
   E queta sovra i tetti e in mezzo agli orti
   Posa la luna, e di lontan rivela
   Serena ogni montagna.   Leopardi.

ing birds and the tepid breezes whisper it. Even that swart night, daguerreotyped on memory, the long mountain waves, the forked and vivid flash, the labouring ships and the toiling crews, bespoke it. Patience, in truth, is urged by all the things of earth and heaven, patience to wait, to be, to do, and to endure. For everywhere nature gives utterance to her deep meanings, her sweet relations, truest final causes.[1]

454. ONE FAITH, ONE GOD.

The influence of but a single truth would seem at times sufficient to redeem the world. And can there be a truth greater or more comforting than that as there is but one religion, one faith, one law, so there is but one God. This magnificent reassuring conception has striven, still strives with many an obstacle, to find acceptance among our kind. Yet every evidence, nature's unfaltering accents, the oneness of design and of ceaseless loving care, the very impossibility of the opposite, all proclaim as with trumpet tongue, that there is but one God.

The sublime yet simple doctrines of the spiritual unity and infinite perfection of God, are indeed consonant with the moral sympathies and affections of individual and collective man. For in the divine, as in ourselves, there is a moral unity, a unity of the affections and intelligence, most mighty and salutary truth, which, indifference, fanaticism, and incredulity are continually prompting men to pass by.

[1] Les vraies causes finales ce sont les rapports avec notre âme et avec notre sort immortel. De Stael.

455. THE HIGHEST TRUST.

I read to day, observes the good John Wesley in his journal,[1] the strange account of that John Endicott, governor of New England and his associates there, who beat and imprisoned so many of the poor Quakers, and murdered William Robinson, Marmaduke Stephenson, and others. Oh, who would have looked for father inquisitors at Boston. All true faith, indeed, is beset with influences more or less inimical. There have been, alas there are those, who are more exigent than is religion, more Christian, if we could imagine it, than Christianity itself. They profess deepest concern for God's honour, fear much lest the lofty heavens should be torn away. They persecute, they blame, they utter aspersions, even as their predecessors did before them, against those, who, by ceaseless sacrifice and true nobility of soul, fain would benefit their kind. For the path of the just is as a shining light, that shineth more and more unto the perfect day.[2] Yet these,

> The teachers shall shine
> As the brightness of the firmament,
> And they that turn many to righteousness,
> As the stars for ever and ever.[3]

When, indeed, we believe that God is with us, then are we clear as to our convictions. For every truth that flashes through the heart is also written on the skies. No era of intense personal confidingness has

[1] April, 1744.
[2] Proverbs iv. 18.
[3] Daniel xii. 3. Inscribed on Fichte's monument.

ever proved a persecuting one.[1] The bigotry that would identify its cruel will with that of God, is at utter variance with a holy faith, a living trust, as with man's great estate as a personal spirit, destined, as Neander sublimely expresses it, throughout eternity, to become conscious of God, and it is only when creeds leave the boundaries of experience, that they stiffen into it.

456. LIFE, A SACRED EXPERIENCE.

Life is not an expiation merely, but an experience, a trial often, but above all, a development, radiant with truths divine, a real cardiphonia, cravings after the infinite, the better life to come. Death is not a punishment, but a sacred ordinance, a heavenly discipline, the cessation of this life indeed, but a new birth unto another and a better, the expansion of the affections, in fine the sacrament and salvation of the world. For literature, religion, science, art, indeed a purified literature, religion unalloyed with error, truest science, and exalted art, with every better pursuit, each social joy, and spiritual affection, must prove of the very pasture of heaven.

Religion, Christianity well understood, shall one day dethrone the spectre which in our ignorance and our weakness we have set up instead. Every deep and holy quality, our innate dignity, the disinterested affections, all suffice to overcome our unbecoming and unmanly dread. For heaven, in removing the outward and visible, shows that our love is not to attach to it

National Review, Jan. 1858.

alone, but to the inward and spiritual, that which
endures when the material passes away.

> God says 'tis time to die,
> And bids us go up higher.[1]

Our sympathies, our moral powers, our reason, all
should lead us to look upon death not as a dispensation
of dread, but the provision of an all-wise beneficent
God.[2] It is the portal to the eternal, the better life,
the falling asleep of the body indeed, but the spirit's
awakening.[3] It is in perfect keeping with the holy
purposes and calm earnestness of nature, and of nature's
God. Death's angel, then, bears no scourge, but is
crowned with roses and amaranths, nepenthe indeed
and nectar in his hand. And he will conduct us to
the divine presence and the serene land, the infinite
universe and all angelic things.

457. OVERCOMING EVIL WITH GOOD.

It is, indeed, a command most sovereign and divine,
to overcome evil with good. But what if the evil be
stronger, more forceful than the good. Could the
ignorant, the vicious, the deceitful, only be brought to
feel, to know, that any body or thing were in any respect better than themselves, then might they arrive at
excellence. But rightly to overcome evil with good,
divinest utterance, is to be stronger than the evil, to
shew it an adamantine front, to oppose it in life

---

[1] E. B. B.   [2] *Philosophy of Human Nature.* Lond. 1837, *passim.*

[3] Faute de connaitre la mort, nous l'environnons d'épouvante. C'est
un bienfait, une délivrance, et non une punition imposée au genre
humain. Aimé Martin, *Education des Mères de Famille.*

and in death alike.[1] For this is the true sublimity of moral, I do not say passive courage, nothing short of an overflowing measure of which, can enable us to slay the lion in our path, or confront him in his den.

458. THE INNER KINGDOM.

It is not the profession merely, but the practice that makes the man. For of what avail is the profession, if we love nor God nor man. The religious affections, along with worth of character, and consequently God's acceptance, are not necessarily connected with any particular set of opinions, may, indeed, be associated with every error. Formulas, even when least objectionable, are simply as means to ends, a possible road to loftier excellence. Else, what have certain doctrines to do with our inward spiritual life, the soul's service, the immutable and glorious God. It is in the individual consciousness, if anywhere, that progress is to be made. Sectaries would consign dissentients, even the tortured, perishing children and confessors of God, not merely to temporal but eternal suffering. It is impossible, exclaims the wise and gentle Schleiermacher, in a letter to his father, bearing date 21 Jan. 1787.[2] Oh, best of

[1] Tu ne cede maeis sed contra audentior ito.

[2] Bester Vater, Ich kann nicht glauben, dass der ewiger, wahrer Gott war, der sich selbst nur den Menschensohn nannte, ich kann nicht glauben dass sein Tod eine stellvertretende Versöhnung war, weil er es selbst nie ausdrücklich gesagt hat, und weil ich nicht glauben kann dass sie nöthig gewesen, denn Gott kann die Menschen die er offenbar nicht zur Vollkommenheit sondern nur zum Streben nach derselben geschaffen hat, unmöglich darum ewig strafen wollen weil sie nicht vollkommen geworden sind. *Leben in Briefen*, Berlin, 1858, B. i, S. 45.

Fathers, it is impossible that God, who has evidently created men, not for perfection, but for the pursuit of it, should will their eternal punishment for not attaining to it. For religion is joy, indeed, not sadness, not dreariness, not gloom. Spiritual wealth and spiritual arrogance cannot subsist together. Since heavenly-mindedness consorts best with everlasting truth, a religion without illusions, and free from contradictions. For what is religion, rightly understood, but the inner kingdom, the love of God, his reign in faithful hearts. Every moral spiritual truth is the utterance of the divine, a revelation from within. Life, glorious, ineffable, now and for ever, free gift of a spiritual God, has been imparted to us. And not life only, but glimpses of paradise, glories transcending earth and time, celestial goodness, purity ineffable, in fine, the angelic amenities of the visible and invisible worlds. True it is that a lofty faith should bind us yet more closely with God and the unseen life, the ceaseless presence of the infinite, and spirits of the invisible.

459. CHARLOTTE MONTEFIORE.

The tendency of the ages is to merge faiths in one. There will be no fresh sects in Christendom. No new Athanasius, Arius, Socinus, Armenius, Calvin, Luther, or Loyola, shall again perplex the intelligence of our kind. When we converse, indeed, with a really sincere and candid inquirer of almost any communion, we are often surprised, not so much at the greatness as at the paucity of dissent. For the oneness and universality of spiritual truth and of the moral law, the necessity of an unceasing individual development, the spirituality and eternity of the thinking principle, the divine unity, are tenets that must one day actuate the entire family of man.

Despite of cruel oppression and bitter prejudice, the Jews have, in various ways, in the courses of the centuries, approved themselves worthy. In ethics, indeed, not many may take precedence of Mendelssohn, while in speculative acuteness, few have equalled, none perhaps surpassed Spinoza.

Charlotte Montefiore eloquently adverts to the barriers which have been built up, the chains which are forged by superstition and fanaticism.[1] She dwells on the worship of wisdom, and of faith, white-robed spirit which bears the olive-branch of love across life's troubled sea. She speaks of the sympathies without which life is very lonely and very poor. She tells us of one eternal unembodied Being filling space and time, author of the starry spheres, the delicate beauty of the flowers, the green trees' early bloom, shedding joyousness and glory, diffusing sanctity and calm over the surface of the world. God, she calls a Spirit, radiating through all things, a mercy and a love whose depths know no soundings. She urges consecration to virtue, a humanity moulded in the image of the divine. She dilates on the spiritual life, the mind's progress, communings with the holy, the beautiful, the eternal, and the true. Every man she asseverates, however poor and fallen, is a child of God. And she commends brave and earnest words, brave and earnest deeds,

[1] *A Few Words to the Jews*, 2nd ed. Lond. John Chapman.

sacrificing all other interests to the mind's integrity, the soul's truth, with immutable faith in God's perfection, planting the seed which is to yield fruitage in eternity, beginning here what there shall have no end.

460. ANTONINUS, EPICTETUS.

Marcus Antoninus, Niebuhr, as he was wont to do by any great and good man, terms a saint. Why should I be wanting to myself, exclaims Antoninus, who never yet was wanting to another.[1] I seek but the truth, he repeats, which injures no one.[2] For there is but one world, one God,[3] one law, one truth, one reason common to all thinking beings, and one perfection for them to aim at. Plato, thou sayest well, to live or die is of no account, but only how we live and how we die. And this is best, to spend each day as it were the last. A man, he adds, may be in a measure divine, though unknown to all. In saving others, the gain indeed is ours. For hath not God, who is immortal, put up for ages with the folly and impiety of the world. Look within. There, lies the fountain of good, which will flow for ever if you will. If it be not right, he intreats, do not do it, if it be not true do not say it.[4] Oh thou, he exclaims, who livest in this great city of the universe, although thy years be few, if justly spent and well, it is the same. No unjust tyrant, but God himself, who gives and takes away, leads you hence.

[1] Οὐδὲ γὰρ ἄλλον πώποτε ἑκὼν ἐλύπησα. *Meditations*, Book viii.
[2] Ζητῶ γὰρ τὴν ἀλήθειαν ὑφ᾽ ἧς οὐδεὶς πώποτε ἐβλάβη. *Id*. vi.
[3] Θεὸς εἷς διὰ πάντων. *Id*. Book vii.
[4] Εἰ μὴ καθήκει μὴ πράξης, εἰ μὴ ἀληθές ἐστι μὴ εἴπης. *Id*. Book xii.

Epictetus drove the same truths home, but in a yet shorter, pithier strain. He was one of those philosophers, observes Pascal, who in this world best knew the duties of man,[1] and the vanity of seeking happiness in outward things, instead of giving ourselves up to God alone. Bear, he for ever says, and forbear, it is the keystone of his doctrine. Events, he looked upon as phantasms, but greatness and goodness he esteemed divine. Never say thou hast lost anything, he continues, but only restored it. Wouldst control that which is not within thy control, desire what is not thine to desire.[2] Do not wish events to be otherwise than they are, and it shall be well with thee.[3] It is the stamp of the vulgar to set exclusive value on what is without, whereas the wise make themselves the only centres of praise and blame.[4] Heaven and providence are our only guides. Wherever these lead let us follow, for willingly or unwillingly we must still follow. But he who yields a cheerful assent is justly reckoned wise, his knowledge is indeed divine. Stoicism, although, as Cicero[5] says, somewhat more exacting than what nature or truth requires, was nevertheless a noble doc-

---

[1] Qui ait le mieux connu les devoirs de l'homme.

[2] Immer weise ich dich auf dich selbst zurück. Du sollst der Schöpfer deines Glückes sein. Zschokke, *Stunden der Andacht*.

[3] Μη ζήτει τα γινόμενα γίνεσθαι ώς θέλαις, άλλα θέλε γίνεσθαι τα γινόμενα ύς γίνεται, και ίυροήσεις. M'Cormac, *Manual of Epictetus and Antoninus*.

[4] Quomodo animus semper aequalis secundoque cursu eat, propitiusque sibi sit et sua laetas adspiciat. Seneca.

[5] Nec moderata nec mitis, sed, ut mihi apparetur, paulo asperior quam aut veritas aut natura patiatur.

trine, a not unworthy precursor of a yet higher life, still loftier aims.

461. SPIRITUAL UNITY.

Spiritual unity is fostered by many things. Life's affections and realities here, tend to the yet greater realities of the life to come. How striking are the results of culture, developing the native excellencies of the soul, revealing spiritual beauty various as it is exquisite. To witness features grow radiant with sensibility, intelligence, and worth, souls casting aside prejudice after prejudice, with every base unworthy thing, is as if angels were to take us by the hand and lead us straight to heaven.

462. SHELLEY, ROUSSEAU.

Some parallel might be traced between Shelley and Rousseau. Both had the poet's ardent temperament, both struggled with the abuses of their time, both, too, were impetuous and not seldom mistaken in speculation. Few writers have reached the extreme beauty of Rousseau's periods. Shelley, indeed, was born to a position. Rousseau achieved one through the vigour of his fervid pen. He it was who pointed out the extreme inconsequence of a church professing to be for the poor, yet freeing souls from purgatory for gain. The discourse of the Savoyard vicar, and the fifth book of the Emile, are in a sense divine. Let the shortcomings of the man then be forgotten, and his obsequies performed to the music of his own wild dream. As for Shelley, he met his death amid the wash and the welter of the wild wide sea, and his own lines fitly enough record his memory.

> 'Tis like the wondrous strain that sweeps
> Around a lonely ruin,
> When west winds sigh and evening waves respond
> In whispers from the shore.

463. ELEVATION OF THE MASSES.

The practical conception of training and elevating the masses belongs to modern times. Inculcated with intense energy by the divine democracy of Christ, it has not been fitly realised even now. For Christianity alone has enlarged enough on the priceless worth of every single soul. When Telemachus the monk, descended into the arena at Rome, to rescue men condemned to battle with the brute, he sealed the great achievement with his blood, gave reality and name to the mighty truth that men are indeed equal in the eye of God and of enlightened humanity, equal in their claims for sustenance, for spiritual and material culture, and fitting preparation for the life to come. For in that one act, issuing as does all true bravery from the heart, did Telemachus inaugurate a new era for his kind.

In the very lowest there is an infinite capacity that needs but culture for its development. Turgot's ideal, indeed, was founded on the universality of education, the admixture of all classes in early childhood, sole basis, as he conceived, of the self-respect which insures the respect of others, and the real dignity of man. Is there a soul so debased, as never even to have faintly felt that all goodness and excellence and beauty come from God, thrice divine conviction, which, if duly fostered, would one day change the fortunes of our kind. For man's capacities, in very truth, are divine. We are greater, observes Augustin, than we can comprehend, greater sings Wordsworth than we seem. For in nature there are neither slaves nor tyrants, no English, French, or Russ, but only men, children of one father and one God. To be good, to be wise then, depends much upon ourselves, for, God's kingdom in truth is within.[1] Love is the very life of man, and not until love, freed from slavery to error, spring up within the soul, can man's real life begin.[2] The heart and affections, like human speech and intelligence, all our faculties in fine, are developed by effort and continuous exercise. Aspirations mean and low, alone impoverish. We are only rich in the treasures which accompany us from this life. For thoughts of God and man's eternal destiny are not fitted merely to shorten idle hours,[3] but to elevate and quicken the immortal spirit.

464. STANDING ARMIES.

Armed multitudes, diverted from the peaceful culture of the soil, encumber the surface of Europe and the world. Yet everywhere there are deserts, some Mantchou or Australian wilderness, to reclaim, districts to fertilise, material wealth to develop, women to relieve

---

[1] 'Ιδού γὰρ ἡ βασιλεία τοῦ Θεοῦ ἐντὸς ὑμῶν ἐστίν.

[2] La veritable vie de l'homme ne commence qu'avec la pensée de Dieu, et la pensée de Dieu seul nous fait libre.

[3] Gedanke an Gott, Ewigkeit, und Bestimmung der Seele, ist nicht geschaffen nur die Langweile zu verkürzen. *Stunden der Andacht.*

from penury and toil. Armed citizens can alone abate this tyranny, and render a country really impregnable. An ignorant, uncivic peasant force is, at this moment, throughout most parts of Europe, the potent instrument of despotism. Military monachism, so to term it, is the further source of excessive immorality and frightful mortality, while discipline, itself, is enforced by the scourge. When, oh when, shall some new Telemachus, standing out before the ranks, tear down the hideous triangle, and, sacrificing himself for his fellows, bring the blood-stained infamy to a close.

465. A PRAYER.

Thou who dost so wisely order the issues of life and death, oh rich, and great, and various God, hast within thyself the ideas of all things. Full of tenderness, and goodness, and compassion, in thee is all excellence, whatever the furthest extent of nature, the fruitful womb of the possible can bring forth.[1] Thou art the centre and mainspring of the universe. For, in thee the rays of all perfection rise, and in thee meet again.

466. ETERNITY.

Here, now, for us, is eternity. It begins with the first moment of consciousness, and never ends. Time, space, all transition, in fine, are divine expedients for realising the material, evoking the spiritual and moral. What men term death, in itself is a development, wherein we shall live, and love, and hope for ever. For the one object of death as of life,

[1] Norris, *On the Ideal, Intelligible World.* Lond. 1701.

with every aspiration and shade of energy, in this great, rich, magnificent universe, nature with all its marvels, art with all its treasures, is to enable the soul to grow. Not a moment, then, should be lost in weakness, irresolution, or delay. Either we must sink into apathy, or sow seed for the blossoms and fruitage of eternity.[1] For outside of the spiritual law are anarchy and slavery, but within, life and freedom, and progress to come.

467. KEY TO HEAVEN.

There is no approach for the sinner to God save through penitence and purity, goodness at heart and holiness of life, alone. Else, no mass will do it, no formulary, no prayer, no doctrine or profession, whatever. But tears, the masses of the heart will do it, resolute to reject each weakness, every shortcoming and stain. Dost thou think that God will sell his mercies for gold, that gold which he has made, and which to him is but as dust in the hollow of the hand. For he, indeed, is love, and would rather forgive than punish, were it the most erring if penitent of our kind. Yet, penitence must not exhale itself in idle words and tears, but in firmest welldoing, best passport to divine favour, and key to heaven. There needs no other payment to secure the remission of sins. And short of this, the blood of martyrs, and ah how many have languished on the tree and quivered at the stake, cannot in the least avail. Yet never must we forget those great souls

[1] Il n'y a de satisfaction çi bas que pour les ames ou brutales ou divines.

who have died that we might live, died for the advancement of us all, and the safety of our kind.

Nay, heaven itself has no other or better healing. Trespass no more, and we delight not only our fellows on earth, but the heavenly cohorts, the great Author of their existence and our own. Every spiritual potency, nature in her sweetest moods, would then become the servitors of our souls. We should enter into the common harmony, become as members of the celestial choir which hymns continually the praises of God. For all that is great and good, in heaven as on earth, is on the side of the soul's amendment and welldoing, the only real salvation and reform.

468. SELF-ESTEEM.

Much has been said of excessive, but what of deficient self-esteem. Numbers, indeed, have arrived at that pitch of self-depreciation, as to seem, I had almost said, to be incapable of any excellence. Well does Zschokke declare that man's greatest persecutor is himself.[1] A rational self-appreciation is absolutely requisite to the realisation of all well-sustained, well-directed effort. A rational, not an insane self-confidingness, justifies success, perhaps realises it. Yet, on one pretext or another, instead of being duly fostered, every spark of self-respect is too often trodden under foot. A false humility, the belief, unnatural and forced at best, maintained by want of self-loyalty and faith in our intellectual and moral worth, is at this moment eating out the spiritual stamina and resources of millions.

[1] Der Mensch hat auf Erde kein grossern Verfolger als sich selbst.

469. A TRUE REVEALING.

The test of a true revealing, the right appreciation of the good, the beautiful, the holy, the pure, is its spiritual character, its recognition of the infinite perfections of God. It is a true revealing that evil should be grappled with and overcome.[1] For all evil shuts or tends to shut us out from God, interferes with his revealings. It is a true revealing that man should confer happiness on man. For God, indeed, is a spirit, and can only be approached spiritually.[2] And purity of soul is the highest possession, cynosure of all excellence. Habitual cheerfulness, too, that cheerfulness of which the little child is the tireless evangel, interpreter, and exemplar, is also spiritual, a true revealing.[3] For day by day, to realise all great and good things, is not less the dictate of true religion than of sound philosophy.

470. THE GREAT REALITY.

The great reality is the spiritual reality. What we term suns, stars, continents, oceans, plants, heat, cold, night, day, with space and time, are but names for our perception of the forces which subsist within us and around. This, then, is the great ideal faculty which teaches us what are realities and what are not,

[1] Je grösser das Uebel, je grösser der Muth.
[2] Πνεῦμα ὁ Θεός, καὶ τοὺς προσκυνοῦντας αὐτὸν εν πνεύματι και ἀληθεία δει προσκυνεῖν.
[3] Sei froh des Tags, den Gottes Hand
Dir reicht vom Lebensbaum,
Was Morgen kommt ist unbekannt,
Was gestern war ein Traum.

in so far as it is given to man to know. The material, indeed, flits away and disappears, but the ideal, the one, the only real, never flits away, cannot, for a moment, disappear. For the feelings and affections, whose home and special birthplace is the soul, are the very, the spiritual life, the life of life, which having once lived, we become assured that seeds of purity, and holiness, and truth take root within us, and can never die. This, then, is the chief good, arcanum and white stone, continual consolation and flower of paradise, the celestial aura and breath divine, which renews existence, animates it as with a perennial spring. This, indeed, is the sun that never sets, the orient star that never pales. It is the soul's infinite riches, the deep and earnest longing which prophecies its own accomplishment, the great reality which every seeker, every child of heaven, is eventually sure to find. And the spirit that has gained it, freed from slavery and chains, casts joyous glances across the infinite, spreads abroad its pinions in glad anticipation of its eternal flight and final happy home.

471. THE SECURE HAVEN.

It is not every one that finds at once admission into the havens of the better life. Many sail past them, do not even know that such havens subsist. Oh world most beautiful and bright, harbours of securest refuge, how is it conceivable that any one should be ignorant of, or indifferent to you. But it is with spiritual as with all truth, that to the soul which is unworthy of admission within its sacred precincts, it is as though it were not. Yet how full of interest is its dawn on the as yet imperfectly conscious soul. It is like the sun's ascent on the great horizon of the world. The red and ruby light darts its tall spires aloft. Gleam succeeds gleam, and flash follows flash, till the glorious day reveal itself at last. And thus is it with the soul on which truth's bright effulgence, indeed the light celestial, breaks, flames, flashes, till the whole man become filled with its celestial splendour, and the affections and intelligence know no will, no purpose, save the divine.

472. SPINDRIFT OF TIME.

In what is termed civilisation, the party of progress and the party of delay stand continually opposed. As neither, however, will yield, society, to borrow a mechanical illustration, moves in the diagonal between. About modes of government and belief, men's affections, hopes, fears, constitute so many mooring chains, mighty anchors, intended to avert change and driftway. But nothing human, forms of faith, though happily not faith itself, inclusive, remains stationary. Creeds, by degrees, run into each other, and, but for the establishments, might have ceased to be distinctive long ago.

Yet, men will not always be kept apart. Spiritual despotism does not last for ever. Everything unworthy of beautiful human nature, of God's truth, and light, and love, must needs perish, and each sweet and gentle thing resume its elevating blessed sway. The real shall be preserved, but the illusory, the merely provisional and traditional, cannot, may not stand. The exquisitely sweet rose of to-day, does not differ from the rose of a thousand years agone, and faith, and hope, and charity, angelic three, true types of flowers in heaven, have been the same from the beginning, and so shall remain till the close.

473. SOCRATES.

Socrates looms forth a giant through the mists of time. His moral dimensions, in truth, hardly lessen with the flight of years. He impressed on all about him, still impresses, the conviction of irrefragable sincerity and truth.[1] His temper was imperturbable. Conduct he based on a divine obligation and reverence. Virtue he founded on self-respect, the voice of conscience, and not the mere verdict of the world. His, indeed, was the catholic mind to which all truth was congenial. He did not believe in an interruptive providence, or that divine truth could be otherwise realised than through the well-sustained operation of the faculties and affections. The religion of Socrates was not the mere utilitarianism of Aristotle or Plato's mysticism. He advised men to look around for proof of wisdom, and goodness, and power, and into themselves for moral capacity. He showed that there was a work for all, which, if neglected, events enforced. He inferred obedience to God, convictions from which conscience and reason derived unfaltering hope. In anticipation of the spiritual philosophy of Christianity, he taught that to gain the approbation of the great Taskmaster was reasonable service, sweetened by many and great rewards, alleviations numberless. An air of heavenly

[1] *Phaedo. Grote's Greece. Religion of Socrates*, Lond. 1831.

truth, indeed, pervades his utterances. As he himself
was most sincere, so did he insist upon sincerity and
truth in others. He pleaded his cause, the cause of
humanity and of truth, with firmness, and bore the
issue unmoved. It seems impossible, almost, to exaggerate the importance of this one man's example in
aid of the principles for which he so greatly contended
and consistently fell. He fought, indeed, the battle
always beginning, never ending, and which never can
end, till, happily, all men shall enjoy the blessing of
pure uninterrupted culture.

474. JEAN PAUL.

We cannot overrate the moral influence of a magna-
nimous spirit, some Phocion or Aristides, upholding
a nation's very life and being, revealing, indeed, the
possible greatness of humanity, redeeming one's country
and one's time.

Jean Paul, surnamed Richter, was an honour, a
glory, and a delight at once to Germany and the world.
The poor, he pithily observes, hope incredibly more
than the rich.[1] The time, he tells us, must come when
morality shall command us to cease tormenting others
and ourselves with the enervating poison of grief, as if
there were no better fortune yonder and nothing better
here. Many, he says, have died to regenerate the world,
whom one day Christ shall take by the hand, and say,
ye too have suffered under Pilates. Man, whom Jean
Paul calls the darling child of the infinite mother,
may believe twenty years in immortality and only on

[1] *Blumen, Frucht und Dornenstücke.*

the twenty-first, be astonished at the richness of this belief. Death, he terms the last rapture and joy of earth, matter a prison-grating between soul and soul, symbol of immortality. And every journey, he adds, lessens our provincialism, makes us feel members of God's city.[1] The last best fruit, he tells us, which ripens in man's warm soul, is gentleness towards the brutal, patience with the impatient, warmth towards the egotist, philanthropy by the cynic. Oh thou measureless brightness, he calls out in Hesperus, fall from the sun upon this narrow earth, and on thy light-flood conduct the heavy ashy heart towards the eternal throne. For the soul is heaven's ante-chamber, and therein is thy whole elysium and thy God. Ah, dear one, he again exclaims, what were harder, more painful, to discover than a heart.[2] Thou hast here, oh soul, ended thy life's last storm, and the evening sun plays upon thy breast, and has filled it with roses and gold. For the true life, ah words divine, knows not death, and we must not so much prepare for God and eternity, as implant them within. Here, indeed, we are in the forecourts of the eternal, and heaven is full of suns with the countenances of men.

Jean Paul dwells much on moral courage even in face of the scaffold and pile. Thrice happy, he says, is he to whom God has vouchsafed a great idea, for which he alone lives and holds higher than any joy.[3] He de-

[1] Stadt Gottes.
[2] Ach du Lieber, was wird den länger gesucht als ein Herz.
[3] O selig ist der welcher Gott eine grosse Idee bescheert, für die allein er lebt, die er höher achtet als seine Freuden, die immer jung und wachsend ihm die abmattende Eintönigkeit des Lebens verbirgt.

scribes a joyous dream, wherein, bereft of body and form, all was sound, and bloom, and the odour of flowers. The bier, he terms the cradle of heaven. To one whose worth was unacknowledged, he said, thou wearest a crown of thorns, but eternal roses bloom within thy breast. He tells the enemies of freedom that were they even to crush all opposition, put down every book, like the image of the sun on troubled waters, each fragment would reflect the truth.

Oh thou gentle and nigh God, he exclaims,[1] sun of suns and of spirits, hardly is the eye of man's soul unclosed, ere thou dost beam therein. The evening shades are long, but they point to the morning's dawn. Sweetest, fairest child, he makes a mother say, I bear the key of thy deep, dark house, but open it never. Then, the blooming transfigured daughter stands before the stars, and exclaims, mother, cast away the key, for I am above in heaven, and not on earth below. He adverts to terrific superstitions, instilled with earnest care. He upheld man's sacred interests and dignity, with faith in a personal God, free ruler and preserver of the world. November 14, 1825, Jean Paul surrendered his spirit to that future, into which, to use his own thrice beautiful words, he had aimed to open fresh lights and new kingdoms for a thousand veiled and tearful eyes.

475. THE TRUE PARADISE.

Although there be subtle essences difficult to appreciate, man's mastery over material nature increases

[1] *Flegeljahre. Titan. Kampaner Thal. Levana.*

with the ages. Yet, were such the alternative, we should prefer to witness moral progress alone, rather than material progress alone. For the heart and intellect, and not the senses, are the soul's eternal empire, and whatever imparts to them range and potency, is of infinite moment to our kind. There is not, indeed, a truth which has not a basis in the soul's receptivity. Man passes through and above the panorama of earthly life, from the mystery which antedates his being, to that which receives him at its close. Nevertheless, the changing scenes of the inner life, the satisfaction of noble desires, receive from culture indefinite expansion and strength. The development of our perception of the beautiful, of literature, religion, science, art, is as means to mightiest ends. The capacities, however, in some sense infinite of man's soul, continually transcend his greatest achievement. Yet, there is not a spot in which there may not be peace, a state of life wherein we may not realise heaven.[1] Our divine endowments, our thrice admirable capacities and affections, were predetermined ere ever we were born, and justify, what do they not justify, unceasing exultation and joy. For God has imparted to us of his own, the inner kingdom, that kingdom of which he is the ceaseless indweller, that we should not banish him from our affections and from our thoughts, but cherish him in our consciousness for ever.

476. MEDISANCE.

A determined stand should be made against unjust ridicule. The tongue of the satirist is steeped in false-

[1] Senza brama sicura ricchezza.

hood, his pen in venom and gall. He takes precedence of his fellows, he who should place himself beneath them. This mean and vicious addiction is adverse to every good, and generous, and noble thing. Satire, at least of this stamp, was not the weapon of a Shakspeare or a Jean Paul. Slander, in truth, is the pasture of low and petty souls, baleful weed of Erebus that too much infests our social life and literature. That religion has been infected by this dreary vice, let the annals of sectarianism declare. The soul with any strain of magnanimity, has no place for medisance, but casts it out, abjures it for ever.

477. A THANKSGIVING.

Life should be a hymn of thanksgiving, the discharge of every duty, the development of all our powers. There is, however, a virtue which resumes most others, and that is the perpetual abnegation of self.[1] The delicate spirits of the world also compose its chivalry. For envy, hatred, malice, and uncharitableness, with all wickedness and ignorance, are the real demons, mighty enemies, indeed, of souls, impeding moral greatness, in short, distorting the feelings, converting the bosom which harbours them into a desolation and a hell.

Nature, religion, warn man alike against wedding too much his affections to earthly things. We might, indeed, become as angels of light, and would prove so too, if we only thought, felt, and acted up to our almost boundless capacities. A strain of infinite tenderness, deepening into a wail, when he falls short

[1] Il n-y-a qu'une vertu, l'éternel sacrifice de soi-meme.

or goes astray, seems to pervade creation in behalf of man. For every sweet and precious interest, all the gracious realities of earth and heaven, prescribe moral truthfulness and disinterestedness, the great, the mighty necessity of the spirit's freehold of the soul. We must discipline ourselves, else be disciplined by the exigencies of nature and of things. Yet, since excellence is a jealous thing, calls for a man's whole soul, how lovely were it to forestall constraint, and to live by anticipation the blessed, the celestial life. As some rose-hued arch or heavenly aurora, some silver moon or star, is in goodliest keeping with visible nature, so moral beauty itself is in truest harmony with every noble characteristic, the spiritual loveliness of earth and heaven.

478. RELIGION, FAITH, PHILOSOPHY.

Disastrous was the error to separate religion from philosophy. Twin sisters both, they cannot live alone. Apart from religion's gentler influences, philosophy becomes hard and stern, falls short of the mighty aim, while without philosophy, religion itself degenerates, is sullied with puerilities, trivialities, superstition, and even crime. Philosophy reasons but does not feel, faith feels but does not reason, therefore is one the indispensable complement and correlative of the other. But religion, itself, through some strange calamity, has too often lapsed into a faith without love. If, indeed, faith without works be dead, what, alas, is faith without love.

Each century, says Richter, develops new views even in beliefs the least progressive. A spiritual creed lighted up by knowledge and intelligence, consummating and combining faith, and works, and love, is perhaps the especial evolution and development of our times. The necessity of conjoining true faith with true philosophy, springs from the essence of both as derived from God.[1] For the absence of truth and love, one or both, leads to disaster and decay. But of the two, it were perhaps better to have a false faith with love, than a true faith without love. But ah, let us have a true faith, and a true love, firmly bonded in one, revealing God as the ever-present, inward witness, father, comforter, guide, and friend. Here, genius, philosophy, and religion are at one, for genius, akin to goodness, also announces God.

479. DOING ARIGHT.

That man is a free agent in the work of his spiritual safety, his turning to God, is of the truths that grow with the growth of the ages. Work out your safety, says Paul to the Philippians.[2] Work out your safety, in goodness and beneficence, sayeth heaven to all men.

Dialectic hair-splitting, traditional dogmatism, have proved of infinite disservice in obscuring a truth so plain. There must be mental and moral, in a word spiritual effort, in order to insure spiritual progress. We are indeed nothing of and by ourselves, but everything through the goodness and graciousness of God.

---

[1] Essendo Iddio il principio vitale della scienza come della natura, il pensiero umano in tanto ha forza e vigore, in quanto riceve i benefici influssi dello spirito creatore e animatore dell'universo. Gioberti, *Introduzione allo Studio della Filosofia.* Brussels, 1840.

[2] Τὴν ἑαυτῶν σωτηρίαν κατεργάζεσθε.

He has yielded to us the mighty power by which, through love and faith, we realise the beautiful things of earth and heaven. For man, let us ever repeat, is a free agent, in the furtherance of his own regeneration and advancement, within the prescribed range of holiness, and purity, and truth. Heaven, itself, has bestowed the means, and through every precious sacred influence incites us to apply them. And creeds, confessions, churches, can only avail as setting forth this most intelligible and comforting of all formulas, that God has imparted to every man the power of doing well. This, then, is the potent life-bestowing element, which, duly worked out and developed in religious and secular culture, shall one day redeem the world. It is, in truth, our birthright, the great conception and element of the free right of private judgment which characterised the Reformation, and which, in its degree, has imparted spiritual life and liberty to all, but which, if quashed or tampered with, millions have fought, and bled, and struggled in vain.

480. A HEALTHY SOUL.

An undeveloped heart, an unhealthy mind, can treat no subject healthily. Whole schools, so to speak, there are, of philosophy, literature, theology, politics, art, unfitted for supplying healthy moral nutriment, as a worn and tattered garment is unfitted for healthy use and wear. For moral and religious truth is only fitly assimilated and appreciated, when uttered by, and received into, pure hearts and upright souls which alone draw light and love from heaven. Our conceptions of the life celestial, indeed, are coloured by our earthly life. The inflictions of a cruel tribunal are only to be paralleled by the decrees of reprobation that would consign our hapless species to wretchedness beyond the tomb. But as the cruel practice has mainly died out, so must the cruel dogma itself expire. There is no eternal evil, there can be no eternal suffering. For as only love appreciates love, so man's affections, however finite, alone suffice to fathom the infinite affections of God.

481. MENTAL AFFLUENCE.

The intellectual poverty, the paucity of knowledge, of feeling, and ability of some, are yet more inconceivable than is the mental affluence of others. Thought, indeed, expires, in the first instance or the last, without just relations with the outer material world, primary element of human consciousness. For God having thought the world, it became the object of his contemplation, and man can only follow the divine thought as manifested. Therefore, must thought's beginning consist in the observation of creation, and the correspondence between thoughts and things.[1] Creation has been laid open to us, with all its grand phenomena, nature's wondrous laws, best safeguard against prejudice,[2] the great realities of earth and heaven, the wealth

[1] Daher muss das erste Princip des Denkens ein solches sein, dass in die Anschauung führt und die Möglichkeit derselben erzeugt. Ohne ein solches giebt es keine Gemeinschaft zwischen dem Denken und den Dingen. Trendelenborg, *Logische Untersuchungen*, Berlin, 1840. Zweiter Band, Rückblick.

[2] *Arago's Astronomy*, Book xvii. cap. 35.

of the understanding and the heart, literature, science, religion, social polity, and art. For there is not a thing which God has left undone to serve us, short of doing our work for us, and that he will not do, either in this rich and various life, or that yet more beautiful and glorious existence which the divine transfiguration, by men termed death, lays open to us.

482. RELIGION, PAST AND TO COME.

The time has surely come for conjoining in one harmonious whole, the things of reason, of sense, and of love. That reason only is insufficient, is discernible in the churches of the Reformation. That the affections alone, do not avail, we perceive in the church which they have left. Religion, indeed, must comprise the whole man, his workings and his doings, his knowledge and his belief, become his infinite hope and possible stay. The sectaries will not yield to each other, but they can and must yield to a faith, which, at once loving, earnest, truthful, pure, omitting no single item of precious truth, shall reconcile their differences, resume their perfections. For the intelligence is not opposed to the heart, the heart to the intelligence. They are at once complementary and essential to each other. And together, they shall yet rescue our suffering humanity, and render it angelic in the sight of God and of our own souls.

483. TRUE GENIUS.

Were we to strive for ever, never could we exaggerate the mighty efficacy of true genius, that winged power which raises man above the dust and sere of common things. For genius is of the interpreters of God to man, fulfiller of the gospel of the beautiful, harmoniser of the else perchance discordant elements of earth and heaven. True genius is calm because full of power, truthful because God, whom true genius imitates, is all truth. It has a holy definiteness, a sacred energy of purpose and of will that nothing can subdue or quell.

Was it not genius that upheld Howard in his course of mercy, causing him calmly to breathe his last when his work of love was done. Were not Pestalozzi's simplicity, power, and greatness of heart, Arnold's goodness, generosity, and devotion, also genius. Who can read Niebuhr's letter to a young philologist, and say that he had not the genius of culture. The inexpressible dignity, delicacy, and courtesy, which shone forth in Christ's demeanour, surely savoured of this divine infusion. The wisdom, truth, and faith culminating in the Phaedo, Theaetetus, and others of Plato's discourses, suggest indeed thoughts of heaven. And when we consider the grace of Guido's angels, the exquisite sweetness and purity of Sasso Ferrato's virgin and child, the unspeakable grace and innocence of Murillo and Raphael's female portraitures, we acknowledge the celestial effluence, and feel drawn towards the great, wise Being, who, originating such types of loveliness, goodness, and truth, has imparted to us power to appreciate and imitate them.

484. FEAR, NOT RELIGION.

The frightful element of fear must one day be eliminated from religion, wherein love alone must reign.

Let us, indeed, act as beseems those who are ever present with themselves, as they are with God. There is, else, in religion no finality. It goes from conception to conception, and from holiness to holiness, for ever. There are not seven heavens, merely, but seventy times seven, or rather countless heavens, each revealing fresh aspects of the inner, the divine life, open to us in succession if we will. For every great and good thought, each sweet, loving impulse, generous act, and true affection, are of the very reality and seed of paradise.

The martyr on his mission, Kosciusko leading his perishing hosts to battle, some captain with firm foot planted on the brine-washed plank about to descend with him into the abyss, the negro plunging sheer into the depths to yield boat-room for his master's child, Grace Darling, on her errand of mercy, heading her frail skiff into the trough of the seething sea, and countless other instances of purest, most perfect sacrifice, realise in conception and in act, even in this life, the many-voiced, angelic ecstasies of eternity.

He, says Arnold, who believes conscience to be God's law, by obeying it obeys God. It is merest fanaticism, he adds, to oppose faith to reason. For, with united faith and reason, holy and noble thoughts and principles spring up in the soul as in a garden planted by God, beautiful, fresh, and full of aspiration, for this life and also for heaven.

485. MAN'S CAPACITY.

Man is made in the image of God. His conceptions, in truth, are oft divine. Most momentous, is his capacity for greatness, and goodness, and freedom, and all excellence. Ah, did we but act up to it, then should it be well with us for ever. The smallest acquisition of truth and energy, of the nobler affections, thoughts, and aspirations, which refine not merely the material but the moral world, is so much realised for the commonwealth of souls. For all genius and excellence are as one. And the spirit-life opens the gates of the universe, reveals regions compared with which material glories seem faint indeed, and dim.

486. SUFFERING, TERMINABLE.

Where the the worm dieth not, and the fire is not quenched.[1] This refers only to man's soul, for there and there only, lies his weal and his woe, his heaven and his hell. Yet, goodness, divine goodness, quenches the fire, love, divine love, annihilates the worm. Thus is it written in characters of light, registered ere ever was time. That sin and the suffering which flows from sin, do not, cannot last, is of the truths, in which, as in every celestial illumination, man has an infinite stake. To the sincere, indeed, God yields the entire creation, the great eternities of space and time. As He is all truth, all sincerity, so does he require truth, sincerity, and directness in his creatures. For as the boundless universe and the spiritual empire are made for all, even the very humblest soul, so truth demands no slack, precarious utterance, but our intensest reverence and regard. Here, we must have no halfness, no paltering between the truth, the entire truth, and

[1] Ὅπου ὁ σκώληξ αὐτῶν οὐ τελευτᾷ, καὶ τὸ πῦρ οὐ σβέννυται.

what is not truth at all, but acknowledge it without hesitancy or pause for ever.

Anxiety and fear, as Schiller has somewhere said, reside too much in our first acquaintance with the spiritual life. Joy, only, should attend truth's faintest dawnings on the soul, that truth whose ceaseless expansions are among the celestial miracles of God. For, let us only consider, every truth which we may or can discover, has waited, must wait, to find deliverance, from the beginning. If any one, then, be so happy as to experience some new and beneficent revealing, and such is all truth, how precious is the charge of first imparting it to his kind. If it were not, indeed, for the divine, the inextinguishable energy of earnest thinkers, there would be neither safety nor solace in this world.

487. ABELARD.

Abelard was acute, in truth, and learned,[1] the restless advocate of spiritual liberty. Yet, his highest claim to fame is the affection which he inspired in one faithful woman's breast. I know not if the crumbling stone that spans a portion of soil in the Paris burying ground, do, indeed, cover the remains of Abelard and Eloisa, but assuredly it did once cover them, and marble canopy or cinerary urn never came nigher the ashes of more faithful or heroic hearts. Eloisa's passionate confession of love and constancy,[2] must ring

---

[1] *Petri Abaelardi et Heloissae conjugis ejus opera.* M. de Remusat, Paris, 1614.

[2] Testor Deum omnipotentem—

for ever in the ears, and vibrate in the memories of men.

All records saving thine, come cool, and calm,
And shâdowy through the mist of passed years.[1]

And so long as our race endures, her name shall recal a heroism not too often paralleled in the history of our kind.

488. THE PURE SHALL SEE GOD.

The pure in heart shall see God,[2] can indeed see him on no other terms or conditions whatever. Outside the beauty of holiness and truth, with the material forms which, so to speak, are its living exponent and investiture, life would be a filmy vapour, a sorry dream. Death stands like a saviour at the entrance of the life unseen. The myriad voices of eternity, of all excellence and goodness and truth, pealing from the infinite, from God, assure us of the sweetest, brightest of all certainties, the imperishable grandeur and elevation of the human soul. Faith, guided by reason, conscience directed, leads us through the labyrinth, conquers death's enigma with thoughts like quickening dew. Each moral purpose and lofty affection, cherished in the soul, become as it were a centre of the spiritual universe, blessed means to celestial ends, the seed in short of heaven.

For here, the finite and the infinite, faith and works, God and his children, giving and receiving, meet in unison and truth together. Deep in the soul abides

[1] Keats.
[2] Μακάριοι οἱ καθαροὶ τῃ καρδίᾳ· ὅτι αὐτοί τον Θεον ὄψσονται.

the bright conviction of life's infinite significance, that man's better nature shall not always have to submit to the control of the material, but shall be finally set free of it in his proper, his celestial home.[1] Each man

[1] Vorbereitung zur gemeinschaftlichen Andacht.

DIE GEMEINE.

Müde von des Leben's Leiden,
Müder von des Leben's Freuden,
Flüchten wir in eure Stille,
Ob uns hier Erquickung quille.
Frohseyn ist uns nie gelungen,
Wie wir eifrig auch gerungen,
Und wir sind des Treibens müde,
Suchen Ruhe, wünschen Friede.

DIE PFLEGER.

Kommt Belad'ne zur Erquickung,
Kommt Erschöpfte zur Entzückung.
Neue Stärke soll die Matten
Ueberschwänglich überschatten,
Nur dass draussen ihr versenken
Wollet euer Thun und Denken,
Abthun euer altes Streben,
Sterben all dem eig'nen Leben.

DIE GEMEINE.

Und was habt ihr uns zu geben
Zum Ersatz für unser Leben.

DIE PFLEGER.

Solch ein Leben, das gegründet
In sich selber, nimmer schwindet,
Nimmer wandelt, selbst sich gnüget.
Dieses hier euch offen lieget.
Aber nur von euch geschieden
Geht ihr ein in seinen Frieden.

Fichte, *Kleinere Gedichte, Sämmtliche Werke.* Berlin 1846, Band viii. S. 463.

then, is his own, nay, all men's greatest enemy or truest friend. He can infinitely serve or as infinitely disserve, not merely the poorest, meanest, but the loftiest, most spiritually elevated of his kind. In our inmost hearts lies a yearning for the unchangeable, the divine, for all the sacraments, union with the better life and with heaven.

489. A FALSE SECURITY.

Next to actual sin, is perhaps the danger of a false security. Ceaseless must be our advance if we would have a place amid the star-crowned angels, a home in the sunny heavens. Let us but seek for it, and God shall not only sustain and purify us, but yield security and immunity for ever. We may not falter in resolve, recoil in act, since, recipients of a mighty faith, we are to become as a very revelation to our kind. For all true spirits, and hope, and memory, nay God himself, are with every great and good resolve.

490. LEOPARDI.

The greatest of men are sometimes little known. How many, in truth, have heard of Leopardi. Yet, was he wise and good, worthy of deepest honour and renown. Christ, said Leopardi, was the first to denounce that scoffing hypocrite and servile tyrant, the world. During his later years, like Dante, he was rarely seen to smile. Warm in his attachments, most moderate in his wants, he was nobly free from greed of gain. All-conquering was his assiduity.[1] Leopardi's

[1] *Quarterly Review*, March 1850.

tomb adds yet fresher interest to that glorious Italian bay, on whose enchanting strand it stands, and must for ever stand. Like the withered leaf in his lovely version from the French,[1] he himself, a withered leaf, has translation found to heaven.

491. THE DEAD CHILDREN.

> But God gives patience, love learns strength,
> And faith remembers promise,
> And hope itself can smile at length
> On other hopes gone from us.

Thus graciously hymns Barrett Browning of her treasure lost at Florence. Any one, in truth, who has seen a child, his own perchance, its little face turned star-ward, coffined, still, and cold, will understand it all. Its erewhile bright features are at rest, its eyes are all closed, its prattle has ceased, the perfume of its

[1] FOGLIA FRALE.

Lungo dal proprio ramo.
Povera foglia frále
Dove vai tu. Dal fággio
Là dov' io naque, mi divise il vento
Esso, tornando, a volo
Dal bosco alla montagna
Seco perpetuamente
Vo pellegrina, e tutto l'altro ignoro.
Vo dove ogni altra cosa,
Dove naturalmente
Va la foglia di rosa
E la foglia d'alloro.
  Opere, Tom. i. p. 160.

LA FEUILLE DE CHENE.

Do ta tige détachée
Pauvre feuille desséchée,
Où vas-tu. Je n'en sais rien.
L'orage a brisé le chêne
Qui seul était son soutien.
De son inconstante haleine
Le zéphyr ou l'aquilon,
Depuis ce jour me promène
De la forêt à la plaine,
De la montagne au vallon,
Je vais où le vent me mène
Sans me plaindre ou m'effrayer,
Je vais où va toute chose,
Où va la feuille de rose
Et la feuille de laurier.
  Anonyme.

presence is at an end. Yet, the dead child speaks with perchance diviner power than when living, not so much of past endearments perhaps, the fulness of confiding love and dependent helplessness, as of a celestial home and angelic presences, gardens whose blossoms do not wither, joys which experience no decay.

Alas, I have seen the innocents, whom men term children, swept away, like those white blossoms which some plants shed, almost without a notice or a tear. Heaven, indeed, must be peopled with such, for half our race but leave the cradle for the tomb. And I have known them, too, when expiring, to utter such things, to pass away, so sweetly, so uncomplainingly, that one could ill brook their departure at all, or without tears behold the trail of heavenly light and purity which they left behind.

Yes, they are mirrors of the better life, realise embodied grace, and goodness, and excellence, in fine, a paradise, but without or stain or soil. For the baby's warmth transfigures the mother's bosom, the lustre of its sunny eyes, the pressure of its lips and arms, conduct her straight to regions whose sweetness it helps to bring very nigh. Without children, and sometimes losing them too, I fear, we could hardly aspire on earth as we do, much more realise the higher excellencies of heaven.

492. GOD'S PROVIDENT LOVE.

Every thing is made ready to our hand. Parents' fondest love, the very honey of ages, in literature, religion, science, art, await our requirements and our will. Every man, indeed, bears within him an ideal man, in correspondence with his capacity and destination.[1] The same reason has ever prevailed,[2] one truth that through every age has rescued human intelligence from sophistry and chains. No part of nature is too mean for the divine presence, and the visible world is but the portraiture of celestial archetypes. Sensible objects, although themselves insensible, rouse man's dormant energies.[3] Yet mind, both the human and the divine mind, must be congenial, else there were no intercourse between man and man, or what is of yet greater moment, between man himself and heaven.

499. GODWIN, ROLAND, FULLER.

O I wish
That I were some great princess,
I would build
Far off from men a college
Like a man's.
And I would teach them all that
Men are taught.
We are twice as quick.

Thus, in effect, with Tennyson, has spoken many a woman to herself, and thus, isolation apart, should be the culture of each single woman, till like unto some lovely garden, her soul, as Cervantes has divinely said,[4] should overflow with fragrance and with flowers.

[1] Die Natur handelt für dem Menschen wo er als freie Intelligenz noch nicht selbst handeln kann. Schiller, *Aesthetische Erziehung des Menschen*, Dritter Brief.

[2] *Harris' Hermes*, Book iv.

[3] Νουν δὲ οὐδὲν σωμα γεννᾶ, πως γὰρ ἄν τα ανοητα νουν γεννεσαι.

[4] Estimar la muger come se guarda y estima, un hermoso jardin lleno de flores y rosas, de fragrancia y hermosura.

Mary Wolstonecraft Godwin was remarkable for her attainments and force of character. Her letters from Norway contain the sweetest reflections on men and things. She speaks of the wild plants, the melody of the pines, the balm which the open air has for aching hearts. She tells us how energy is undermined by dread of censure, how men labouring to be prudent lose sight of rectitude. Her thoughts on education are often excellent. She dwells much on the celestial expression which the culture of the intellect and affections bestows. She would conquer all things through spiritual insight and determination. Her book on woman's rights, indeed, is a wail in behalf of the tortured, the suffering, and the degraded of her sex.

Mme Roland was not less an honour to her nation than her time. I appreciate life, she tells us, in her memorable confession from the Abbaye, and have only feared to do wrong. Injustice and death, she says, I despise.[1] They shall not hinder me from living to the end. Before the world she sustained herself, but alone she wept for hours.[2] This admirable and accomplished creature, clothed in white, her long hair flowing to her waist, passed from this life through the wicket opened by a violent death, with all the sweetness and serenity with which she had ever lived.

Margaret Fuller Ossoli shewed what a soul bent on self-culture might become.[3] She loved the ideal from

---

[1] J'apprecie la vie, je n' ai jamais craint que le crime, je méprise l'injustice et la mort, *Appel à l'Impartielle Posterité.*

[2] Appuyée sur sa fenêtre à pleurer.

[3] *Woman in the Nineteenth Century. Memoirs*, Boston, 1852.

her childhood, nature's shifting shows, the spiritual issues of the sunbeam and the wave, the shadows on the hill. Children, she repeated, should not be forced on reflection, but suffered to run fallow till thought came to them. We inspire the impossible, she repeated, and find it. God she spoke of as loving eternally, man as shaking off ignorance and sin. Love, she termed the soul's desire to realise the whole, seeking in another what it finds not in itself. Only through aspiration, she exclaimed, was she able to vanquish unpropitious circumstances and save her soul alive. Aiming ever at thoughts divine, she was alone intolerant of faithlessness and sin. Flowers, she said, brought her into harmony with creation, soothed every irritation away. The Italian spring with its anemones, crocuses, and cowslips, its glorious sunshine and gently-flowing airs, was good to her as paradise. This noble-hearted woman, with husband and child, breathed her last amid the wash and surge on Fire-Island beach, the place where the ship she sailed in from Europe, was cast away.

494. CULTURE'S OBJECT.

Man is prone to retrograde, but then he is also prone to advance. The grand, the final aim, is progress.[1] But freedom alone confers freedom, the freedom to do well, and to be satisfied with it, as Quevedo has urged, for our reward.[2] Man, observes Schiller, develops his in-

[1] Erkühne dich weise zu sein. Schiller, *Aesthetische Erziehung*.

[2] Basta por temor la fealdad del mal obrar, basta por premio la hermosura del bien hacer, y si despues el hombre quesiere considerar que se reciben premios, podria considerar los premios ya recibidos, cuando sacada de la nada, fué creado à la inmortalidad. *El Romulo*.

tellect and his sensuous powers in order to subject nature to his will.¹ But freedom would expire were he only susceptible of physical development. For the man of moral culture alone is free. He either conforms to physical nature, or withdraws to a region to which she has no access. For there, he is a true member of the invisible church, not only receives, but reproduces the spiritual ray.

495. AUGUSTIN, CALVIN.

Augustin, of Hippo, was an earnest, loving soul. His devotion to God, and affection for Monica his mother, shine forth in his somewhat melancholy confessions. Multifarious, indeed, are the topics on which the good Bishop dilates in his ample tomes.²

Very different was Calvin from Hippo's gentle saint. A possible eye-witness when Francis I. cast heretics into the flames in Paris streets,³ and a dissentient from the faith of Rome, Calvin himself was intolerant of all dissent. An earnest, striving, though mistaken inquirer, he was doubtless anxious for the weal of souls, desirous to rescue them from spiritual death. But so, likewise, we may not question it, were the Inquisitors of Spain. We are not, however, at liberty to rack men's

¹ *Ueber Anmuth und Würde.*
² An infantes in suo sexu resuscitanda. *De Civitate Dei*, Paris, 1838, Lib. xxii. cap. 17. An amicitia coelestium deorum per intercessionum daemonum possit homini provideri. *Id.* Lib. ix. cap. 9. De ampulla sanguinis famulae Dei per somnium ostensa. *De Miraculis sancti Stephani*, Lib. i. cap. 1. De muliere caeca quae pallam cum reliquiis contigit et visum recipit. *Id.* cap. 3.
³ Quia multis piis hominibus in Gallia exustis. Prefat. Psalm.

bodies under plea of rescuing their souls. Calvin's intellect was developed, but his heart was cold.¹ The gentler affections, apparently, had no place in his bosom. The Manichean opinions of the hapless Servetus, he terms devilish errors, foul and gross absurdities.² Our whole humanity, both as to the sense and the higher nature, he describes as corrupt, voluntarily lapsing into sin,³ and man, as regards life and happiness, perishing utterly.⁴ Yet, God desires the holiness of all, that all may have life.⁵ There is no freezing limitation, but a mercy, boundless as space, open as the firmament.⁶ For the real gospel is unlike the views of some of its interpreters, and heaven's liberality has been strained through an artificial theology, instead of falling in a universal shower upon the world.⁷

Yet, in Calvin as in Augustin,⁸ whom indeed he often cites,⁹ great truths are also adumbrated, gleams and glimpses of that happy final state in which the wicked cease from troubling and the weary are at rest. Our very being, he tells us, is subsistence in God, whose blessings distil like streams conducting us to the

¹ Balmez, *On European Civilisation*, chap. i. and x.
² *Institutio Christianae Religionis*. Lib. i. cap. 15.
³ *Id.* Lib. ii. cap. 3.
⁴ *Id.* cap. 5.
⁵ *Bledsoe's Theodicy*. New York, 1854, p. 234.
⁶ *Chalmers' Institutes of Theology*, vol. ii. chap. 8. ⁷ *Id.*
⁸ Ibi vacabimus et videbimus, videbimus et amabimus, amabimus et laudabimus. Ecce quod erit in fine sine fine. *De Civitate Dei*, Lib. xxii. cap. 30.
⁹ Responsio ad Versipellem. *Calvini Tractatus Theologici Omnes*. Genevae 1597, p. 414.

fountain.[1] Blessings, he repeats, consist in the knowledge of God, who regards not outward appearance, but only purity of heart.[2] Would that they had but pervaded his own heart, inspired him with sentiments of love and mercy to his kind.

Ah, there is a yet loftier city than that imagined by Augustin, heavenlier institutes than any Calvin penned. Faith, a purer faith, love, a mightier love, hand in hand must join, and Calvin and Augustin become as one. For God's true city is the universe, with all the sentient creatures that inhabit it. His institutes comprise a higher hope, the brief though simple formula of love and charity. And all shall yet be brought within his mantle folds, and the blessed precincts of his perfect day.

496. WOMAN'S WRONGS.

Every day fresh pages would seem added to the sad register of woman's mighty wrongs and sufferings. A provincial paper[3] has just recorded the last moments of Marianne. She died from poison taken by her own hand. In the lines which she traced, she blesses the man for whom she died. Another journal describes the tenderness and devotion of the wives of the Portland prisoners, as something affecting in the extreme.[4] They rarely upbraided these men, when they wrote, urging only prayer and reconciliation with God.

[1] *Institutio*, Lib. i. cap. 5.
[2] *Id.* Lib. ii. cap. 8.
[3] *Manchester Guardian*, Sept. 24, 1858.
[4] *Times*, Sept. 20, 1858.

497. CELESTIAL ARMIES.

There are, so to speak, whole armies of mercy and excellence, onlookers, we may not doubt it, of our every effort for the good, the beautiful, the true. For there is never a sacrifice or suffering for a spiritual object, that has not mightiest suffrage and sympathy, at once in earth and heaven. Next to God, the spirits of the celestial armies are ever nigh, rejoicing, let us hope, in whatever cleanses and exalts the earnest striving heart of man. In the culture of the holy, the beautiful, the true, resides alike the angelic tillage of this life and of the life to come. We are all through nature nurselings of God. And the beautiful is ever in closest relation with the good.

Not for nothing is each revelation of loveliness stamped with ecstasy on the soul. It is not for nothing that the wild rose blows, that the foxglove and the wallflower dance with every wind, and that chorusses from heaven are borne upon each breeze. They are, indeed, revealings from the infinite, utterances of man's celestial destinies, of a not to be questioned reversion of every glory of earth and time.

498. INSANITY, CRIME.

It is but recently that insanity has ceased to be looked upon as an immediate providential award, nay, a demoniacal possession, and tacitly relegated to the dominion of science. The asseveration that insanity was of material origin,[1] or that brain has mind for its

---
[1] Forbes Winslow, *Psychological Journal*, passim.

principal function,¹ throws no light on the subject, in effect is not true. It has again and again been asserted that the brain was mind,² and that its functions were the mental faculties.³ The brains of maniacs and criminals, unless in cases complicated with incidental disease, are not less healthy than those of other men. Cerebral disease has no necessary connexion with insanity and crime, which are alone ascribable to vicious, perverted training, and neglected individual culture.

It is all-important to cultivate the intellect and the affections, since this would be to realise the divine idea, to prevent both insanity and crime, the insanity of thought with that of word and act. For, as Porphyry has said,⁴ the ruling mind, though manifold, is one, and needs development, not in a single direction only, but in all. Perverted habits, undeveloped powers and affections, uncontrolled appetites, uncorrected lawless trains of thought and feeling, these, and not the material changes, vainly imagined by materialistic physiologists and divines, are the single sources of insanity and crime. To a pure and highly disciplined will, indeed, under the guidance of divine law, moral health and well-being, avoiding both insanity and crime, are practicable as they are certain. And, thus, by progress on progress, ascent upon ascent, developing at once the individual and the race, man's soul might rise till it came

[1] Bain, *On the Senses and the Intellect.*
[2] Keine Kraft ohne Stoff, kein Stoff ohne Kraft. Buchner, *Kraft und Stoff*, Frankfurt, 1855.
[3] Der so-genannten Seelanthätigkeiten nur Functionen der Gehirnsubstanz sind. Vogt, *Physiologische Briefe*, Giessen, 1854, S. 325.
[4] Πολλὰ γάρ ἐστιν ὁ νοῦς· πρὸ δὲ τῶν πολλῶν ἀνάγκη εἶναι τὸ ἕν.

to dwell habitually in that Presence, before which no conceit or craze is possible, and in face of which evil cannot live.

499. THE TEST OF EXISTENCE.

The value of existence resides in its quality, not merely in its quantity. Were it otherwise, life would be a deception, and the deceived would be those who had lived for something better than their own happiness, who had spent themselves in the race or fallen at the altar of human good.[1] The great philosophical and Christian truth, the truth of truths, is that religious unity and perfection are independent of theological opinions, consist in the moral and religious affections.[2] That religion resides in spiritual states, is indeed our great present need and continually augmenting conviction. All religion, assumes the natural law, and is at one with it.[3] But, then, all science is also divine.[4]

The truest, is also the safest creed, since from truth there is nothing to fear, indeed no appeal. It is only untruth that is unsafe. For every truth, all law and all order, are as it were continually upheld and uttered by God, and with the same spiritual energy, and love, and skill, as on the first day.[5] The soul is the arena of every truth. There, and no other where, lies God's great appeal to man, the first appealing and also the last, of the great I am. In the heart, and in the heart

[1] *Martineau's Endeavours after the Christian Life*, vol. i. p. 185.
[2] *Arnold's Life*, vol. i. p. 188.
[3] *Ward's Ideal of a Christian Church*.   [4] Bishop Cumberland.
[5] Omnis gratia ab uno fonte descendit, et omnis illuminatio ab uno lumine. Hugo de St. Victor.

only, abides all faith, all charity, the inner light and life, and as coupled with these, all truth. But spiritual knowledge cannot be fully compassed without an infinite and painstaking care, our own efforts coupled with the fruits of the efforts of those who are no more. And thus perfected, and as it were inspired, conscience and reason would assume more perfect sway, until man at length became a member of the hierarchy of heaven.

500. LAW, DIVINE.

One law pervades creation, all the realms of space and time. There is nowhere anarchy. There never was anarchy, either on this earth of ours, or yet in the remotest heavens. Without law, indeed, how could there be holiest thought or rule divine. There is no interruptive providence or interruptive inspiration, either. Everything and all things are regulated by preconcerted fiat. Glimpses of this mighty truth have pervaded the world, but mixed up with errors, feeble, distorted, confused. There is law throughout all nature. Chaos is a dream. The most distant sun or comet, starry galaxy or nebulous mass, is regulated by laws, if not identical, at least in strictest harmony with those of earth. God and nature, order and law, are not separate influences, but one influence. For all is science and all is law.

Chemistry, astronomy, geology, physics, anatomy, physiology, life, death, health, disease, so termed, refer to conditions, which, in their degree, not the minutest fragment of matter here or in other realms of space, escapes. On the other hand, metaphysics, psychology,

2 B

logic, philosophy, theology, religion, politics, history, jurisprudence, art, poesy, all literature, all culture, are founded on revealings, expansions more or less perfect, of the moral law. Never was there a religious influence, an historical, poetical, artistic or social fact, that did not owe its genesis to the operation, more or less wisely, more or less unwisely interpreted, of this law. To conjoint physical and spiritual law, as regulated by the habits, the ethos in fine, of nations, is owing their position, social and otherwise. For there is not a capacity or an affection in man, that does not acknowledge the divine.

Universal physical law immutably regulates material things. And in like manner must it be conceded that all moral changes and phenomena obey, and ever have obeyed, one supreme head, one inflexible and unerring law. If God conform, as assuredly he does conform, to the law which he has given, so should man also conform, not indeed as slave or hireling, but as a well-loved child. For here, too, is liberty, liberty in obedience. This, then, is the saving truth which is to liberate our kind, perfect liberty, obedience perfect. For, on God's earth, as in God's heaven, there is law, divine law. Everywhere there is law, and with law liberty, the liberty of obedience, divine liberty and unity with the divine, liberty to obey and to love the God of thought and love, in whose spiritual image we are made, liberty to grow in knowledge, and goodness, and capacity, and love, for ever, and for ever, and for ever.

www.ingramcontent.com/pod-product-compliance
Lightning Source LLC
Chambersburg PA
CBHW021336300426
44114CB00012B/977